NORTHAMPTON SAINTS
OFFICIAL YEARBOOK 2006/07

Editorial
Caroline Moore, Graham Reid

Sidan Press Team
Simon Rosen, Julian Hill-Wood, Marc Fiszman, Mark Peters, Karim Biria, Robert Cubbon, Marina Kravchenko, Anette Lundebye, Gareth Peters, Janet Callcott, Trevor Scimes, John Fitzroy, Jenny Middlemarch, Anders Rasmussen, Lim Wai-Lee, Emma Turner, Charles Grove, Tim Ryman, Ronen Dorfan, Humphrey Badia

Statistics
Stuart Farmer Media Services, OPTA

Kick Off Editorial
Amanda Chatterton

Photography
Getty Images

Copyright © 2006 Northampton Saints

Sidan Press, 63-64 Margaret St, London W1W 8SW
Tel: 020 7580 0200
Email: info@sidanpress.com

sidanpress.com

Club Directory

Chairman and Directors

Chairman
Keith Barwell

Commercial director
Allan Robson

Finance director
Richard Deane

Board of directors
Leon Barwell, Richard Deane, Jon Drown, Tony Hewitt,
Murray Holmes, Colin Povey, Jon Raphael and Allan Robson.

Company secretary
Andrew Cozzolino

President
Jon Raphael

Rugby Management

Director of Rugby
Budge Pountney

Head Coach
Paul Grayson

Assistant Coaches
Paul Larkin, Frank Ponissi and Peter Sloane

Academy
James Sinclair and Rob Hunter

Rugby Administration
Lennie Newman
Phone: 01604 751543
Email: lennienewman@northamptonsaints.co.uk

Ros Hargreaves
Phone: 01604 599139
Email: roshargreaves@northamptonsaints.co.uk

Contacts

Communications
Caroline Moore
Phone: 01604 599125
Fax: 01604 599110
Email: carolinemoore@northamptonsaints.co.uk

Commercial, Sales and Sponsorship
Andrew Kendrick
Phone: 01604 599137
Email: andrewkendrick@northamptonsaints.co.uk

Annmaire Kulakowski
Phone: 01604 599128
Email: annmariekulakowski@northamptonsaints.co.uk

Graham Caldecott
Phone: 01604 599103
Email: grahamcaldecott@northamptonsaints.co.uk

Shobha Aranha
Phone: 01604 599115
Email: shobhaaranha@northamptonsaints.co.uk
Fax: 01604 599110

Marketing
Brian Facer
Phone: 01604 599131
Email: brianfacer@northamptonsaints.co.uk
Fax: 01604 599110

Community and Promotions
Sian Haynes
Phone: 01604 599113
Email: sianhaynes@northamptonsaints.co.uk

Andy Regan
Phone: 01604 599116
Email: andyregan@northamptonsaints.co.uk

Ross Stewart
Phone: 01604 599116
Email: rossstewart@northamptonsaints.co.uk
Fax: 01604 599110

Conferencing and Events
Nicola Clark
Phone: 01604 599114
Email: nicolaclarke@northamptonsaints.co.uk

Janice Newall
Phone: 01604 599136
Email: janicenewall@northamptonsaints.co.uk

Rebecca Worth
Phone: 01604 599166
Email: rebeccaworth@northamptonsaints.co.uk

Merchandising
Jo Norman
Phone: 01604 599111
Email: shop@northamptonsaints.co.uk

Ticket Office
Denise Davies
Phone: 01604 581000
Email: ticketoffice@northamptonsaints.co.uk

Ground
Franklin's Gardens
Weedon Road
Northampton
NN5 5BG
Phone: 01604 751543
Fax: 01604 599110

Thank you to Graham Reid for his excellent contribution

Contents

four packages
that make choosing
a phone plan simple

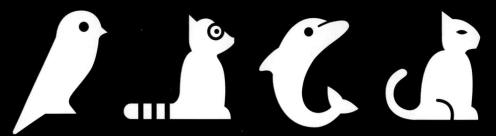

love to chat?

Canary
for nature's
born talkers

want no-nonsense
basics?

Racoon
for the industrious
and resourceful

text a lot?

Dolphin
for the fun-loving
and highly sociable

want all
the extras?

Panther
for people who are
always on the go

the future's bright orange™

EBS MOBILE PHONES

Established in 1985, the EBS group of companies offer a varied choice for all communication solutions.

EBS Corporate offer mobile/PDA/Blackberry contracts, Pay as you go, in-car hands free kits, an extensive range of mobile accessories, landline services, comprehensive insurance and all data solutions. They also provide an in-depth mobile phone tariff analysis - simply supply a set of fully itemised bills and the Corporate Team will compare your call usage and advise you of what savings can be made. To take advantage of this service please contact either Hayley Morris or Suzanne Coburn on the Corporate number below.

EBS UK Limited - the distribution arm of the business - is the largest Orange distributor within the UK.

Retail
92 Wellingborough Rd, NORTHAMPTON
Car Park in St Edmunds Rd
01604 604444

Corporate
01604 602244

Retail
3 Sheep Street, RUGBY
01788 577055

Retail
41 High Street, Harborne, BIRMINGHAM
0121 428 4445

Chairman's notes
Keith Barwell

No sooner is the season over before we have to prepare for next year.

What are the prospects? I am cautiously optimistic. The team performed well, particularly in the second half; that is, from January 1, 2006, onwards. We played 12 games, won eight, drew one and lost three. The three we lost were against three of the top four teams. We also managed to get five bonus points during those weeks too. However, the GUINNESS PREMIERSHIP is not played over 12 games; it's played over 22. If we are going to achieve our targets, we need to play well for the whole season, not just the second half. We have the players, or at least, most of them. We might move to strengthen out squad further during the summer months and early autumn. This will partly depend on how people recover from injuries.

One of the most pleasing aspects of last year was our style of play. We want to play fast, attacking rugby and this style will continue for the 2006/07 season. Fasten your seatbelts.

The coaching and backroom staff is strong. We now employ 19 people at a cost of more than £1 million. This is double some Premiership clubs and no-one has a bigger staff. We intend to substantially increase money we spend on the Academy. These two items alone give cause for optimism. Although no-one is under any illusions. The time to deliver has come. What then are our targets and expectations for next season?

Well, consider a few things. Firstly, we are halfway through a two-year rebuilding exercise. In 12 months, we should have a team capable of winning everything. At the moment, we are not quite the finished article. However, we shall be striving to win some silverware. In the league, the minimum requirement is to finish in the top four. In the Heineken Cup, a competition of 24 teams, 16 drops out after the pool stages; it is our target to qualify for the quarter-finals. That is, to become one of the best eight teams in Europe. After that, everything is a bonus and, to a certain extent, in the lap of the gods. But we will be trying 110 per cent. We can win the Anglo-Welsh Cup, but a realistic target, is to get to the final.

The GUINNESS PREMIERSHIP final will be played at Twickenham, as will be the Heineken Cup final, as will be the Anglo-Welsh final. I believe we have a realistic chance of going to Twickenham twice next year, as well as having some wonderful trips to Europe.

Of course, there will be some disappointment along the way. Of course, the pressure will be massive. But the pressure of trying to win something at the top is a lot more pleasant than the pressure when you are struggling to avoid relegation. It will be tight next year and the little things will matter. A referee's decision, a missed penalty, getting the crowd behind you and paying attention in detail to everything we do may determine the outcome of a few games. I promise you that if we fall short, it will not be for the lack of trying.

Green Shoots
By head coach Paul Grayson

Standing on the pitch at Sixways stadium in the immediate aftermath of our last day defeat to Worcester not knowing for a few brief seconds that Quins had gone down, was one of the most bizarre rugby moments of my life.

Up until that point the consequences of relegation had been largely ignored, but for those few seconds it looked like the unthinkable had happened. As the news filtered through, in what seemed like a lifetime, all the strain and heartache of the last few months started to drift away. Budge and I had taken on an almost impossible task with a squad that was on its knees and club that looked a pale shadow of the one that had lifted the European and been a regular fixture in the play-offs and domestic cup finals. We had somehow managed to find six wins in the league and make it to the quarter-finals of the Heineken Cup, but I was filled with a sense of guilt that for the first time in a long time the club was at the wrong end of the table and had severely bruised its reputation as one of the most successful clubs of the modern era.

As a fledgling management and coaching staff, we had hurled ourselves headlong into our roles and being appointed for the next season was a big risk for the board of directors. They had however responded well to our call for pride in our colours and our history and were in favour of our insistence on understanding just how lucky we all were to be involved with this great club. Our first job was to organise and implement a pre-season training plan and with our own experiences still fresh in our minds we put the players through an enjoyable but brutal few months. Along with Tim and Cliff we picked all the best bits from previous pre seasons that had given us, as players, the best results added a few new ideas and we were to reap the rewards of such a good foundation later in the year. The first harsh lesson I learned as a coach was that pre-season is the best time of year, full of hope and expectation, lateral thinking and new ideas and most importantly no games of rugby to get in the way!

Leicester 32 Northampton 0. Honeymoon over! We knew we had a tough start to the season with three away games while the stadium development was completed, but a real hiding at Welford Road made it clear where our immediate problems lay. An immediate bounce back saw us win away to Bath and set us up for a first home game and chance to make a good start in our newly extended facility. Billed as Carlos versus Jonny it was a damp squib of a game and we went down tamely, negating the progress made the week before. A robust display at Gloucester saw us lose a game we should have won, but with four to the sin-bin and a stream of penalties it was only an intercepted pass that saved the Cherries' blushes. What was clear was that we were making progress in our style of play, but we had a serious discipline problem. October saw further progress with Challenge Cup wins over Worcester and Newport and a nail-biting win in the GUINNESS PREMIERSHIP at home to London

Irish (not the last we would see). Viadana were dispatched at Franklin's and we were given a lesson at Bristol, but all in all a good month and the first green shoots of recovery were beginning to show. Or so we thought.

Although we had a tough start, we saw November as a real chance to get some league points and establish ourselves in a healthy position. It was not going to turn out that way. Beaten by 10 men at Sarries, unlucky not to take Wasps at home, appalling at Leeds and ill-disciplined at home to Worcester, November was over and we were winless. The Anglo-Welsh Cup should have provided solace but the mighty Tigers took the tries and the win and the place in the semi-finals and our misery was just about complete. We were in a hole and we knew it. It was time to stop digging and start climbing and back to back games against Narbonne were a good opportunity to recover some dignity away from the glare of the Premiership. Two fine performances, particularly away in the south of France, showed commitment and pride and gave us a hint of self belief. We set off for Sale on Boxing Day with a horrendous injury list and were never likely to win; thankfully spirit and determination were there in spades. So at the end of 2005 we nearly qualified for the quarter-final of the Challenge Cup, we were out of the Anglo-Welsh and, worst of all, we were second bottom of the league with a meagre 13 points. Something had to change.

We decided not to wait until the end of the season to do our end of season review and instead we did an end of year review. It was a very positive experience and the players set some very challenging goals, one of which was to go through January unbeaten. 01/01/06 seemed like a good starting point to redefine ourselves and a heart stopper saw us overcome Bristol at home then Worcester away as the forwards started to hold their collective hand up. Bristol again in the Challenge Cup and the Viadana fiasco saw us reach crunch time at home to Leeds. Not a classic by any stretch of the imagination but yet again a thrilling encounter which saw us try to throw the game away in the last stages and only a late penalty saved our bacon. However we had achieved our first target and started to look like a side that, with a bit of confidence, were looking to give someone a hiding. We should have won at Wasps but never the less a draw was good reward and then came the day where it all came together. Sarries at home

started nervously for our supporters as we trailed early on but then the first try came and from then on it was all about the Saints. We were showered with praise from both the written media and even the Sky commentators. It was a fantastic advert for the club and I felt for the first time that we were starting to recover our reputation. A loss to an in-form London Irish backed up by another nail-biting win against Gloucester put us in a position where we could, once and for all, put fears of relegation behind us. Five points and five tries at Kingston Park in our most complete display of the season and the ghost that had haunted every step for a season and a half was almost gone. A collective sigh of relief saw us under-perform for the first time in 2006 and exit the Challenge Cup to Worcester. A bonus point win at home against Bath in a tremendous game suddenly made the playoffs an outside possibility, which was both astonishing and a sign of just how far we had come. What better than a local derby to test ourselves. It was the best game of the season and only a couple mistakes cost us dear. Play -offs out of reach it was time to try and get a place in Europe for players and fans alike and so to Bristol for one of the strangest games I have seen. Down 16-nil with only injury-time to play, we were dead and buried, but as our loyal supporters know, we do leave it late sometimes. A blistering three-try burst and the game was ours and with that a place in the Heineken Cup. It was our ultimate destination and although we had strayed from the path for a while we were finally there.

If you wanted to know how Northampton's season had gone then the last game of the season, against champions elect Sale, was a perfect microcosm. In the first half of the season we were pushed around up front, as in the Sale game. In the second half of the season we were breathtaking and put many sides to the sword, just like the Sale game and just like the Sale game we came up just short at the end. There were many outstanding performances by many players this season and I deliberately mention no-one in particular for during the course of the season it is our desire to be and live as a team that has seen us through. I thought I had detected the first green shoots of recovery early in the season but by the end they were well and truly established and with care and attention they may just flourish. The whole staff at the playing end would like to thank every one who has stuck with us and believed in our way from the beginning.

Leicester Tigers 32
Northampton Saints 0

Premiership Away Record vs Leicester Tigers					
Played	Won	Drawn	Lost	For	Against
9	**2**	**1**	**6**	**156**	**217**

The Saints were given a rude introduction to the new GUINNESS PREMIERSHIP season as Leicester piled on 32 points without reply.

The game will also be remembered for its dismal kicking, especially from Leicester fly-half Any Goode, who missed seven from eight attempts in the first half alone and Saints' new co-captain Bruce Reihana also failed with his two attempts. When Goode eventually decided to opt for the corner in the 15th minute, Leicester managed to shove their driving maul over the try line with James Hamilton scoring.

On 33 minutes, Leicester managed to cross Saints' line for the second time, again with a driving maul. This time prop Michael Holford came up with the ball. Goode added two points from the boot to make the score 12-0.

Saints' were doing their best to compete, with the backs doing a lot of running. Big summer signing Carlos Spencer tried to make inroads but to no avail. It never appeared like it would be Northampton's day. This rhetoric was consolidated when a loose pass from Damien Browne was intercepted by wing Alesana Tuilagi, who raced the length of the field to score. Northampton turned around 19-0 down after Goode slotted over the conversion.

In the second half, Leicester piled on 13 more points through tries from centre Dan Hipkiss and wing sensation Tom Varndell, as well as Goode's only successful penalty conversion of the day.

▶ Did you know?

Six new players played for Saints on the first day of last season: Lamont, Mallon, Spencer, Hartley, Rae, Lewitt.

Venue:	Welford Road	Referee:	Roy Maybank - Season 05/06		**Leicester Tigers**
Attendance:	16,815	Matches:	0		**Northampton Saints**
Capacity:	16,815	Yellow Cards:	0		
Occupancy:	100%	Red Cards:	0		

Starting Line-Ups

O Leicester Tigers		Northampton Saints O
Vesty	15	Reihana (c)
Tuilagi	14	Rudd
Hipkiss	13	Clarke
Gibson	12	Mallon
Varndell	11	Cohen
Goode	10	Spencer
Ellis	9	Robinson
Holford	1	Smith
Chuter	2	Hartley
Moreno	3	Sturgess
Hamilton	4	Lord
Cullen	5	Dm Browne
Johnson	6	Rae
Jennings	7	Fox
Corry (c)	8	Dn Browne

Replacements

Lloyd	22	Lamont
Broadfoot	21	Davies
Healey	20	Howard
Abraham	19	Lewitt
White	18	Boome
Kay	17	Budgen
Taukafa	16	Richmond

Match Stats

Tackles	76	86
Missed Tackles	7	9
Ball Carries	78	61
Metres	475	394
Defenders Beaten	9	7
Passes	113	67
Clean Breaks	1	0
Pens Conceded	6	17
Turnovers	13	17
Breakdowns Won	61	53
% Scrums Won	100%	88%
% Line-Outs Won	100%	82%

Premiership Table

Team	P	W	D	L	F	A	BP	Pts
10 Saracens	1	0	0	1	11	23	0	0
11 Leeds Tykes	1	0	0	1	11	27	0	0
12 Northampton Saints	1	0	0	1	0	32	0	0

Event Line

TC	Try Converted		P	Penalty
T	Try		DG	Drop Goal

Min	Score Progress		Event	Players
15	5	0	T	O Hamilton
27	5	0		O Smith
29	5	0	⇄	O Budgen > Rae
33	12	0	TC	O Holford / Goode
36	17	0	T	O Tuilagi
40	17	0	⇄	O Rae > Budgen
Half time 17-0				
41	17	0	⇄	O Boome > Rae
44	24	0	TC	O Hipkiss / Goode
49	24	0	⇄	O Abraham > Corry
49	24	0	⇄	O Lloyd > Hipkiss
56	24	0	⇄	O Kay > Cullen
58	24	0	⇄	O Hipkiss > Gibson
59	24	0	⇄	O Budgen > Smith
59	24	0	⇄	O Lewitt > Fox
60	24	0	⇄	O White > Holford
64	27	0	P	O Goode
67	27	0	⇄	O Healey > Ellis
68	27	0	⇄	O Broadfoot > Goode
71	27	0	⇄	O Taukafa > Chuter
72	27	0	⇄	O Lamont > Rudd
78	27	0	⇄	O Richmond > Hartley
79	27	0	⇄	O Holford > Moreno
85	32	0	T	O Varndell
Full time 32-0				

Scoring Statistics

O Leicester Tigers				O Northampton Saints			
by Situation		by Half		by Situation		by Half	
TC:	14	first:	53%	TC:	0	first:	0%
T:	15	second:	47%	T:	0	second:	0%
P:	3			P:	0		
DG:	0			DG:	0		

11

Bath Rugby 9
Northampton Saints 17

Premiership Away Record vs Bath Rugby					
Played	Won	Drawn	Lost	For	Against
9	**4**	**0**	**5**	**135**	**188**

The match against Bath was a world away from the performance of Saints' previous fixture at Leicester.

Northampton were given an instant advantage when Bath wing Salesi Finau was sin-binned for a high tackle. Captain Bruce Reihana duly slotted over the resulting penalty but Olly Barkley got Bath on the score sheet with a penalty of his own just a few minutes later.

▶ Did you know?

This was the first game that Sean Lamont started for Northampton Saints.

In torrid rain, Reihana and Barkley traded three more kicks, with the Saints' captain edging his team three points ahead. The remainder of the half was most notable for Daniel Browne's sin-binning for obstructing Bath back-rower James Scaysbrook. At half-time the scores stood at 9-6 to Northampton.

The second half began with England hooker Steve Thompson making his first appearance of the season, only days after signing a new four-year contract with his home club. It was the backs making the difference on the scoreboard, however, as Barkley clawed back three points following another kick from Reihana.

The game-breaking move came after 73 minutes when new centre Seamus Mallon threw a dummy and rushed through a gap, crossing for Saints and scoring their first try of the season. That made it 17-9 to Northampton, and no more scores were made. Danny Grewcock still managed to take some of the attention from Saints' first victory though when he was sin-binned at the death for stamping.

Venue:	Recreation Ground	Referee:	David Rose - Season 05/06		**Bath Rugby**
Attendance:	10,060	Matches:	1		**Northampton Saints**
Capacity:	10,600	Yellow Cards:	1		
Occupancy:	95%	Red Cards:	0		

Starting Line-Ups

Bath Rugby		Northampton Saints
Perry	15	Reihana (c)
Finau	14	Lamont
Higgins	13	Clarke
Barkley	12	Mallon
Welsh	11	Cohen
Malone	10	Spencer
Wood	9	Robinson
Barnes	1	Smith
Mears	2	Hartley
Bell	3	Sturgess
Borthwick (c)	4	Lord
Grewcock	5	Dm Browne
Beattie	6	Soden
Scaysbrook	7	Fox
Feau'nati	8	Dn Browne

Replacements

Davis	22	Rudd
Dunne	21	Davies
Walshe	20	Howard
Fidler	19	Lewitt
Delve	18	Rae
Stevens	17	Budgen
Dixon	16	Thompson

Match Stats

Tackles	81	95
Missed Tackles	8	6
Ball Carries	69	58
Metres	244	310
Defenders Beaten	6	7
Passes	88	93
Clean Breaks	12	12
Pens Conceded	6	16
Turnovers	22	18
Breakdowns Won	50	45
% Scrums Won	88%	87%
% Line-Outs Won	86%	56%

Premiership Table

Team	P	W	D	L	F	A	BP	Pts
6 Bristol Rugby	1	1	0	0	19	16	0	4
7 Northampton Saints	2	1	0	1	17	41	0	4
8 Worcester Warriors	1	0	1	0	15	15	0	2

Event Line

TC	Try Converted	P	Penalty
T	Try	DG	Drop Goal

Min	Score Progress		Event	Players
3	0	0	■	Finau
4	0	3	P	Reihana
7	3	3	P	Barkley
11	3	6	P	Reihana
17	3	6	■	Browne
22	6	6	P	Barkley
32	6	6	⇄	Fidler > Borthwick
33	6	9	P	Reihana
Half time 6-9				
41	6	9	⇄	Borthwick > Fidler
41	6	9	⇄	Davis > Perry
41	6	9	⇄	Thompson > Hartley
48	6	9	⇄	Perry > Davis
55	6	12	P	Reihana
58	6	12	⇄	Fidler > Borthwick
59	6	12	⇄	Stevens > Barnes
60	6	12	⇄	Lewitt > Browne
61	9	12	P	Barkley
62	9	12	⇄	Borthwick > Fidler
63	9	12	⇄	Budgen > Sturgess
69	9	12	⇄	Delve > Feau'nati
73	9	17	T	Mallon
74	9	17	⇄	Dunne > Malone
80	9	17	■	Grewcock
86	9	17	⇄	Howard > Robinson
Full time 9-17				

Scoring Statistics

Bath Rugby
by Situation   by Half

TC:	0	first:	67%
T:	0	second:	33%
P:	9		
DG:	0		

Northampton Saints
by Situation   by Half

TC:	0	first:	53%
T:	5	second:	47%
P:	12		
DG:	0		

Northampton Saints 9
Newcastle Falcons 16

Premiership Home Record vs Newcastle Falcons					
Played	Won	Drawn	Lost	For	Against
9	**7**	**0**	**2**	**257**	**150**

In the shadow of the new South Stand development, a sold-out Franklin's Gardens was disappointed to see Saints beaten in a game they could have won.

It was the Falcons who scored first when Dave Walder collected the ball and touched down after his own chip had bounced out of the reach of Bruce Reihana. Matt Burke converted and suddenly Saints were seven points down.

Carlos Spencer was causing havoc with his running lines and silky skills, and Saints were still having the most of the ball in the first quarter. Ben Cohen and Jon Clarke were making the most of the space Spencer has created for them. Clarke's break earned a penalty which Reihana converted to make the score 7-3.

Northampton dropped off the pace in the second quarter, and Newcastle made the most of the territory and Northampton indiscipline as Walder dropped a goal and Burke converted a penalty.

In the second half, Saints were first to score with a Reihana penalty, but they could not get back into the game due to Walder's tactical kicking. He added a further three points to his tally with another drop-goal. Saints only managed a third penalty conversion, leaving the game to finish 16-9 to Newcastle. It was a disappointing end to a promising first 20 minutes.

▶ Did you know?

Saints requested their first home match be delayed to assist with the building schedule of the extended South Stand.

Venue:	Franklin's Gardens	Referee:	Roy Maybank - Season 05/06		**Northampton Saints**
Attendance:	12,018	Matches:	2		**Newcastle Falcons**
Capacity:	13,591	Yellow Cards:	4		
Occupancy:	89%	Red Cards:	0		

Starting Line-Ups

○ Northampton Saints		Newcastle Falcons ○
Reihana (c)	15	Burke
Lamont	14	May
Clarke	13	Noon
Mallon	12	Mayerhofler
Cohen	11	Tait
Spencer	10	Walder
Robinson	9	Charlton
Smith	1	Ward
Hartley	2	Long
Sturgess	3	Morris
Lord	4	Perry
Dm Browne	5	Parling
Soden	6	Finegan
Fox	7	Woods
Easter	8	Charvis (c)

Replacements

Myring	22	Flood
Davies	21	Grindal
Howard	20	Grimes
Lewitt	19	McCarthy
Rae	18	Paoletti
Budgen	17	Mackie
Thompson	16	Wilson

Event Line

TC	Try Converted		P	Penalty
T	Try		DG	Drop Goal

Min	Score Progress	Event	Players
11	0 — 7	TC	○ Walder / Burke
16	3 — 7	P	○ Reihana
25	3 — 10	DG	○ Walder
26	3 — 10	⇄	○ Grimes > Perry
31	3 — 13	P	○ Burke
36	3 — 13	⇄	○ Perry > Grimes
40	3 — 13	⇄	○ Thompson > Hartley

Half time 3-13

43	6 — 13	P	○ Reihana
50	6 — 13	⇄	○ Paoletti > Morris
53	6 — 13	⇄	○ Budgen > Sturgess
59	6 — 13	⇄	○ Wilson > Ward
59	6 — 13	⇄	○ Grindal > Charlton
68	6 — 16	DG	○ Walder
69	6 — 16	⇄	○ Davies > Mallon
69	6 — 16	⇄	○ Lewitt > Soden
71	6 — 16	⇄	○ Howard > Robinson
80	9 — 16	P	○ Reihana

Full time 9-16

Match Stats

Tackles	80	134
Missed Tackles	15	23
Ball Carries	111	70
Metres	617	415
Defenders Beaten	24	15
Passes	130	126
Clean Breaks	3	9
Pens Conceded	9	15
Turnovers	17	10
Breakdowns Won	87	54
% Scrums Won	89%	100%
% Line-Outs Won	77%	90%

Scoring Statistics

○ Northampton Saints

by Situation | by Half

▶ TC:	0	▶ first:	33%
▶ T:	0	▶ second:	67%
▶ P:	9		
▶ DG:	0		

○ Newcastle Falcons

by Situation | by Half

▶ TC:	7	▶ first:	81%
▶ T:	0	▶ second:	19%
▶ P:	3		
▶ DG:	6		

Premiership Table

Team	P	W	D	L	F	A	BP	Pts
9 London Irish	3	1	0	2	45	60	2	6
10 Northampton Saints	3	1	0	2	26	57	1	5
11 Bath Rugby	3	0	0	3	51	76	1	1

Gloucester Rugby 28
Northampton Saints 24

Guinness Premiership
24.09.05

Premiership Away Record vs Gloucester Rugby					
Played	Won	Drawn	Lost	For	Against
9	**3**	**0**	**6**	**184**	**200**

In a penalty-ridden game, four yellow cards proved to be the undoing of Saints, despite being eight points up at the break.

Steve Thompson touched down after 14 minutes thanks to the mercurial skills of Carlos Spencer. The good start seemed to be consolidated as Gloucester's Rob Thirlby was sin-binned for offside only metres from the home side's line. Bruce Reihana missed the penalty, and a possible 10-point lead was cut to nothing when almost immediately scrum-half Peter Richards scored from a quick tap penalty.

▶ Did you know?

Damien Browne's try was his first and only try for Northampton Saints... so far.

Ludovic Mercier gave Gloucester a six-point lead with two penalties. Thankfully, Gloucester's three-quarters gifted Jon Clarke a score after fumbling in midfield. Despite a sin-binning for hooker Dylan Hartley, a 14-man scored again through Damien Browne and at half-time, Saints were 21-13 ahead.

The second half proved to be a horror show for Saints as first Tom Smith and then Dan Richmond were both yellow-carded. Gloucester capitalised with a try from Jake Boer, although a missed conversion meant Saints were still three points ahead. It did not last long though as wing James Simpson-Daniel intercepted a pass to dive in under the post leaving a simple conversion for Mercier. Two minutes later things went from poor to worse when Thompson became the fourth Northampton player to sit out for 10 minutes. Each team added a penalty to their scores, with the match finishing at 28-24 to Gloucester.

Venue:	Kingsholm
Attendance:	11,156
Capacity:	13,000
Occupancy:	86%

Referee:	Dave Pearson - Season 05/06
Matches:	3
Yellow Cards:	5
Red Cards:	0

Gloucester Rugby
Northampton Saints

Starting Line-Ups

○ Gloucester Rugby		Northampton Saints ○
Thirlby	15	Reihana (c)
Foster	14	Lamont
Tindall (c)	13	Clarke
Paul	12	Quinlan
Simpson-Daniel	11	Cohen
Mercier	10	Spencer
Richards	9	Robinson
Collazo	1	Smith
Azam	2	Hartley
Powell	3	Budgen
Eustace	4	Lord
Brown	5	Dm Browne
Buxton	6	Thompson
Boer	7	Fox
Forrester	8	Easter

Replacements

Goodridge	22	Mallon
Davies	21	Davies
Thomas	20	Howard
Hazell	19	Soden
Cornwell	18	Boome
Sigley	17	Sturgess
Davies	16	Richmond

Match Stats

Tackles	85	87
Missed Tackles	17	13
Ball Carries	83	79
Metres	458	572
Defenders Beaten	12	14
Passes	80	114
Clean Breaks	2	10
Pens Conceded	4	18
Turnovers	19	11
Breakdowns Won	53	55
% Scrums Won	100%	93%
% Line-Outs Won	80%	64%

Premiership Table

Team	P	W	D	L	F	A	BP	Pts
9 Newcastle Falcons	3	1	0	2	55	51	2	6
10 Northampton Saints	4	1	0	3	50	85	2	6
11 Bath Rugby	3	0	0	3	51	76	1	1

Event Line

TC	Try Converted		P	Penalty
T	Try		DG	Drop Goal

Min	Score Progress		Event	Players
13	0	7	TC	○ Thompson / Reihana
16	0	7		○ Thirlby
19	7	7	TC	○ Richards / Mercier
26	10	7	P	○ Mercier
33	13	7	P	○ Mercier
36	13	14	TC	○ Clarke / Reihana
39	13	14		○ Hartley
40	13	14	⇄	○ Richmond > Easter
40	13	21	TC	○ Browne / Reihana
	Half time 13-21			
48	13	21	⇄	○ Richmond > Hartley
48	13	21	⇄	○ Easter > Richmond
51	13	21	⇄	○ Thomas > Richards
53	13	21		○ Smith
54	13	21		○ Richmond
56	13	21	⇄	○ Boome > Lord
58	13	21	⇄	○ Sturgess > Easter
59	18	21	T	○ Boer
67	25	21	TC	○ Simpson-Daniel / Mercier
68	25	21	⇄	○ Sturgess > Budgen
69	25	21		○ Thompson
70	25	21	⇄	○ Easter > Sturgess
70	25	21	⇄	○ Soden > Easter
75	25	21	⇄	○ Goodridge > Thirlby
75	25	21	⇄	○ Hazell > Boer
76	25	21	⇄	○ Davies > Azam
76	25	24	P	○ Reihana
81	25	24	⇄	○ Sigley > Collazo
81	28	24	P	○ Mercier
	Full time 28-24			

Scoring Statistics

○ Gloucester Rugby		Northampton Saints
by Situation by Half		by Situation by Half

○ Gloucester Rugby		
TC:	14	first: 46%
T:	5	second: 54%
P:	9	
DG:	0	

○ Northampton Saints		
TC:	21	first: 88%
T:	0	second: 13%
P:	3	
DG:	0	

Worcester Warriors 7
Northampton Saints 22

New signing Sam Harding could not have made a bigger impact when a try from his first touch in a Northampton jersey secured a convincing win. Ben Cohen had earlier grabbed two tries of his own, reminding Andy Robinson not to leave him out of England's autumn internationals.

The first came after just five minutes, when Cohen found himself on the end of a move that involved Carlos Spencer, David Quinlan and No 8 Mark Soden. Winger Sean Lamont handed Cohen a second score seven minutes later after making a blistering break down the touchline. The dominant start was dampened by the sight of prop Colin Noon being helped off the field, who was playing in his first top-flight game since returning from a six-month ban.

Neither side could add to the scoreboard for the remainder of the first half, but Saints continued their form into the second and were rewarded with Harding diving over only a minute after stepping onto the field. Saints were now a healthy 22 points to the good.

▶ Did you know?

This was the first time Saints had beaten Worcester Warriors since they were promoted to the Premiership.

As expected, Worcester rallied to save some face and, after Soden was sin-binned for a high tackle, Sione Tuamoheloa crossed for the home side. Shane Drahm, one of Saints' relegation saviours from the 2004/05 season, added two more points with a conversion.

The remainder of the game was noted for the injury to Andre Van Niekerk, who was carried from the field on a stretcher. Centre Dale Rasmusen also had to go off as the game neared its end, which finished 7-22 with Cohen being named Powergen Man of the Match.

Venue:	Sixways	Referee:	Martin Fox

Attendance: 7,561
Capacity: 9,726
Occupancy: 78%

**Worcester Warriors
Northampton Saints**

Starting Line-Ups

⚪ Worcester Warriors		Northampton Saints ⚪
Le Roux	15	Reihana (c)
Hylton	14	Lamont
Rasmussen	13	Clarke
Trueman	12	Quinlan
Tucker	11	Cohen
Drahm	10	Spencer
Powell	9	Robinson
Windo	1	Smith
Van Niekerk	2	Richmond
Taumoepeau	3	Noon
Collier	4	Boome
Gillies	5	Dm Browne
Horstmann	6	Thompson
Sanderson (c)	7	Fox
Hickey	8	Soden

Replacements

Lombard	22	Mallon
Whatling	21	Davies
Gomarsall	20	Howard
Tu'amoheloa	19	Harding
Murphy	18	Lord
Clunis	17	Budgen
MacDonald	16	Hartley

Event Line

TC	Try Converted		P	Penalty
T	Try		DG	Drop Goal

Min	Score Progress		Event	Players
9	0	7	TC	⚪ Cohen / Reihana
20	0	7	⇄	⚪ Tu'amoheloa > Hickey
25	0	7	⇄	⚪ Budgen > Noon
28	0	12	T	⚪ Cohen
Half time 0-12				
49	0	15	P	⚪ Reihana
50	0	15	⇄	⚪ Murphy > Collier
50	0	15	⇄	⚪ Harding > Fox
50	0	22	TC	⚪ Harding / Reihana
56	0	22	⇄	⚪ Howard > Robinson
61	0	22	▦	⚪ Soden
65	7	22	TC	⚪ Tu'amoheloa / Drahm
66	7	22	⇄	⚪ Gomarsall > Powell
66	7	22	⇄	⚪ Lombard > Trueman
66	7	22	⇄	⚪ Lord > Browne
66	7	22	⇄	⚪ Davies > Quinlan
70	7	22	⇄	⚪ Clunis > Van Niekerk
80	7	22	⇄	⚪ Whatling > Rasmussen
81	7	22	⇄	⚪ Mallon > Thompson
Full time 7-22				

Match Stats

Tackles	77	66
Missed Tackles	21	10
Ball Carries	70	105
Metres	376	691
Defenders Beaten	9	22
Passes	94	108
Clean Breaks	9	18
Pens Conceded	11	16
Turnovers	14	17
Breakdowns Won	44	58
% Scrums Won	92%	83%
% Line-Outs Won	59%	67%

Scoring Statistics

⚪ Worcester Warriors
by Situation   by Half

▶ TC:	7	▶ first:	0%
▶ T:	0	second:	100%
▶ P:	0		
DG:	0		

⚪ Northampton Saints
by Situation   by Half

▶ TC:	14	▶ first:	55%
▶ T:	5	second:	45%
▶ P:	3		
DG:	0		

Powergen Cup Table

Team	P	W	D	L	F	A	BP	Pts
1 Northampton Saints	1	1	0	0	22	7	0	4
2 Newport Gwent Dragons	1	1	0	0	24	15	0	4
3 Leicester Tigers	1	0	0	1	15	24	0	0
4 Worcester Warriors	1	0	0	1	7	22	0	0

Northampton Saints 32
Newport Gwent Dragons 7

Northampton faced their first ever Welsh Powergen Cup opponents and succeeded where Leicester had failed the previous week by beating Newport-Gwent Dragons convincingly at Franklin's Gardens.

With the weather playing havoc with any attempts to play rugby, Saints opted to kick with the wind behind them in the first half. The decision was an inspired one, and created a try for wing Sean Lamont when a Bruce Reihana punt was knocked into touch by Dragons' Gareth Wyatt. Darren Fox charged through the midfield from the resulting line-out before the ball was spun wide for Lamont to touch down.

▶ Did you know?

Sean Lamont scored his debut Saints try during this game.

In the 16th minute, Jon Clarke finished off a move involving Carlos Spencer, Mark Soden and Mark Robinson. Saints went 18-0 up when Reihana added the conversion and a penalty, and the Dragons never really looked like scoring. In injury time, Sean Lamont was shown a yellow card for a shove on Hal Luscombe, although the team did not show they were a man down and even scored early in the second period. Only four minutes in, Robinson broke from the base of a scrum and ran 60 metres to claim a fantastic solo try. Two points from Reihana gave Saints a 25-0 lead.

David Gerard, who had recently been signed from Toulouse, came on with Sam Harding for their home debuts and with those fresh legs on the field Saints pushed for a bonus point and a killer blow. The all important fourth try came from captain Reihana who finished off work from Ben Cohen, Spencer and David Quinlan to go in between the posts.

Newport managed to save some pride at the death with a try from Sione Tuipulotu, which proved to be the last act of a match which Saints had won comfortably.

Venue:	Franklin's Gardens	Referee:	Tony Spreadbury

Attendance: 11,695
Capacity: 13,591
Occupancy: 86%

Northampton Saints
Newport Gwent Dragons

Starting Line-Ups

○ Northampton Saints		Newport Gwent Dragons ○
Reihana (c)	15	Tuipulotu
Lamont	14	Wyatt
Clarke	13	Luscombe
Quinlan	12	Bryant
Cohen	11	Breeze
Spencer	10	Sweeney
Robinson	9	Baber
Smith	1	Maddocks
Richmond	2	Brown
Budgen	3	Thomas
Boome	4	Charteris
Dm Browne	5	Sidoli
Thompson	6	Bryan
Fox	7	Ringer
Soden	8	Owen (c)

Replacements

Mallon	22	Cooper
Davies	21	Warlow
Howard	20	Morgan
Harding	19	Forster
Gerard	18	Gough
Sturgess	17	Black
Hartley	16	Jones

Match Stats

Tackles	68	74
Missed Tackles	8	19
Ball Carries	92	63
Metres	444	233
Defenders Beaten	16	7
Passes	92	94
Clean Breaks	14	5
Pens Conceded	14	8
Turnovers	17	17
Breakdowns Won	67	46
% Scrums Won	100%	100%
% Line-Outs Won	82%	73%

Powergen Cup Table

Team	P	W	D	L	F	A	BP	Pts
1 Northampton Saints	2	2	0	0	54	14	1	9
2 Leicester Tigers	2	1	0	1	57	40	1	5
3 Newport Gwent Dragons	2	1	0	1	31	47	0	4
4 Worcester Warriors	2	0	0	2	23	64	0	0

Event Line

TC	Try Converted		P	Penalty
T	Try		DG	Drop Goal

Min	Score Progress		Event	Players
3	3	0	P	○ Reihana
7	8	0	T	○ Lamont
16	15	0	TC	○ Clarke / Reihana
29	18	0	P	○ Reihana
40	18	0	▦	○ Lamont
Half time 18-0				
41	18	0	⇄	○ Warlow > Bryant
41	18	0	⇄	○ Morgan > Tuipulotu
44	25	0	TC	○ Robinson / Reihana
49	25	0	⇄	○ Gough > Sidoli
49	25	0	⇄	○ Forster > Ringer
50	25	0	⇄	○ Gerard > Soden
52	25	0	⇄	○ Cooper > Baber
55	25	0	⇄	○ Tuipulotu > Morgan
56	25	0	⇄	○ Harding > Thompson
72	25	0	⇄	○ Black > Thomas
72	25	0	⇄	○ Sturgess > Budgen
72	25	0	⇄	○ Howard > Robinson
72	25	0	⇄	○ Jones > Brown
80	32	0	TC	○ Reihana / Reihana
82	32	0	⇄	○ Davies > Spencer
82	32	0	⇄	○ Hartley > Richmond
82	32	0	⇄	○ Mallon > Cohen
88	32	7	TC	○ Wyatt / Warlow
Full time 32-7				

Scoring Statistics

○ Northampton Saints		○ Newport Gwent Dragons	
by Situation	by Half	by Situation	by Half

Northampton Saints
- TC: 21
- T: 5
- P: 6
- DG: 0
- first: 56%
- second: 44%

Newport Gwent Dragons
- TC: 7
- T: 0
- P: 0
- DG: 0
- first: 0%
- second: 100%

Northampton Saints 25
London Irish 23

Premiership Home Record vs London Irish					
Played	Won	Drawn	Lost	For	Against
9	**5**	**0**	**4**	**195**	**190**

Northampton Saints sneaked a third win in a row with an 89th-minute try from wing Ben Cohen.

Once again it was Saints who set the early pace, with a chance from David Quinlan that went begging. He made up for his mistake when he was involved in a move that ended with Bruce Reihana touching down near the posts. Sam Harding, who made his first start for the club, also featured in the score. Saints appeared to be settling in to a rhythm until Riki Flutey, who had just converted a penalty, intercepted a pass from Carlos Spencer and ran in unopposed for a try. With the conversion added, Irish were three points ahead.

▶ Did you know?

This was the last Saints game that would feature South African lock Selborne Boome after he ruptured his Achilles tendon as he stepped back into a lineout.

It seemed as though Saints were crumbling again when winger Dominic Feau'nati scored to help Irish to a 10-point lead. Reihana, who traded penalties with Flutey, managed to score his second try of the game to take Saints to within five points. He added another penalty to make the half-time score a closely contested 18-20.

Early in the second half Saints put on all the pressure but could not score, while Irish managed three more points from the boot of Flutey. But missed chances from Flutey and Juan Miguel Leguizamon meant Irish could not finish the game off, and Saints took advantage of the fact.

Reihana took the ball quickly and a pass from Harding put Cohen over to level the scores. Reihana added the conversion, and Northampton snatched the game from the fingertips of the visiting Exiles.

Venue:	Franklin's Gardens	Referee:	Chris White - Season 05/06		**Northampton Saints**
Attendance:	13,262	Matches:	2		**London Irish**
Capacity:	13,591	Yellow Cards:	0		
Occupancy:	98%	Red Cards:	0		

Starting Line-Ups

○ Northampton Saints		London Irish ○
Reihana (c)	15	Horak
Lamont	14	Staniforth
Clarke	13	Penney
Quinlan	12	Catt (c)
Cohen	11	Feau'nati
Spencer	10	Flutey
Robinson	9	Willis
Smith	1	Hatley
Richmond	2	Flavin
Budgen	3	Skuse
Gerard	4	Casey
Dm Browne	5	Kennedy
Fox	6	Danaher
Harding	7	Dawson
Boome	8	Murphy

Replacements

Rudd	22	Everitt
Davies	21	Hodgson
Howard	20	Armitage
Soden	19	Leguizamon
Lord	18	Roche
Sturgess	17	Hickie
Thompson	16	Rautenbach

Event Line

TC	Try Converted			P	Penalty
T	Try			DG	Drop Goal

Min	Score Progress		Event	Players
4	7	0	TC	○ Reihana / Reihana
11	7	3	P	○ Flutey
13	7	10	TC	○ Flutey / Flutey
19	7	17	TC	○ Feau'nati / Flutey
23	10	17	P	○ Reihana
26	10	20	P	○ Flutey
30	15	20	T	○ Reihana
38	18	20	P	○ Reihana
Half time 18-20				
41	18	20	⇄	○ Armitage > Staniforth
41	18	20	⇄	○ Leguizamon > Murphy
56	18	20	⇄	○ Howard > Robinson
56	18	20	⇄	○ Thompson > Richmond
59	18	23	P	○ Flutey
60	18	23	⇄	○ Rautenbach > Skuse
61	18	23	⇄	○ Lord > Gerard
63	18	23	⇄	○ Soden > Boome
70	18	23	⇄	○ Sturgess > Budgen
73	18	23	⇄	○ Davies > Quinlan
84	18	23	⇄	○ Rudd > Lamont
89	25	23	TC	○ Cohen / Reihana
Full time 25-23				

Match Stats

Tackles	33	135
Missed Tackles	6	15
Ball Carries	140	44
Metres	658	330
Defenders Beaten	15	6
Passes	138	53
Clean Breaks	15	6
Pens Conceded	10	5
Turnovers	17	7
Breakdowns Won	108	33
% Scrums Won	100%	91%
% Line-Outs Won	75%	92%

Scoring Statistics

○ Northampton Saints

by Situation		by Half	
▶ TC:	14	▶ first:	72%
▶ T:	5	second:	28%
▶ P:	6		
▶ DG:	0		

○ London Irish

by Situation		by Half	
▶ TC:	14	▶ first:	87%
▶ T:	0	second:	13%
▶ P:	9		
▶ DG:	0		

Premiership Table

Team	P	W	D	L	F	A	BP	Pts
7 Bath Rugby	5	2	0	3	96	108	2	10
8 Northampton Saints	5	2	0	3	75	108	2	10
9 Bristol Rugby	4	2	0	2	66	95	1	9

Northampton Saints 47
Arix Viadana 25

England hooker Steve Thompson returned to captain a Saints side that disposed relatively easily of Italian side Viadana. It would be the only time the two teams met in the season as Viadana conceded their home tie later in January.

Former All Black Sam Harding was first to claim five points, sliding over after collecting a loose lineout throw. Bruce Reihana added five points through a conversion and a penalty and it looked like Saints would cruise away with the game.

To Viadana's credit, they did not lose heart and, even though for large periods they never threatened to score, they managed to work a try for Roberto Pedrazzi using a myriad of dummy runners. A penalty from Jaques Shutte drew the Italians to within two points. Before the break, Cohen kicked off his scoring rout with a typical cross-field kick collection, taking the half-time score to 20-11.

▶ Did you know?

This was the only match that lock Damien Browne did not start throughout the 2005/06 season.

In the second half, Saints began to pull away when a clever kick from Carlos Spencer fell to John Rudd, who ran in to score his first of the season. Cohen doubled his scoring tally for the match on the hour. Wing Paul Diggin came on as replacement to join fellow Academy debutant Mark Hopley, who was making his first start for Saints with fellow Academy player Charlie Beech. Viadana took advantage of the inexperience on the field and Callie Wannenburg grasped an interception try, although this was cancelled out by a Jon Clarke effort just three minutes later.

Confident of their win, Saints began to take risks on their own line. This was punished when Peitro Travagli pulled back a score, but the game was finished off with Cohen's hat-trick, before Rudd consolidated the victory with his try.

Venue:	Franklin's Gardens	Referee:	Romain Poite
Attendance:	10,802		
Capacity:	13,591		
Occupancy:	80%		

Northampton Saints
Arix Viadana

Starting Line-Ups

○ Northampton Saints		Arix Viadana ○
Reihana (c)	15	Durston
Rudd	14	Accorsi
Clarke	13	Pedrazzi
Quinlan	12	Spadaro
Cohen	11	Pace
Spencer	10	Schutte
Howard	9	Mazzantini
Beech	1	Aguero
Thompson	2	Daly
Budgen	3	Nieto
Gerard	4	Bezzi (c)
Lord	5	Geldenhuys
Hopley	6	Lopez
Harding	7	Wannenburg
Dn Browne	8	Sole

Replacements

Diggin	22	Fernandez-Rouyet
Mallon	21	Travagli
Robinson	20	Tonni
Dm Browne	19	Benatti
Sturgess	18	Fotofili
Smith	17	Ferraro
Richmond	16	Savi

Euro Challenge Cup Table

Team	P	W	D	L	F	A	BP	Pts
1 Northampton Saints	1	1	0	0	47	25	1	5
2 Narbonne	1	1	0	0	20	13	0	4
3 Bristol Rugby	1	0	0	1	13	20	1	1
4 Arix Viadana	1	0	0	1	25	47	0	0

Event Line

TC	Try Converted		P	Penalty
T	Try		DG	Drop Goal

Min	Score Progress		Event	Players
8	7	0	TC	○ Harding / Reihana
24	10	0	P	○ Reihana
25	10	5	T	○ Pedrazzi
32	10	8	P	○ Schutte
37	13	8	P	○ Reihana
38	13	11	P	○ Schutte
40	20	11	TC	○ Cohen / Reihana
Half time 20-11				
48	20	11	⇄	○ Travagli > Durston
51	25	11	T	○ Rudd
55	25	11	⇄	○ Savi > Aguero
59	32	11	TC	○ Cohen / Reihana
60	32	11	⇄	○ Ferraro > Daly
60	32	11	⇄	○ Diggin > Reihana
60	32	11	⇄	○ Smith > Beech
60	32	11	⇄	○ Mallon > Spencer
60	32	11	⇄	○ Richmond > Browne
63	32	11	⇄	○ Tonni > Mazzantini
63	32	18	TC	○ Wannenburg / Schutte
66	32	18	⇄	○ Fernandez-Rouyet > Nieto
66	37	18	T	○ Clarke
67	37	18	⇄	○ Fotofili > Bezzi
67	37	18	⇄	○ Benatti > Lopez
72	37	25	TC	○ Travagli / Schutte
77	42	25	T	○ Cohen
82	47	25	T	○ Rudd
Full time 47-25				

Scoring Statistics

○ Northampton Saints			○ Arix Viadana		
by Situation		by Half	by Situation		by Half

▶ TC:	21	▶ first:	43%	▶ TC:	14	▶ first:	44%
▶ T:	20	second:	57%	▶ T:	5	second:	56%
▶ P:	6			▶ P:	6		
DG:	0			DG:	0		

Bristol Rugby 36
Northampton Saints 28

Saints' perfect record in the cup competitions was spoilt with some impeccable David Lemi finishing at Bristol's Memorial Stadium.

Defence kept the first 40 minutes' total to single-figure points. In the first quarter, fortunes were mixed, with both sides having chances before Danny Gray slotted over a penalty. A second penalty was added with two minutes to spare in the first half, in which no-one could really make a mark.

With Bristol, in particular winger Lemi, pushing for a score before the half-time whistle, Saints managed one of their own with a break from their own half. The move was fuelled by Ben Cohen. Bruce Reihana and Carlos Spencer combined to finish off the score to leave a slender lead of 7-6.

In the second half, Bristol took control, scoring two tries while Sam Harding was in the sin-bin. The home side used their forward advantage to send over Jake Rauluni before Lemi claimed his first. Veteran lock Gareth Llewellyn added to the misery ahead of Lemi's second, thanks to some great forward work from the West Country club.

The game looked impossible for Saints until two tries in as many minutes offered a lifeline. Reihana and Spencer were both the benefactors of some skilful Northampton handling, and when the former converted both, Saints looked like they had a shout.

Centre Rhodri Davies scored for Saints to create a nervous last few minutes, before Lemi, who had taken on the kicking duties, slotted over his second penalty to deny Northampton a losing bonus point.

▶ Did you know?

Both Carlos Spencer and Rhodri Davies scored debut tries for Saints in this game.

Venue:	Memorial Stadium	Referee:	Jean-Pierre Matheu		**Bristol Rugby**
Attendance:	5,662				**Northampton Saints**
Capacity:	12,000				
Occupancy:	47%				

Starting Line-Ups

○ Bristol Rugby		Northampton Saints ○
Going	15	Reihana (c)
Lima	14	Lamont
Higgitt	13	Clarke
Cox	12	Quinlan
Lemi	11	Cohen
Gray	10	Spencer
Rauluni	9	Robinson
Hilton	1	Smith
Regan	2	Thompson
Crompton	3	Noon
Winters	4	Gerard
Llewellyn	5	Dm Browne
Salter (c)	6	Fox
El Abd	7	Harding
Ward-Smith	8	Dn Browne

Replacements

Robinson	22	Rudd
Denney	21	Davies
	20	Howard
Lewis	19	Soden
Kohn	18	Lord
Clark	17	Budgen
Clarke	16	Richmond

Euro Challenge Cup Table

Team	P	W	D	L	F	A	BP	Pts
1 Narbonne	2	2	0	0	40	27	0	8
2 Northampton Saints	2	1	0	1	75	61	2	6
3 Bristol Rugby	2	1	0	1	49	48	2	6
4 Arix Viadana	2	0	0	2	39	67	1	1

Event Line

TC	Try Converted		P	Penalty
T	Try		DG	Drop Goal

Min	Score Progress		Event	Players
23	3	0	P	○ Gray
37	6	0	P	○ Gray
40	6	0	⬛	○ Harding
40	6	0	⇄	○ Denney > Gray
40	6	7	TC	○ Spencer / Reihana
Half time 6-7				
41	6	7	⇄	○ Robinson > Lima
42	11	7	T	○ Rauluni
47	18	7	TC	○ Lemi / Lemi
49	18	7	⇄	○ Budgen > Noon
53	18	7	⇄	○ Lewis > El Abd
54	18	7	⇄	○ Richmond > Thompson
54	18	7	⇄	○ Lord > Gerard
56	25	7	TC	○ Llewellyn / Lemi
61	25	7	⇄	○ Clarke > Hilton
61	25	7	⇄	○ Clark > Regan
61	25	7	⇄	○ Kohn > Llewellyn
64	25	7	⇄	○ El Abd > Ward-Smith
65	30	7	T	○ Lemi
67	30	7	⇄	○ Soden > Harding
67	30	7	⇄	○ Davies > Quinlan
69	30	14	TC	○ Reihana / Reihana
72	30	21	TC	○ Spencer / Reihana
74	30	21	⇄	○ Hilton > Crompton
80	33	21	P	○ Lemi
82	33	28	TC	○ Davies / Reihana
86	36	28	P	○ Lemi
Full time 36-28				

Scoring Statistics

○ Bristol Rugby			○ Northampton Saints		
by Situation	by Half		by Situation	by Half	

Bristol Rugby				Northampton Saints			
TC:	14	first:	17%	TC:	28	first:	25%
T:	10	second:	83%	T:	0	second:	75%
P:	12			P:	0		
DG:	0			DG:	0		

Saracens 28
Northampton Saints 22

Premiership Away Record vs Saracens					
Played	Won	Drawn	Lost	For	Against
9	**2**	**0**	**7**	**176**	**241**

Saints' current longest serving player Grant Seely returned to the squad for this game but his presence could not give Northampton a win, despite the visiting side scoring three tries to Saracens' one.

Two misplaced Saracens' kicks both came back with interest as the Northampton backs made use of some running space. All of the Saints backline were involved to hand an easy finish to scrum-half Mark Robinson, and the same sequence of events reoccurred just five minutes later to give Northampton a 14-nil lead.

▶ Did you know?

Prop Pat Barnard made his Saints debut against Saracens in this match.

It seemed like Saints would run away with the game, but Saracens then took advantage of a David Gerard sin-binning. Richard Haughton linked with Dan Scarbrough to cut the deficit to seven points. Two Glen Jackson penalties following one from Bruce Reihana which meant Saints' half-time lead was 13-17.

Jackson was forced time and time again to his boot as Saints' defence refused to let a Saracens player through. Pressure inevitably led to penalties and Jackson did not miss any of his chances. Disappointingly, the Saracens' fly-half added five penalties to his two in the first half to take the home side's total to 28.

Carlos Spencer who saved some blushes for Northampton, grabbing a try in the corner, and more importantly a bonus point for his side. But not for the first time this season, Saints had failed to capitalise of early good work.

Venue:	Vicarage Road		Referee:	Sean Davey - Season 05/06		**Saracens**
Attendance:	8,524		Matches:	4		**Northampton Saints**
Capacity:	20,000		Yellow Cards:	4		
Occupancy:	43%		Red Cards:	0		

Starting Line-Ups

○ Saracens		Northampton Saints ○
Scarbrough	15	Reihana (c)
Haughton	14	Lamont
Bartholomeusz	13	Clarke
Sorrell	12	Davies
Bailey	11	Rudd
Jackson	10	Spencer
Dickens	9	Robinson
Yates	1	Smith
Cairns	2	Richmond
Visagie	3	Noon
Raiwalui	4	Dm Browne
Fullarton	5	Gerard
Vyvyan (c)	6	Seely
Seymour	7	Fox
Skirving	8	Dn Browne

Replacements

Powell	22	Mallon
Russell	21	Quinlan
Bracken	20	Howard
Armitage	19	Harding
Chesney	18	Lord
Broster	17	Barnard
Kyriacou	16	Hartley

Match Stats

Tackles	73	45
Missed Tackles	15	8
Ball Carries	44	85
Metres	201	484
Defenders Beaten	7	15
Passes	48	101
Clean Breaks	2	11
Pens Conceded	9	19
Turnovers	8	12
Breakdowns Won	38	49
% Scrums Won	90%	88%
% Line-Outs Won	78%	75%

Event Line

TC	Try Converted		P	Penalty
T	Try		DG	Drop Goal

Min	Score Progress	Event	Players
5	0 — 7	TC	○ Robinson / Reihana
10	0 — 14	TC	○ Robinson / Reihana
21	0 — 14	▪	○ Gerard
24	7 — 14	TC	○ Scarbrough / Jackson
28	7 — 17	P	○ Reihana
32	10 — 17	P	○ Jackson
37	13 — 17	P	○ Jackson
Half time 13-17			
41	13 — 17	⇄	○ Barnard > Smith
42	16 — 17	P	○ Jackson
48	16 — 17	⇄	○ Quinlan > Davies
49	16 — 17	⇄	○ Bracken > Dickens
49	19 — 17	P	○ Jackson
52	19 — 17	⇄	○ Lord > Gerard
57	19 — 17	⇄	○ Chesney > Raiwalui
57	19 — 17	⇄	○ Broster > Yates
57	22 — 17	P	○ Jackson
60	22 — 17	⇄	○ Harding > Seely
68	25 — 17	P	○ Jackson
77	25 — 17	⇄	○ Yates > Visagie
77	25 — 17	▪	○ Lord
78	28 — 17	P	○ Jackson
80	28 — 22	T	○ Spencer
Full time 28-22			

Scoring Statistics

○ Saracens				○ Northampton Saints			
by Situation		by Half		by Situation		by Half	
▪ TC:	7	▪ first:	46%	▪ TC:	14	▪ first:	77%
▪ T:	0	second:	54%	▪ T:	5	second:	23%
▪ P:	21			▪ P:	3		
▪ DG:	0			▪ DG:	0		

Premiership Table

Team	P	W	D	L	F	A	BP	Pts
7 London Irish	6	3	0	3	128	120	4	16
8 Northampton Saints	6	2	0	4	97	136	3	11
9 Bath Rugby	6	2	0	4	109	144	2	10

Northampton Saints 13
London Wasps 21

Premiership Home Record vs London Wasps					
Played	Won	Drawn	Lost	For	Against
9	**5**	**0**	**4**	**180**	**184**

Memories of Saints' good run in October were fast being forgotten as they fell to their third defeat on the bounce.

▶ Did you know?

This was the first time Wasps' director of rugby Ian McGeechan has returned to Franklin's Gardens as an opposition coach since his departure to Scotland in 1999.

The sides were level at the break, with only two penalties each to show for good efforts from both teams. Wasps had opened up brightest, and could have scored had centre Ayoola Erinle held onto an inside pass from John Rudd to Bruce Reihana.

The Wasps' defence was immense as Saints came on the attack. Alex King had already kicked two goals for the London side, so Carlos Spencer chose to drop a goal to get Northampton on the scoreboard, and it seemed things were looking up when Wasps were reduced to 14 men following a yellow card for Rob Hoadley. With the advantage, Saints pressured for a score, but to no avail. Hoadley returned, and all Saints could add was a penalty to level the scores.

In the second half, the game remained on a knife-edge. Wasps had taken advantage of an injured Rudd to score in the corner. King added a penalty against the run of play and Wasps opened up an eight-point lead. Saints started to press for a score and chances were created but not finished. The cause looked lost until a moment of brilliance from Rhodri Davies slashed the lead to one point when he scored his debut home try. Spencer then went all out for the win. From his own 22, he chipped the chasing line and collected. However, his pass from the tackle went awry, leaving Hoadley to intercept and hold off Matt Lord to score. King converted and Saints were denied a bonus point.

Venue:	Franklin's Gardens	Referee:	Rob Debney - Season 05/06		**Northampton Saints**
Attendance:	13,585	Matches:	5		**London Wasps**
Capacity:	13,591	Yellow Cards:	4		
Occupancy:	100%	Red Cards:	0		

Starting Line-Ups

○ Northampton Saints		London Wasps ○
Reihana (c)	15	Voyce
Diggin	14	Sackey
Clarke	13	Erinle
Quinlan	12	Abbott
Rudd	11	Hoadley
Spencer	10	King
Robinson	9	Reddan
Budgen	1	Payne
Richmond	2	Ward
Barnard	3	Bracken
Gerard	4	Skivington
Dm Browne	5	Birkett
Fox	6	Hart (c)
Harding	7	Rees
Dn Browne	8	Lock

Replacements

Davies	22	Staunton
Vilk	21	Baxter
Howard	20	Fury
Lewitt	19	Dallaglio
Lord	18	Shaw
Harbut	17	McKenzie
Hartley	16	Gotting

Match Stats

Tackles	74	129
Missed Tackles	14	24
Ball Carries	124	74
Metres	777	495
Defenders Beaten	25	14
Passes	174	81
Clean Breaks	12	12
Pens Conceded	10	9
Turnovers	21	13
Breakdowns Won	90	59
% Scrums Won	100%	94%
% Line-Outs Won	77%	73%

Premiership Table

Team	P	W	D	L	F	A	BP	Pts
7 Saracens	6	3	0	3	152	137	4	16
8 Northampton Saints	7	2	0	5	110	157	3	11
9 Newcastle Falcons	7	1	1	5	127	144	4	10

Event Line

TC	Try Converted			P	Penalty
T	Try			DG	Drop Goal

Min	Score Progress		Event	Players
2	0	3	P	○ King
7	0	6	P	○ King
24	3	6	DG	○ Spencer
27	3	6	■	○ Hoadley
38	6	6	P	○ Reihana
Half time 6-6				
41	6	6	⇄	○ Lord > Gerard
45	6	6	⇄	○ Vilk > Diggin
46	6	6	⇄	○ McKenzie > Bracken
46	6	6	⇄	○ Shaw > Birkett
46	6	6	⇄	○ Dallaglio > Lock
54	6	11	T	○ Reddan
56	6	11	⇄	○ Davies > Rudd
65	6	11	⇄	○ Gotting > Ward
67	6	11	⇄	○ Harbut > Budgen
68	6	14	P	○ King
71	6	14	⇄	○ Lewitt > Browne
72	6	14	⇄	○ Hartley > Richmond
72	6	14	⇄	○ Baxter > Erinle
76	6	14	⇄	○ Howard > Robinson
77	13	14	TC	○ Davies / Reihana
78	13	21	TC	○ Hoadley / King
79	13	21	⇄	○ Staunton > Abbott
79	13	21	⇄	○ Fury > Reddan
Full time 13-21				

Scoring Statistics

○ Northampton Saints		○ London Wasps	
by Situation	by Half	by Situation	by Half

▶ TC:	7	▶ first:	46%
▶ T:	0	second:	54%
▶ P:	3		
DG:	3		

▶ TC:	7	▶ first:	29%
▶ T:	5	second:	71%
▶ P:	9		
DG:	0		

Leeds Tykes 28
Northampton Saints 25

Premiership Away Record vs Leeds Tykes					
Played	Won	Drawn	Lost	For	Against
5	**2**	**0**	**3**	**122**	**101**

After two disappointing losses, Saints wanted to make a good start against bottom-placed Leeds.

Gordon Ross had handed Leeds an early lead from a penalty, but centre Chris Jones handed the advantage away with a loose pass that fell to Spencer. He off-loaded the ball to Daniel Browne who then returned the favour for Spencer to score. Saints gained a second try through a crafty chip over the defence from Jon Clarke. Andy Vilk, making his first start of the season, collected the ball and ran over the whitewash to touch down.

▶ Did you know?

Andy Vilk's try was his first and only try in 22 first team appearances.

Just one minute after Vilk's score, Tykes' David Doherty tried a chip of his own and the bounce fell into the hands of full-back Roland De Marigny for an easy try. Chips were the order of the day and Leeds' second was gained similarly when Andre Snyman lobbed Browne to touch down. Spencer's sin-binning added to Saints' changing fortunes and a Gordon Ross conversion and penalty gave Tykes a 23-17 lead at half-time.

A penalty from Bruce Reihana in the 62nd minute made it anyone's game, but Leeds replied with the seemingly killer blow when replacement Tom Palmer crashed over after only three minutes on the field. Centre Seamus Mallon went over from a scrum set-piece to cut the lead to just three points. Reihana had the chance to level but, amid the boos from the crowd, sent a last penalty effort wide. Saints had one last chance to win the game from an attacking lineout but Leeds held firm to record their first GUINNESS PREMIERSHIP win of the season.

Venue:	Headingley Carnegie		Referee:	Martin Fox - Season 05/06		**Leeds Tykes**
Attendance:	4,564		Matches:	3		**Northampton Saints**
Capacity:	24,000		Yellow Cards:	4		
Occupancy:	19%		Red Cards:	0		

Starting Line-Ups

Leeds Tykes			Northampton Saints
De Marigny	15		Reihana (c)
Snyman	14		Rudd
Vickerman	13		Clarke
Jones	12		Quinlan
Doherty	11		Vilk
Ross	10		Spencer
Marshall	9		Robinson
Lensing	1		Budgen
Rawlinson	2		Richmond
Gerber	3		Barnard
Hooper (c)	4		Dm Browne
Morgan	5		Lord
Dunbar	6		Fox
Parks	7		Harding
Crane	8		Dn Browne

Replacements

McMillan	22		Davies
Palmer	21		Mallon
Care	20		Howard
Hyde	19		Lewitt
Reid	18		Gerard
Bulloch	17		Harbut
Cusack	16		Hartley

Match Stats

Tackles	115	102
Missed Tackles	10	8
Ball Carries	90	102
Metres	557	512
Defenders Beaten	10	10
Passes	169	124
Clean Breaks	6	2
Pens Conceded	13	11
Turnovers	17	14
Breakdowns Won	61	70
% Scrums Won	75%	100%
% Line-Outs Won	82%	85%

Premiership Table

Team	P	W	D	L	F	A	BP	Pts
9 Bath Rugby	8	2	1	5	141	184	2	12
10 Northampton Saints	8	2	0	6	135	185	4	12
11 Newcastle Falcons	8	1	1	6	145	171	4	10

Event Line

TC	Try Converted		P	Penalty
T	Try		DG	Drop Goal

Min	Score Progress		Event	Players
2	3	0	P	Ross
12	3	7	TC	Spencer / Reihana
17	6	7	P	Ross
20	6	10	P	Reihana
23	6	17	TC	Vilk / Reihana
25	13	17	TC	De Marigny / Ross
28	20	17	TC	Snyman / Ross
34	20	17		Spencer
34	20	17	⇄	Harbut > Budgen
36	23	17	P	Ross
37	23	17	⇄	Davies > Quinlan
40	23	17	⇄	Budgen > Harbut
Half time 23-17				
46	23	17	⇄	Howard > Robinson
62	23	17	⇄	Hyde > Dunbar
62	23	17	⇄	Palmer > Parks
62	23	20	P	Reihana
65	28	20	T	Palmer
67	28	20	⇄	Lewitt > Harding
67	28	20	⇄	Mallon > Clarke
70	28	25	T	Mallon
71	28	25	⇄	Gerard > Browne
71	28	25	⇄	Harbut > Budgen
Full time 28-25				

Scoring Statistics

Leeds Tykes

by Situation — by Half

TC:	14
T:	5
P:	9
DG:	0

first:	82%
second:	18%

Northampton Saints

by Situation — by Half

TC:	14
T:	5
P:	6
DG:	0

first:	68%
second:	32%

Northampton Saints 21
Worcester Warriors 22

Premiership Home Record vs Worcester Warriors					
Played	Won	Drawn	Lost	For	Against
2	0	0	2	27	39

Former Saint Shane Drahm was Worcester's hero, scoring all of their points in this see-saw battle.

The Aussie fly-half opened his scoring spree in the sixth minute, supporting Thomas Lombard when the centre swept through a hole in the defence. With a superb touchline conversion, Drahm gave Worcester a seven-point lead. Three points were later added, following a ruled out touchdown from Thinus Delport.

Now 10 points down, Saints eventually shifted up a gear. Bruce Reihana took three points when Saints could not find the Warriors' line. The balance of play began to shift slightly in the home side's favour, and when Darren Fox was pushed over the line, Saints were right back in the game. A yellow card for Kai Horstmann a minute earlier had helped the Saints with their efforts. Ten minutes of sin-binning followed when Seamus Mallon and Drew Hickey were carded for persistent offside and killing the ball. The half ended 13-16 with only 27 players on the field.

▶ Did you know?

Saints did not win any of their games in November – this was their fourth defeat in as many games.

In the second half, Saints dominated the play. Carlos Spencer made magical breaks and created a try for man of the match Rhodri Davies. With Saints now ahead, they should have gone for the jugular. Sadly, all they had to show for their continued dominance was one Reihana penalty.

At 21-16, Northampton still looked in control, but two more penalties from Drahm gave Worcester a slender lead. A red card for Horstmann gave Reihana a chance to win the game, but his effort sailed wide and the Warriors claimed the points.

Venue:	Franklin's Gardens	Referee:	Wayne Barnes - Season 05/06	**Northampton Saints**
Attendance:	12,481	Matches:	1	**Worcester Warriors**
Capacity:	13,591	Yellow Cards:	1	
Occupancy:	92%	Red Cards:	0	

Starting Line-Ups

○ Northampton Saints		Worcester Warriors ○
Reihana (c)	15	Le Roux
Clarke	14	Havili
Mallon	13	Rasmussen
Davies	12	Lombard
Cohen	11	Delport
Spencer	10	Drahm
Howard	9	Gomarsall
Budgen	1	Windo (c)
Richmond	2	C Fortey
Barnard	3	Taumoepeau
Dm Browne	4	Murphy
Lord	5	Gillies
Lewitt	6	Horstmann
Fox	7	Tu'amoeloa
Dn Browne	8	Hickey

Replacements

Myring	22	Hinshelwood
Vilk	21	Brown
Robinson	20	Powell
Harding	19	Mason
Gerard	18	O'Donoghue
Harbut	17	L Fortey
Hartley	16	Hickie

Match Stats

Tackles	62	84
Missed Tackles	10	25
Ball Carries	89	70
Metres	559	375
Defenders Beaten	26	10
Passes	108	81
Clean Breaks	10	8
Pens Conceded	15	11
Turnovers	8	12
Breakdowns Won	67	56
% Scrums Won	75%	88%
% Line-Outs Won	67%	88%

Premiership Table

Team	P	W	D	L	F	A	BP	Pts
9 Bath Rugby	9	2	1	6	153	200	3	13
10 Northampton Saints	9	2	0	7	156	207	5	13
11 Newcastle Falcons	8	1	1	6	145	171	4	10

Event Line

TC	Try Converted		P	Penalty
T	Try		DG	Drop Goal

Min	Score Progress		Event	Players
7	0	7	TC	○ Drahm / Drahm
14	0	10	P	○ Drahm
18	3	10	P	○ Reihana
24	3	13	P	○ Drahm
31	3	13	▧	○ Horstmann
32	10	13	TC	○ Fox / Reihana
36	10	13	▧	○ Mallon
37	10	16	P	○ Drahm
40	10	16	▧	○ Hickey
40	13	16	P	○ Reihana
Half time 13-16				
48	18	16	T	○ Davies
52	18	16	⇄	○ Harbut > Budgen
54	18	16	⇄	○ Harding > Fox
54	18	16	⇄	○ Robinson > Howard
57	18	16	⇄	○ Powell > Gomarsall
58	18	16	⇄	○ Vilk > Mallon
60	18	16	⇄	○ O'Donoghue > Murphy
60	18	16	⇄	○ Hickie > Fortey
60	21	16	P	○ Reihana
63	21	19	P	○ Drahm
66	21	19	⇄	○ Hartley > Richmond
69	21	22	P	○ Drahm
70	21	22	⇄	○ Budgen > Barnard
73	21	22	⇄	○ Gerard > Browne
80	21	22	■	○ Horstmann
Full time 21-22				

Scoring Statistics

○ Northampton Saints

by Situation — by Half

▶ TC:	7	▶ first: 62%
▶ T:	5	second: 38%
▶ P:	9	
DG:	0	

○ Worcester Warriors

by Situation — by Half

▶ TC:	7	▶ first: 73%
▶ T:	0	second: 27%
▶ P:	15	
DG:	0	

Leicester Tigers 29
Northampton Saints 16

Saints must have thought revenge was in the offing when they racked up an 11-point lead in the first half of this Powergen Cup pool decider.

Within five minutes, Mark Robinson gave the visitors a perfect start, dropping on a hack ahead from John Rudd. Points on the scoreboard were already a change from the previous meeting. As ever, in the hotly contested derby, tempers flared. Alex Moreno was penalised for fighting with Ben Cohen, and Bruce Reihana punished the indiscipline to create an eight-nil lead. Another penalty meant Saints led 11-0, and this was how it looked like heading into half-time.

If Saints had made it to the break without conceding, the match could have ended very differently. However Leicester showed their resolve with a try just before half-time from Leon Lloyd. Andy Goode converted to make the score 7-11.

▶ Did you know?

This was the only game centre Jon Clarke missed all season as he was laid up in bed with flu.

Tigers began the second half with vigour and Ollie Smith came close to scoring straight away. Instead, a penalty was earned and Ben Kay earned his team five points when he drove over from the resulting lineout.

Carlos Spencer made sure the lead was short-lived when he claimed a loose kick-off, and chipped into space to give John Rudd an immediate reply for Saints. But rather than give Saints a platform to victory, the try spurned on the Tigers and they found another gear. Shane Jennings pounced on a charge-down from Spencer's kick to regain Leicester's lead, and then Leon Lloyd touched down a second. The hosts were now 10 points ahead.

Even though Saints threw everything at Leicester, then could not manage another score. Their hopes of a Cardiff final had disappeared and the game ended 26-16.

Venue:	Welford Road	Referee:	Chris White
Attendance:	11,072		
Capacity:	16,815		
Occupancy:	66%		

Leicester Tigers
Northampton Saints

Starting Line-Ups

○ Leicester Tigers		Northampton Saints ○
Vesty	15	Reihana (c)
Lloyd	14	Lamont
Smith	13	Cohen
Cornwell	12	Davies
Murphy	11	Rudd
Goode	10	Spencer
Ellis	9	Robinson
Holford	1	Budgen
Chuter	2	Thompson
Moreno	3	Barnard
Deacon	4	Dm Browne
Kay	5	Gerard
Deacon	6	Lewitt
Jennings	7	Harding
Corry (c)	8	Dn Browne

Replacements

Rabeni	22	Mallon
Hipkiss	21	Myring
Cole	20	Howard
Abraham	19	Fox
Hamilton	18	Seely
Young	17	Noon
Buckland	16	Hartley

Event Line

TC	Try Converted	P	Penalty
T	Try	DG	Drop Goal

Min	Score Progress		Event	Players
5	0	5	T	○ Robinson
8	0	8	P	○ Reihana
38	0	11	P	○ Reihana
40	7	11	TC	○ Lloyd / Goode
Half time 7-11				
45	14	11	TC	○ Kay / Goode
46	14	11	⇄	○ Rabeni > Vesty
48	14	11	⇄	○ Hartley > Thompson
48	14	16	T	○ Rudd
55	19	16	T	○ Jennings
58	19	16	⇄	○ Fox > Harding
60	19	16	⇄	○ Abraham > Jennings
66	19	16	⇄	○ Hamilton > Deacon
70	26	16	TC	○ Lloyd / Goode
71	26	16	⇄	○ Seely > Gerard
71	26	16	⇄	○ Howard > Robinson
72	26	16	⇄	○ Noon > Barnard
73	26	16	⇄	○ Hipkiss > Cornwell
73	26	16	⇄	○ Cole > Ellis
74	26	16	⇄	○ Buckland > Chuter
76	26	16	⇄	○ > Moreno
78	29	16	P	○ Goode
Full time 29-16				

Match Stats

Tackles	100	62
Missed Tackles	13	8
Ball Carries	70	85
Metres	378	368
Defenders Beaten	8	12
Passes	70	122
Clean Breaks	6	5
Pens Conceded	10	14
Turnovers	13	9
Breakdowns Won	58	67
% Scrums Won	100%	92%
% Line-Outs Won	100%	71%

Scoring Statistics

○ Leicester Tigers

by Situation   by Half

■ TC:	21	■ first:	24%
■ T:	5	second:	76%
■ P:	3		
DG:	0		

○ Northampton Saints

by Situation   by Half

■ TC:	0	■ first:	69%
■ T:	10	second:	31%
■ P:	6		
DG:	0		

Powergen Cup Table

Team	P	W	D	L	F	A	BP	Pts
1 Leicester Tigers	3	2	0	1	86	56	2	10
2 Northampton Saints	3	2	0	1	70	43	1	9
3 Newport Gwent Dragons	3	2	0	1	64	57	0	8
4 Worcester Warriors	3	0	0	3	33	97	0	0

Northampton Saints 32
Narbonne 20

Saints' return to Europe was a welcome change as they got back to winning ways against tough French outfit Narbonne.

Carlos Spencer was the architect as Northampton gained their first win in six. His clever chip to the corner on 12 minutes put Saints on the offensive and a couple of scrums later No 8 Daniel Browne crossed unopposed for his first competitive try for the side.

Narbonne, who had earlier wasted a four-to-one overlap, were unlucky not to be given a try in the 25th minute when it was disallowed for a knock-on. Narbonne were getting the edge in the forwards, but Spencer still managed to weave magic from behind the ruck when he sped down the blindside to create a scoring move for Sam Harding.

▶ **Did you know?**

This was the second time Saints had played Narbonne after being beaten 22-23 at Franklin's Gardens in the European Shield back in 1997.

Unsurprisingly, Narbonne got themselves on the scoresheet with their pack. Prop Arnaud Martinez took advantage of a good lineout maul to force himself over around the fringes. Saints were still in command, however, and Bruce Reihana added a penalty to make a first half lead of 13.

Spencer again was involved in the second half when two quick inside passes made space for Reihana to score. A conversion made the score a healthy 27-7.

Yellow cards had been given with unwanted regularity for Saints this season, and Johnny Howard's in the 52nd minute gave Narbonne extra manpower and ultimately six points. This was never going to be enough and when Howard returned, he made amends to handle Rhodri Davies's pass and to go over for the fourth try and a bonus point. With the game won, Saints handed Narbonne a consolation when hooker Thibaut Algret touched down in injury time.

Venue:	Franklin's Gardens	Referee:	Carlo Damasco

Attendance: 11,572
Capacity: 13,591
Occupancy: 85%

Northampton Saints
Narbonne

Starting Line-Ups

○ Northampton Saints		Narbonne ○
Reihana (c)	15	Nadau
Lamont	14	Negre-Gautier
Clarke	13	Desbrosse
Davies	12	Mazars
Cohen	11	Patey
Spencer	10	Rosalen
Robinson	9	Mahe
Budgen	1	Martinez
Thompson	2	Rofes
Noon	3	Tournaire
Dm Browne	4	Springgay (c)
Gerard	5	Sierra
Lewitt	6	Hunter
Harding	7	Haare
Dn Browne	8	Bedes

Replacements

Myring	22	Benassis
Rudd	21	Ruiz
Howard	20	Seron
Fox	19	Tomiki
Beattie	18	Martinez
Smith	17	Algret
Richmond	16	Hooper

Euro Challenge Cup Table

Team	P	W	D	L	F	A	BP	Pts
1 Northampton Saints	3	2	0	1	107	81	3	11
2 Bristol Rugby	3	2	0	1	88	71	3	11
3 Narbonne	3	2	0	1	60	59	0	8
4 Arix Viadana	3	0	0	3	62	106	1	1

Event Line

TC	Try Converted			P	Penalty
T	Try			DG	Drop Goal

Min	Score Progress		Event	Players
2	3	0	P	○ Reihana
13	10	0	TC	○ Browne / Reihana
33	17	0	TC	○ Harding / Reihana
37	17	7	TC	○ Martinez / Rosalen
40	17	7	⇄	○ Tomiki > Haare
40	20	7	P	○ Reihana
Half time 20-7				
41	20	7	⇄	○ Haare > Tomiki
41	20	7	⇄	○ Smith > Budgen
41	20	7	⇄	○ Howard > Robinson
47	20	7	⇄	○ Hooper > Tournaire
50	27	7	TC	○ Reihana / Reihana
51	27	7	⇄	○ Tomiki > Haare
52	27	7	▣	○ Howard
53	27	10	P	○ Rosalen
58	27	13	P	○ Rosalen
60	27	13	⇄	○ Budgen > Noon
64	27	13	⇄	○ Fox > Harding
68	27	13	⇄	○ Richmond > Thompson
70	27	13	⇄	○ Martinez > Bedes
70	27	13	⇄	○ Seron > Mahe
70	27	13	⇄	○ Algret > Rofes
70	27	13	⇄	○ Ruiz > Rosalen
74	27	13	⇄	○ Beattie > Gerard
76	32	13	T	○ Howard
77	32	13	⇄	○ Rudd > Lamont
79	32	13	⇄	○ Benassis > Desbrosse
81	32	13	⇄	○ Myring > Spencer
81	32	20	TC	○ Algret / Ruiz
Full time 32-20				

Scoring Statistics

○ Northampton Saints

by Situation		by Half	
▶ TC:	21	▶ first:	63%
▶ T:	5	second:	38%
▶ P:	6		
DG:	0		

○ Narbonne

by Situation		by Half	
▶ TC:	14	▶ first:	35%
▶ T:	0	second:	65%
▶ P:	6		
DG:	0		

Narbonne 7
Northampton Saints 22

There was no danger of Carlos Spencer issuing the same damage as he had the week before when he was ruled out of this fixture due to a hand injury. Academy product Luke Myring stepped into the former All Blacks' boots to make his first start to help Saints prevail for the second time over Narbonne.

Saints began where they had left off when wing John Rudd scored in the second minute. Swirling winds meant kicking was nigh impossible, but Bruce Reihana managed to overcome the problems by slotting over a penalty to give Northampton an early 8-0 lead. Steve Thompson saw yellow for pulling down a player in the lineout, but it did not affect 14-man Saints. Braving the conditions, Reihana added two more penalties and Northampton had a 14-point lead.

Franck Tournaire was shepherded over the line for Narbonne with a maul led by Marco Bortolami. The French side threatened before half-time, but could not emulate their previous efforts and the score stayed at 7-14.

The second half was more notable for cards than points. Heineken Cup winner Christian Labit was first shown the yellow card then the red in a second half that saw Narbonne's discipline crumble. He was joined on the sidelines by Tournaire, who was sin-binned in the 79th minute, leaving Narbonne with just 13-men to finish.

Reihana sent two penalties over in the second half to end the match 7-22, giving Saints a vital win, and leaving them confident of qualifying from their European Challenge Cup group.

▶ Did you know?

This was the second time Saints had won in France in a European competition having beat Agen in the Heineken Cup in 2003.

40

Venue:	Parc des Sports	Referee:	Hugh Watkins

Attendance: 9,000
Capacity: 10,000
Occupancy: 90%

Narbonne
Northampton Saints

Starting Line-Ups

Narbonne		Northampton Saints
Nadau	15	Reihana (c)
Negre-Gautier	14	Rudd
Benassis	13	Clarke
Mazars	12	Quinlan
Patey	11	Cohen
Rosalen	10	Myring
Mahe	9	Howard
Martinez	1	Smith
Rofes	2	Thompson
Tournaire	3	Noon
Springgay	4	Dm Browne
Bortolami (c)	5	Gerard
Tomiki	6	Lewitt
Haare	7	Harding
Labit	8	Dn Browne

Replacements

Desbrosse	22	Budgen
Ruiz	21	Diggin
Balue	20	Hartley
Hunter	19	Lord
Hooper	18	Fox
Bisaro	17	
Algret	16	Richmond

Euro Challenge Cup Table

Team	P	W	D	L	F	A	BP	Pts
1 Bristol Rugby	4	3	0	1	177	76	4	16
2 Northampton Saints	4	3	0	1	129	88	3	15
3 Narbonne	4	2	0	2	67	81	0	8
4 Arix Viadana	4	0	0	4	67	195	1	1

Event Line

TC	Try Converted		P	Penalty
T	Try		DG	Drop Goal

Min	Score Progress		Event	Players
2	0	5	T	O Rudd
6	0	8	P	O Reihana
16	0	11	P	O Reihana
21	0	11		O Thompson
24	0	11	⇄	O Richmond > Harding
30	0	14	P	O Reihana
32	0	14	⇄	O Harding > Richmond
34	7	14	TC	O Tournaire / Rosalen
Half time 7-14				
41	7	14	⇄	O Hooper > Tournaire
41	7	14	⇄	O Bisaro > Tomiki
48	7	17	P	O Reihana
51	7	17		O Labit
55	7	17	⇄	O Budgen > Noon
55	7	17	⇄	O Hunter > Haare
58	7	17	⇄	O Fox > Harding
59	7	22	T	O Cohen
63	7	22	⇄	O Balue > Mahe
66	7	22	⇄	O Lord > Gerard
68	7	22	⇄	O Desbrosse > Benassis
68	7	22	⇄	O Ruiz > Rosalen
68	7	22	⇄	O Hartley > Smith
71	7	22	⇄	O Tournaire > Martinez
76	7	22	⇄	O Diggin > Quinlan
78	7	22	■	O Labit
79	7	22		O Tournaire
Full time 7-22				

Scoring Statistics

Narbonne				Northampton Saints			
by Situation		by Half		by Situation		by Half	

Narbonne			Northampton Saints		
TC:	7	first: 100%	TC:	0	first: 64%
T:	0	second: 0%	T:	10	second: 36%
P:	0		P:	12	
DG:	0		DG:	0	

Sale Sharks 34
Northampton Saints 14

Premiership Away Record vs Sale Sharks					
Played	Won	Drawn	Lost	For	Against
9	**2**	**1**	**6**	**204**	**263**

Saints travelled to Manchester missing talisman Ben Cohen, who had been ruled out for four weeks with a fractured cheekbone.

They also missed injured Carlos Spender as Saints failed to cope with Sale's attack, commanded by Charlie Hodgson who put Sharks ahead from a penalty. His cross-field kick was then caught by Chris Mayor who charged overs. Bruce Reihana gained Saints' first points after Paul Diggin forced an infringement, which was followed by a second penalty conversion seven minutes later. Two more penalties were traded in the half, which ended 17-9.

In the second period, Hodgson was again involved as he planted Sale deep in Northampton territory from a penalty. The Sharks, who were a man up due to Damien Browne's sin-binning, sent Ignacio Fernandez Lobbe in for a score. Hodgson duly converted and Sale were a comfortable 15 points ahead. Saints were holding out and a mistake from Hodgson gave them a chance to clear. Only a couple of minutes later, his opposite number Luke Myring finished off a phase involving Darren Fox, Reihana, John Rudd and Rhodri Davies.

Hodgson gave his forwards a fantastic platform on the hour. They made the most of their position near the Saints' line and replacement hooker Sebastian Bruno was underneath the pile of bodies that were pushed over. The home side survived a late flurry of attack from Northampton as they searched for some consolation, and showed why they were leading the way in the GUINNESS PREMIERSHIP.

▶ Did you know?

Luke Myring's try was his first for Northampton Saints.

Venue:	Edgeley Park	Referee:	Dave Pearson - Season 05/06		Sale Sharks
Attendance:	10,641	Matches:	7		Northampton Saints
Capacity:	10,641	Yellow Cards:	15		
Occupancy:	100%	Red Cards:	2		

Starting Line-Ups

Sale Sharks			Northampton Saints
Robinson (c)	15		Reihana (c)
Cueto	14		Rudd
Taylor	13		Clarke
Todd	12		Davies
Mayor	11		Diggin
Hodgson	10		Myring
Courrent	9		Howard
Sheridan	1		Smith
Titterrell	2		Richmond
Stewart	3		Barnard
Fernandez Lobbe	4		Dm Browne
Jones	5		Lord
White	6		Lewitt
Lund	7		Fox
Chabal	8		Dn Browne

Replacements

Foden	22	Vilk
Wigglesworth	21	Robinson
Day	20	Easter
Bonner-Evans	19	Harding
Coutts	18	Rae
Turner	17	Budgen
Bruno	16	Hartley

Match Stats

	Sale	Northampton
Tackles	111	78
Missed Tackles	11	13
Ball Carries	71	93
Metres	310	496
Defenders Beaten	13	11
Passes	82	78
Clean Breaks	3	8
Pens Conceded	11	12
Turnovers	11	12
Breakdowns Won	54	77
% Scrums Won	100%	63%
% Line-Outs Won	100%	75%

Event Line

TC	Try Converted		P	Penalty
T	Try		DG	Drop Goal

Min	Score Progress		Event	Players
3	0	0	⇄	Budgen > Barnard
7	3	0	P	Hodgson
10	8	0	T	Mayor
13	11	0	P	Hodgson
16	14	0	P	Hodgson
19	14	3	P	Reihana
25	14	6	P	Reihana
30	17	6	P	Hodgson
37	17	6	■	Todd
38	17	9	P	Reihana

Half time 17-9

41	17	9	⇄	Wigglesworth > Courrent
48	17	9	■	Browne
49	24	9	TC	Fernandez Lobbe / Hodgson
54	24	9	⇄	Turner > Stewart
56	24	9	⇄	Hartley > Richmond
58	24	14	T	Myring
59	24	14	⇄	Harding > Fox
62	24	14	⇄	Bruno > Titterrell
62	24	14	⇄	Bonner-Evans > Chabal
62	24	14	⇄	Day > Jones
63	27	14	P	Hodgson
64	27	14	⇄	Robinson > Howard
69	34	14	TC	Bruno / Hodgson
71	34	14	⇄	Foden > Taylor
74	34	14	⇄	Easter > Lewitt
74	34	14	⇄	Rae > Lord
75	34	14	■	Mayor
79	34	14	⇄	Vilk > Davies

Full time 34-14

Scoring Statistics

Sale Sharks

by Situation | by Half

▶ TC:	14	▶ first:	50%
▶ T:	5	second:	50%
▶ P:	15		
DG:	0		

Northampton Saints

by Situation | by Half

▶ TC:	0	▶ first:	64%
▶ T:	5	second:	36%
▶ P:	9		
DG:	0		

Premiership Table

Team	P	W	D	L	F	A	BP	Pts
10 Newcastle Falcons	9	2	1	6	162	186	4	14
11 Northampton Saints	10	2	0	8	170	241	5	13
12 Leeds Tykes	9	2	0	7	146	244	2	10

Northampton Saints 29
Bristol Rugby 22

Premiership Home Record vs Bristol Rugby					
Played	Won	Drawn	Lost	For	Against
6	**4**	**0**	**2**	**170**	**99**

Bristol's David Lemi was again causing problems for Saints, but this time it was Northampton who came out on top.

The visitors pressurised from the off through Gareth Llewelyn and Dave Hilton. Lemi made inroads up the field, rounding Steve Thompson, but it was his loose pass that handed the ball to Jon Clarke who ran 30 metres to score. Lemi went about redeeming his mistake, first charging down a kick, and then latching onto Shaun Perry's break. He finished both times to claim two tries. Aside from a Bruce Reihana penalty, everything seemed to be going Bristol's way.

▶ Did you know?

One of Saints' two drop goals for the entire 2005/06 season was kicked during this game.

Better handling may have produced more points for Bristol but their poor execution cost them and Reihana claimed the lead with another penalty. A series of phases begun by Grant Seely – celebrating his 250th appearance – ended with a Bristol infringement. Reihana added three points to take a 16-12 half-time lead.

Bristol used their forwards to great effect in the second half when they drove over a driving maul. Darren Crompton was awarded the try, edging the away side ahead. Carlos Spencer levelled the scores with an impressive 40-metre drop-goal.

Jason Strange claimed back the lead with a penalty, but the match was won and lost when Chris Budgen was mauled over the Bristol line. Reihana added a conversion and a penalty. It was an end Saints' run of five league defeats – a perfect start to the New Year.

Venue:	Franklin s Gardens	Referee:	Martin Fox - Season 05/06
Attendance:	13,485	Matches:	5
Capacity:	13,591	Yellow Cards:	7
Occupancy:	99%	Red Cards:	0

Northampton Saints
Bristol Rugby

Starting Line-Ups

○ Northampton Saints		Bristol Rugby ○
Reihana (c)	15	Stortoni
Rudd	14	Robinson
Clarke	13	Lima
Vilk	12	Cox
Diggin	11	Lemi
Spencer	10	Strange
Howard	9	Perry
Smith	1	Hilton
Thompson	2	Regan
Budgen	3	Crompton
Dm Browne	4	Winters
Lord	5	Llewellyn
Seely	6	Salter (c)
Lewitt	7	El Abd
Dn Browne	8	Ward-Smith

Replacements

Patston	22	Higgitt
Robinson	21	Hayes
Tupai	20	Rauluni
Harding	19	Lewis
Gerard	18	Sambucetti
Noon	17	Nelson
Hartley	16	Irish

Match Stats

Tackles	89	101
Missed Tackles	14	22
Ball Carries	99	80
Metres	463	451
Defenders Beaten	22	14
Passes	94	100
Clean Breaks	3	8
Pens Conceded	10	16
Turnovers	14	14
Breakdowns Won	81	57
% Scrums Won	93%	100%
% Line-Outs Won	77%	89%

Premiership Table

Team	P	W	D	L	F	A	BP	Pts
10 Bath Rugby	10	3	1	6	189	218	3	17
11 Northampton Saints	11	3	0	8	199	263	5	17
12 Leeds Tykes	11	2	0	9	163	288	3	11

Event Line

TC	Try Converted		P	Penalty
T	Try		DG	Drop Goal

Min	Score Progress		Event	Players
2	7	0	TC	○ Clarke / Reihana
7	7	5	T	○ Lemi
9	7	12	TC	○ Lemi / Strange
14	10	12	P	○ Reihana
21	10	12	⇄	○ Higgitt > Robinson
21	13	12	P	○ Reihana
32	13	12	⇄	○ Robinson > Higgitt
40	16	12	P	○ Reihana
Half time 16-12				
41	16	12	⇄	○ Robinson > Howard
43	16	19	TC	○ Crompton / Strange
50	19	19	DG	○ Spencer
53	19	19	⇄	○ Irish > Crompton
57	19	22	P	○ Strange
58	19	22	⇄	○ Tupai > Browne
65	19	22	⇄	○ Crompton > Hilton
67	19	22	⇄	○ Lewis > Salter
73	19	22	⇄	○ Harding > Lewitt
73	19	22	⇄	○ Hartley > Smith
74	19	22	▪	○ Ward-Smith
75	26	22	TC	○ Budgen / Reihana
77	26	22	⇄	○ Gerard > Seely
77	26	22	⇄	○ Noon > Budgen
80	29	22	P	○ Reihana
Full time 29-22				

Scoring Statistics

○ Northampton Saints

by Situation   by Half

► TC:	14	► first:	55%
► T:	0	second:	45%
► P:	12		
DG:	3		

○ Bristol Rugby

by Situation   by Half

► TC:	14	► first:	55%
► T:	5	second:	45%
► P:	3		
DG:	0		

Worcester Warriors 11
Northampton Saints 15

Premiership Away Record vs Worcester Warriors					
Played	Won	Drawn	Lost	For	Against
2	**1**	**0**	**1**	**34**	**32**

Northampton Saints' transformation into a winning side was becoming more apparent as they edged this encounter with Worcester.

In the heavy conditions, Worcester decided to concentrate on the set piece. It nearly paid dividends in the 10th minute but defence from Bruce Reihana and Mark Robinson kept Aisea Havili at bay. From a resulting penalty, however, James Brown kicked the hosts three points ahead.

Saints decided to attack through the centres. Robbie Kydd, who recently signed for Northampton after a long injury layoff, saw early action in his debut for the club. He combined well with his centre partner Jon Clarke who went close twice and there was some lovely interplay between the backs. Surprisingly, all Saints had to show for their endeavour was a Reihana penalty.

▶ Did you know?

Robbie Kydd lasted for 63 minutes in this game – not bad for a guy who had not played rugby for nine months.

Northampton took the initiative in the second half. Various Worcester kicks were returned with intent, noticeably by the returning Ben Cohen, who wore a partial mask over his cheekbone fracture site. It was the England winger who helped create space by drawing attention across the field to the right. Reihana exploited the left, and sent his co-captain Steve Thompson over. A much quieter Shane Drahm replied with his first penalty of the game, but it only seemed to provoke Saints into action. Clarke beat four tackles before Carlos Spencer chipped into the created space for Cohen to cap off a triumphant return. Drahm put Kai Horstmann over for a late try, but it was not enough and Saints recorded a priceless win.

Venue:	Sixways		Referee:	Chris White - Season 05/06
Attendance:	9,726		Matches:	5
Capacity:	9,726		Yellow Cards:	0
Occupancy:	100%		Red Cards:	0

Worcester Warriors
Northampton Saints

Starting Line-Ups

Worcester Warriors		Northampton Saints
Delport	15	Reihana (c)
Havili	14	Lamont
Rasmussen	13	Clarke
Lombard	12	Kydd
Tucker	11	Rudd
Brown	10	Spencer
Powell	9	Robinson
Windo (c)	1	Smith
C Fortey	2	Thompson
Taumoepeau	3	Budgen
Murphy	4	Dm Browne
Gillies	5	Lord
Horstmann	6	Tupai
Tu'amoheloa	7	Lewitt
Hickey	8	Dn Browne

Replacements

Whatling	22	Cohen
Drahm	21	Vilk
Gomarsall	20	Howard
Harding	19	Seely
O'Donoghue	18	Gerard
L Fortey	17	Emms
Hickey	16	Hartley

Event Line

TC	Try Converted		P	Penalty
T	Try		DG	Drop Goal

Min	Score Progress		Event	Players
10	3	0	P	O Brown
31	3	0	⇄	O Hickie > Fortey
32	3	3	P	O Reihana
35	3	3	⇄	O Cohen > Rudd
Half time 3-3				
41	3	3	⇄	O Fortey > Hickie
51	3	3	⇄	O Drahm > Brown
59	3	3	⇄	O Seely > Browne
59	3	3	⇄	O O'Donoghue > Murphy
59	3	3	⇄	O Gerard > Lord
59	3	3	⇄	O Emms > Smith
61	3	8	T	O Thompson
63	3	8	⇄	O Vilk > Kydd
63	3	8	⇄	O Gomarsall > Powell
65	6	8	P	O Drahm
66	6	15	TC	O Cohen / Spencer
68	6	15	⇄	O Harding > Tu'amoheloa
73	6	15	⇄	O Fortey > Taumoepeau
74	11	15	T	O Horstmann
76	11	15	⇄	O Hartley > Budgen
Full time 11-15				

Match Stats

Tackles	154	92
Missed Tackles	13	10
Ball Carries	73	145
Metres	350	472
Defenders Beaten	8	13
Passes	90	125
Clean Breaks	9	4
Pens Conceded	5	10
Turnovers	11	9
Breakdowns Won	59	112
% Scrums Won	100%	91%
% Line-Outs Won	100%	80%

Scoring Statistics

Worcester Warriors			
by Situation		by Half	
TC:	0	first:	27%
T:	5	second:	73%
P:	6		
DG:	0		

Northampton Saints			
by Situation		by Half	
TC:	7	first:	20%
T:	5	second:	80%
P:	3		
DG:	0		

Premiership Table

Team	P	W	D	L	F	A	BP	Pts
9 Newcastle Falcons	11	4	1	6	196	211	4	22
10 Northampton Saints	12	4	0	8	214	274	5	21
11 Bath Rugby	11	3	1	7	198	239	3	17

Northampton Saints 45
Bristol Rugby 8

In total contrast to the two previous tightly fought encounters this season, Saints took control early in the match.

Smith's break helped Sam Harding score the first of his tries after two minutes, then a second was added just seven minutes later. The ball was spun from wing to wing and back again as almost the whole back line combined to put Harding over for his brace.

Carlos Spencer, who was controlling play from 10, was causing problems with his imagination and skill, and his endeavour was rewarded with a try after 25 minutes. He collected a loose kick from Jake Rauluni and, finding only space ahead of him, ran 40 metres to score.

The initial scoring spree slowed until the 65th minute, when Mark Robinson opened the flood gates. Once again it was Spencer who was the creator, putting the ball into the hands of a rampaging Ben Cohen, who made ground before Harding sent Robinson in for the fourth try.

In the next 10 minutes, Ben Cohen and Johnny Howard added three more scores, the former grabbing a brace and his 10th try of the season. Bristol had been torn to shreds and had only managed three points to Saints' 45.

They did manage to scrape one try back through Mariano Sambucetti, maybe taking the gloss off the win slightly. Saints were happy with their bonus point win though, and when Viadana conceded their fixture the following week, qualification to the next round was complete.

▶ Did you know?

This game was former Lions and Scotland prop Tom Smith's 100th for the club.

Venue:	Franklin's Gardens	Referee:	Eric Darriere

Attendance: 12,227
Capacity: 13,591
Occupancy: 90%

Northampton Saints
Bristol Rugby

Starting Line-Ups

⊙ Northampton Saints		Bristol Rugby ⊙
Reihana	15	Going
Lamont	14	Robinson
Clarke	13	Denney
Myring	12	Contepomi
Cohen	11	Marsden
Spencer	10	Hayes
Robinson	9	Rauluni
Smith	1	Irish
Thompson (c)	2	Nelson
Budgen	3	Thompson
Dm Browne	4	Sambucetti
Lord	5	Hodge
Lewitt	6	Martin-Redman
Harding	7	Short (c)
Dn Browne	8	Lewis

Replacements

Rudd	22	Gray
Howard	21	Higgitt
Soden	20	El Abd
Fox	19	Llewellyn
Gerard	18	Rospide
Sturgess	17	Clark
Hartley	16	Clarke

Event Line

TC	Try Converted		P	Penalty
T	Try		DG	Drop Goal

Min	Score Progress		Event	Players
2	7	0	TC	⊙ Harding / Reihana
5	7	3	P	⊙ Hayes
8	14	3	TC	⊙ Harding / Reihana
22	14	3	⇄	⊙ Rudd > Myring
24	19	3	T	⊙ Spencer
40	19	3	⇄	⊙ Howard > Lamont
Half time 19-3				
49	19	3	⇄	⊙ Hartley > Thompson
61	19	3	⇄	⊙ Gerard > Lord
63	19	3	⇄	⊙ Clarke > Irish
63	19	3	⇄	⊙ Rospide > Nelson
63	19	3	⇄	⊙ Gray > Robinson
64	26	3	TC	⊙ Robinson / Reihana
65	26	3	⇄	⊙ Clark > Thompson
66	26	3	⇄	⊙ Fox > Lewitt
68	33	3	TC	⊙ Cohen / Reihana
69	33	3	⇄	⊙ Sturgess > Budgen
71	33	3	⇄	⊙ Soden > Browne
71	40	3	TC	⊙ Cohen / Reihana
72	40	3	⇄	⊙ Higgitt > Marsden
74	45	3	T	⊙ Howard
78	45	8	T	⊙ Sambucetti
Full time 45-8				

Euro Challenge Cup Table

Team	P	W	D	L	F	A	BP	Pts
1 Northampton Saints	5	4	0	1	174	96	4	20
2 Bristol Rugby	5	3	0	2	185	121	4	16
3 Narbonne	5	3	0	2	96	95	1	13
4 Arix Viadana	5	0	0	5	81	224	1	1

Scoring Statistics

⊙ Northampton Saints

by Situation   by Half

▥ TC:	35	▥ first:	42%
▥ T:	10	▥ second:	58%
▥ P:	0		
▥ DG:	0		

⊙ Bristol Rugby

by Situation   by Half

▥ TC:	0	▥ first:	38%
▥ T:	5	▥ second:	63%
▥ P:	3		
▥ DG:	0		

Premiership Home Record vs Leeds Tykes					
Played	Won	Drawn	Lost	For	Against
5	**5**	**0**	**0**	**149**	**71**

Saints were more rusty than fresh after their two-week break courtesy of Viadana's forfeit.

▶ Did you know?

This win gave Saints four wins out of four for January and a good start to 2006.

The opening period of had more turnovers than sparkling play. Nevertheless, Northampton managed to score first against Leeds when Sean Lamont got on the end of a Carlos Spencer kick to earn his first GUINNESS PREMIERSHIP try. Bruce Reihana hit the upright on the conversion but Saints were five up.

The lead was short lived and Roland De Marigny used a deft boot to put through Tom Biggs. Gordon Ross hit the post leaving the scores level. Biggs was again in good form when his acceleration left Northampton's defence for dead. The score was aided by mistakes from Spencer and Ben Cohen, who spilled the ball to give possession to the Tykes' wing. Saints were having an indifferent day with their handling, with promising moves ending with dropped balls and knock-ons. On 30 minutes Cohen charged through from a lineout. Centre David Quinlan received then passed out of the tackle for Jon Clarke to go over for Saints' second.

After the break, a yellow card to Justin Marshall handed Saints' the initiative. They took three points through Reihana to regain the lead, before Spencer extended the advantage with another penalty. When Danny Care scored with three minutes to go, Ross missed a potential winning conversion. The game looked like it would end a stalemate until Reihana slotted home a last-minute penalty. Saints ended January as they had begun it – with a narrow, priceless Premiership win.

Venue:	Franklin's Gardens	Referee:	Tony Spreadbury - Season 05/06
Attendance:	13,448	Matches:	6
Capacity:	13,591	Yellow Cards:	6
Occupancy:	99%	Red Cards:	2

Northampton Saints
Leeds Tykes

Starting Line-Ups

Northampton Saints		Leeds Tykes
Reihana (c)	15	De Marigny
Lamont	14	Snyman
Clarke	13	Vickerman
Quinlan	12	Bell
Cohen	11	Biggs
Spencer	10	Ross
Robinson	9	Marshall
Smith	1	Shelley
Thompson (c)	2	Rawlinson
Budgen	3	Gerber
Dm Browne	4	Hooper (c)
Lord	5	Palmer
Tupai	6	Morgan
Lewitt	7	Parks
Dn Browne	8	Thomas

Replacements

Rudd	22	Doherty
Kydd	21	Hyde
Howard	20	Care
Harding	19	Crane
Gerard	18	Dunbar
Emms	17	Bulloch
Hartley	16	Lensing

Match Stats

Tackles	103	119
Missed Tackles	16	18
Ball Carries	109	115
Metres	446	653
Defenders Beaten	18	13
Passes	128	103
Clean Breaks	9	11
Pens Conceded	7	10
Turnovers	12	17
Breakdowns Won	84	75
% Scrums Won	100%	89%
% Line-Outs Won	88%	88%

Event Line

| TC | Try Converted | | P | Penalty |
| T | Try | | DG | Drop Goal |

Min	Score Progress		Event	Players
7	5	0	T	O Lamont
11	5	5	T	O Biggs
26	5	8	P	O Ross
29	5	13	T	O Biggs
38	12	13	TC	O Clarke / Reihana
Half time 12-13				
45	12	13	⇄	O Rudd > Cohen
45	12	13	▣	O Marshall
45	15	13	P	O Reihana
46	15	13	⇄	O Bulloch > Rawlinson
46	15	13	⇄	O Crane > Thomas
46	15	13	⇄	O Dunbar > Morgan
48	15	13	⇄	O Harding > Tupai
49	15	13	⇄	O Doherty > Vickerman
50	15	13	⇄	O Cohen > Rudd
54	18	13	P	O Spencer
58	18	13	⇄	O Lensing > Shelley
59	18	13	⇄	O Kydd > Quinlan
65	18	13	⇄	O Care > Marshall
65	18	13	⇄	O Hyde > Parks
73	18	13	⇄	O Emms > Budgen
73	18	13	⇄	O Howard > Robinson
73	18	13	⇄	O Gerard > Lord
78	18	18	T	O Care
79	21	18	P	O Reihana
Full time 21-18				

Scoring Statistics

O Northampton Saints

by Situation   by Half

▶ TC:	7	▶ first:	57%
▶ T:	5	▶ second:	43%
▶ P:	9		
▶ DG:	0		

O Leeds Tykes

by Situation   by Half

▶ TC:	0	▶ first:	72%
▶ T:	15	▶ second:	28%
▶ P:	3		
▶ DG:	0		

Premiership Table

Team	P	W	D	L	F	A	BP	Pts
9 Bristol Rugby	13	5	0	8	251	272	5	25
10 Northampton Saints	13	5	0	8	235	292	5	25
11 Bath Rugby	13	4	1	8	240	280	3	21

London Wasps 19
Northampton Saints 19

Premiership Away Record vs London Wasps					
Played	Won	Drawn	Lost	For	Against
9	**2**	**1**	**6**	**125**	**236**

Wasps threatened Northampton's unbeaten start to 2006 when they included a host of household names in their ranks.

Saints began strongly, with Jon Clarke crossing to cancel out Alex King's early penalty. He collected a loose ball and used a step to round prop Peter Bracken before bypassing Mark Van Gisbergen to score. Bruce Reihana, starting on the wing for the first time in the season, added the extras.

Only a penalty each was added in the remainder of the half, and the teams ran into the changing rooms with Saints the happier. Nearing the end of the half they had squandered a scrum on the Wasps' five-metre line, but were also lucky to still have a four-point lead when almost immediately King missed a penalty.

▶ Did you know?

This was the first time Saints had not been beaten at the Causeway Staduim.

Saints were creating the most pressure in the second half, but failed to pull away from the home side. They managed two more penalties to open up a 10-point gap but Wasps' forwards showed their experience and resolve and forced Saints into their own 22. King slid the ball through to Van Gisbergen and it was game on at 13-16.

Wasps then levelled the match with a Van Gisbergen penalty, but the match looked to be won by Reihana when he kicked the visitors three ahead with just four minutes to go. King then lead the attack as Wasps went for Saints' line. A quick Dawson penalty made space for the Wasps' fly-half to level the sides with a drop-goal and the match ended at stalemate.

Venue:	Causeway Stadium	Referee:	Rob Debney - Season 05/06	**London Wasps**
Attendance:	8,143	Matches:	8	**Northampton Saints**
Capacity:	10,200	Yellow Cards:	9	
Occupancy:	80%	Red Cards:	0	

Starting Line-Ups

O London Wasps		Northampton Saints O	
Van Gisbergen	15	Kydd	
Sackey	14	Rudd	
Hoadley	13	Clarke	
Abbott	12	Quinlan	
Erinle	11	Reihana (c)	
King	10	Spencer	
Reddan	9	Robinson	
Payne	1	Smith	
Barrett	2	Richmond	
Bracken	3	Budgen	
Skivington	4	Dm Browne	
Birkett	5	Lord	
Rees	6	Tupai	
O'Connor	7	Lewitt	
Dallaglio (c)	8	Dn Browne	

Replacements

Laird	22	Pritchard
Staunton	21	Howard
M Dawson	20	Fox
Haskell	19	Harding
Leo	18	Gerard
Va'a	17	Emms
Gotting	16	Hartley

Match Stats

Tackles	81	103
Missed Tackles	16	8
Ball Carries	102	87
Metres	301	349
Defenders Beaten	8	16
Passes	65	48
Clean Breaks	5	3
Pens Conceded	7	15
Turnovers	16	16
Breakdowns Won	84	63
% Scrums Won	100%	94%
% Line-Outs Won	81%	57%

Event Line

TC	Try Converted		P	Penalty
T	Try		DG	Drop Goal

Min	Score Progress		Event	Players
6	3	0	P	O King
7	3	7	TC	O Clarke / Reihana
11	6	7	P	O King
28	6	10	P	O Reihana
Half time 6-10				
42	6	13	P	O Reihana
52	6	13	⇄	O Gerard > Lord
52	6	16	P	O Reihana
54	13	16	TC	O Van Gisbergen / King
57	13	16	⇄	O Va'a > Payne
57	13	16	⇄	O Haskell > Rees
57	13	16	⇄	O Fox > Lewitt
63	13	16	⇄	O Emms > Smith
63	13	16	⇄	O Hartley > Richmond
63	13	16	⇄	O Dawson > Reddan
65	13	16	⇄	O Payne > Bracken
68	13	16	▧	O Spencer
69	13	16	⇄	O Gotting > Barrett
69	13	16	⇄	O Leo > Birkett
69	13	16	⇄	O Harding > Tupai
69	16	16	P	O Van Gisbergen
74	16	19	P	O Reihana
76	19	19	DG	O King
Full time 19-19				

Scoring Statistics

O London Wasps			
by Situation		by Half	
▶ TC:	7	▶ first:	32%
▶ T:	0	▶ second:	68%
▶ P:	9		
▶ DG:	3		

O Northampton Saints			
by Situation		by Half	
▶ TC:	7	▶ first:	53%
▶ T:	0	▶ second:	47%
▶ P:	12		
▶ DG:	0		

Premiership Table

Team	P	W	D	L	F	A	BP	Pts
8 Saracens	14	4	1	9	299	314	9	27
9 Northampton Saints	14	5	1	8	254	311	5	27
10 Bath Rugby	14	5	1	8	274	309	4	26

Northampton Saints 58
Saracens 17

Premiership Home Record vs Saracens

Played	Won	Drawn	Lost	For	Against
9	**5**	**0**	**4**	**252**	**179**

After the first 10 minutes, few spectators would have envisaged the eight-try rout that Saints inflicted upon Saracens.

The result looked ominous after the visitors gained an early 10-point lead through Dan Scarbrough and the boot of Glen Jackson. When Bruce Reihana's second penalty hit the post, the home crowd must have been shifting in their seats.

The disappointment lasted all of 60 seconds. Christmas signing Paul Tupai was on hand to charge down Mark Bartholomeusz's kick and he claimed his first Saints try. The deficit was erased four minutes later when Reihana made up for his earlier misses and slotted over his first penalty. Saints then started to take the game away from Saracens. Tries from Sam Harding and Ben Cohen gave Northampton a healthy 24-10 lead at half-time.

▶ Did you know?

Sky pundit Stuart Barnes awarded Carlos Spencer the Guinness Man of the Match award for this game.

In the second, Sean Lamont claimed a poor kick from Jackson and ran in 65 metres to gain Northampton's first four-try bonus point of the season. Lamont was on the end of a well worked move from Spencer and Jon Clarke to score a deserved hat-trick, before Steffon Armitage grabbed a consolation try for the London side.

With nine minutes to go, Lamont made Saints history by becoming their first GUINNESS PREMIERSHIP player to score four tries in a match. With Saracens on the attack, he grabbed an interception to touch down. Reihana rounded off the scoring and the match ended to a deserved standing ovation.

Venue:	Franklin's Gardens
Attendance:	13,523
Capacity:	13,591
Occupancy:	99%

Referee:	Roy Maybank - Season 05/06
Matches:	11
Yellow Cards:	18
Red Cards:	0

Northampton Saints
Saracens

Starting Line-Ups

○ Northampton Saints		Saracens ○
Reihana (c)	15	Bartholomeusz
Lamont	14	Scarbrough
Clarke	13	Johnston
Quinlan	12	Powell
Cohen	11	Haughton
Spencer	10	Jackson
Robinson	9	Bracken
Smith	1	Yates
Thompson (c)	2	Cairns
Budgen	3	Visagie
Dm Browne	4	Raiwalui
Lord	5	Chesney (c)
Tupai	6	Russell
Harding	7	Armitage
Dn Browne	8	Skirving

Replacements

Rudd	22	Castaignede
Kydd	21	Rauluni
Howard	20	Seymour
Fox	19	Ryder
Gerard	18	Lloyd
Emms	17	Broster
Hartley	16	Byrne

Match Stats

Tackles	94	107
Missed Tackles	12	12
Ball Carries	112	79
Metres	847	509
Defenders Beaten	12	9
Passes	121	109
Clean Breaks	13	11
Pens Conceded	10	11
Turnovers	19	18
Breakdowns Won	66	62
% Scrums Won	100%	82%
% Line-Outs Won	100%	67%

Premiership Table

Team	P	W	D	L	F	A	BP	Pts
6 Worcester Warriors	15	7	1	7	301	345	3	33
7 Northampton Saints	15	6	1	8	312	328	6	32
8 Newcastle Falcons	14	6	1	7	232	254	4	30

Event Line

TC	Try Converted		P	Penalty
T	Try		DG	Drop Goal

Min	Score Progress		Event	Players
3	0	3	P	○ Jackson
8	0	10	TC	○ Scarbrough / Jackson
14	7	10	TC	○ Tupai / Reihana
18	10	10	P	○ Reihana
24	17	10	TC	○ Harding / Reihana
33	24	10	TC	○ Cohen / Reihana
34	24	10	⇄	○ Lloyd > Yates
Half time 24-10				
43	27	10	P	○ Reihana
46	34	10	TC	○ Lamont / Reihana
47	34	10	⇄	○ Broster > Visagie
47	34	10	⇄	○ Rauluni > Bracken
51	34	10	⇄	○ Byrne > Cairns
51	34	10	⇄	○ Castaignede > Bartholomeus
53	39	10	T	○ Lamont
54	39	10	⇄	○ Fox > Tupai
55	39	10	⇄	○ Ryder > Chesney
55	39	10	⇄	○ Emms > Budgen
58	46	10	TC	○ Lamont / Reihana
59	46	10	⇄	○ Hartley > Thompson
59	46	10	⇄	○ Rudd > Cohen
61	46	10	⇄	○ Gerard > Browne
62	46	10	⇄	○ Seymour > Skirving
63	46	10	⇄	○ Howard > Robinson
65	46	17	TC	○ Armitage / Jackson
67	51	17	T	○ Rudd
69	51	17	⇄	○ Kydd > Clarke
70	51	17	⇄	○ Browne > Browne
71	58	17	TC	○ Lamont / Reihana
75	58	17	⇄	○ Budgen > Smith
75	58	17	⇄	○ Yates > Lloyd
Full time 58-17				

Scoring Statistics

○ Northampton Saints

by Situation   by Half

▶ TC:	42	▶ first:	41%
▶ T:	10	▶ second:	59%
▶ P:	6		
▶ DG:	0		

○ Saracens

by Situation   by Half

▶ TC:	14	▶ first:	59%
▶ T:	0	▶ second:	41%
▶ P:	3		
▶ DG:	0		

London Irish 30
Northampton Saints 3

26.02.06

Premiership Away Record vs London Irish

Played	Won	Drawn	Lost	For	Against
9	**6**	**0**	**3**	**218**	**179**

If Saints' backline had fired against Saracens, the opposite was true in a match where the scoring impetus was sparse.

The damage was done in the opening half hour. Irish opened up with intent and Saints' defence had to be solid to repel a number of drives for the line. In the end Delon Armitage broke the Northampton line when he collected a Carlos Spencer kick, booted it back into space, and then outstripped the covering defenders to score.

When Mark Robinson knocked on in an attack involving John Rudd, Armitage picked up the pieces and went on the counter. He drew the defence then involved Nick Kennedy who put David Paice through to achieve a spectacular touch down. All Saints had mustered in the half was a promising Jon Clarke break and three points from the boot of Spencer.

▷ Did you know?

This game was sandwiched by two massive home wins for Saints against Saracens and Gloucester.

Poor handling cost points for Saints in the second half, but when Topsy Ojo was sin-binned for deliberate offside, a man advantage gave a glimmer of hope. Disappointingly, two five-metre scrums were as close as Saints came.

Sailosi Tagicakibau sealed an unassailable lead for London Irish when he touched down in the corner. England veteran Mike Catt piled on the misery with a drop-goal before the match was put to bed by Ojo. He took a pass from Gonzalo Tiesi to squeeze over the line. Four minutes later the match was over and Saints unbeaten record for 2006 was gone.

56

Venue:	Madejski Stadium	Referee:	Wayne Barnes - Season 05/06
Attendance:	9,355	Matches:	5
Capacity:	24,104	Yellow Cards:	9
Occupancy:	39%	Red Cards:	1

London Irish
Northampton Saints

Starting Line-Ups

O London Irish		Northampton Saints O
Horak	15	Kydd
Armitage	14	Rudd
Mordt	13	Clarke
Catt (c)	12	Quinlan
Tagicakibau	11	Vilk
Flutey	10	Spencer
Hodgson	9	Robinson
Hatley	1	Smith
Paice	2	Richmond
Rautenbach	3	Budgen
Casey	4	Dm Browne (c)
Kennedy	5	Lord
Roche	6	Tupai
Dawson	7	Harding
Leguizamon	8	Dn Browne

Replacements

Tiesi	22	Pritchard
Willis	21	Howard
Ojo	20	Noon
Murphy	19	Fox
Gustard	18	Gerard
Flavin	17	Emms
Collins	16	Hartley

Match Stats

Tackles	100	91
Missed Tackles	19	14
Ball Carries	109	122
Metres	612	679
Defenders Beaten	14	19
Passes	127	142
Clean Breaks	14	17
Pens Conceded	11	7
Turnovers	17	23
Breakdowns Won	63	80
% Scrums Won	100%	100%
% Line-Outs Won	100%	70%

Event Line

TC	Try Converted			P	Penalty
T	Try			DG	Drop Goal

Min	Score Progress		Event	Players
13	3	0	P	O Flutey
24	10	0	TC	O Armitage / Flutey
26	10	3	P	O Spencer
31	17	3	TC	O Paice / Flutey
32	17	3	⇄	O Fox > Browne
Half time 17-3				
41	17	3	⇄	O Ojo > Armitage
41	17	3	⇄	O Collins > Hatley
52	17	3	▣	O Ojo
57	17	3	⇄	O Gustard > Casey
58	22	3	T	O Tagicakibau
60	22	3	⇄	O Emms > Smith
60	22	3	⇄	O Tiesi > Mordt
60	22	3	⇄	O Pritchard > Kydd
64	25	3	DG	O Catt
67	25	3	⇄	O Murphy > Leguizamon
67	25	3	⇄	O Hartley > Richmond
67	25	3	⇄	O Noon > Budgen
67	25	3	⇄	O Howard > Quinlan
67	25	3	⇄	O Gerard > Lord
69	25	3	⇄	O Hatley > Rautenbach
73	25	3	⇄	O Flavin > Paice
76	30	3	T	O Ojo
Full time 30-3				

Scoring Statistics

O London Irish

	by Situation		by Half	

TC:	14	first:	57%
T:	10	second:	43%
P:	3		
DG:	3		

O Northampton Saints

	by Situation		by Half	

TC:	0	first:	100%
T:	0	second:	0%
P:	3		
DG:	0		

Premiership Table

Team	P	W	D	L	F	A	BP	Pts
7 Worcester Warriors	16	7	1	8	316	366	4	34
8 Northampton Saints	16	6	1	9	315	358	6	32
9 Bristol Rugby	16	6	1	9	295	320	5	31

Northampton Saints 21
Gloucester Rugby 20

Premiership Home Record vs Gloucester Rugby					
Played	Won	Drawn	Lost	For	Against
9	**5**	**0**	**4**	**221**	**164**

It was a nervous last few minutes but Saints got themselves back into winning ways... just.

After a series of missed kicks from both sides, it was Saints who were first on the scoreboard. With the wind swirling, Northampton looked to the set-piece. Six scrums in succession on the Gloucester line ended in a penalty try being awarded, and Australian-born Canadian international debutant James Pritchard converted an easy two points to begin the second quarter well.

The lead only stood for five minutes however, Terry Fanolua created problems and the big Samoan gave space to Peter Richards who nipped over. Ludovic Mercier added the extras to level the scores. The teams remained level until the break.

▶ Did you know?

This was the only game in which James Pritchard kicked points for Northampton Saints.

Academy product Mark Easter was awarded with a deserved try nine minutes into the second half. Another series of scrums resulted in the No 8 driving over the line and his hands were credited with a debut try. Pritchard gave Saints a seven-point lead, but this was slashed by Mercier's first successful penalty of the game.

Sam Harding appeared to have given Saints a safe cushion when Jon Clarke collected a spill to send the flanker over. Mercier again chipped at the lead immediately and the deficit was only eight points. A penalty try from Gloucester's pack – taking advantage of Easter's sin-binning – meant that the home crowd had yet another gut-wrenching finale. Thankfully they held on to take four valuable points.

Starting Line-Ups

O Northampton Saints		Gloucester Rugby O
Pritchard	15	Goodridge
Rudd	14	Bailey
Clarke	13	Fanolua
Quinlan	12	Davies
Reihana (c)	11	Foster
Spencer	10	Mercier
Robinson	9	Richards
Smith	1	Wood
Richmond	2	Elloway
Barnard	3	Sigley
Dm Browne	4	Pendlebury
Gerard	5	Brown
Tupai	6	Buxton (c)
Harding	7	Hazell
Easter	8	Narraway

Replacements

Kydd	22	Thirlby
Diggin	21	Garvey
Jones	20	Thomas
Fox	19	Forrester
Lord	18	Eustace
Emms	17	Forster
Budgen	16	Parkes

Match Stats

Tackles	58	116
Missed Tackles	11	16
Ball Carries	109	83
Metres	408	353
Defenders Beaten	16	12
Passes	88	81
Clean Breaks	15	12
Pens Conceded	15	15
Turnovers	8	11
Breakdowns Won	81	48
% Scrums Won	81%	92%
% Line-Outs Won	71%	86%

Premiership Table

Team	P	W	D	L	F	A	BP	Pts
7 Newcastle Falcons	17	7	1	9	283	303	6	36
8 Northampton Saints	17	7	1	9	336	378	6	36
9 Bath Rugby	17	7	1	9	340	375	5	35

Event Line

TC	Try Converted			P	Penalty
T	Try			DG	Drop Goal

Min	Score Progress		Event	Players
21	7	0	TC	O Pen Try / Pritchard
26	7	7	TC	O Richards / Mercier
Half time 7-7				
41	7	7	⇄	O Lord > Gerard
41	7	7	⇄	O Budgen > Barnard
49	7	7	⇄	O Fox > Tupai
49	7	7	⇄	O Forrester > Narraway
49	14	7	TC	O Easter / Pritchard
52	14	10	P	O Mercier
54	14	10	⇄	O Parkes > Elloway
54	14	10	⇄	O Forster > Wood
55	14	10	▪	O Buxton
57	14	10	⇄	O Emms > Smith
59	14	10	⇄	O Diggin > Pritchard
62	14	10	⇄	O Eustace > Pendlebury
62	14	10	⇄	O Thirlby > Goodridge
62	21	10	TC	O Clarke / Reihana
64	21	13	P	O Mercier
68	21	13	⇄	O Thomas > Richards
68	21	13	⇄	O Garvey > Bailey
72	21	13	▪	O Easter
77	21	20	TC	O Pen Try / Mercier
Full time 21-20				

Scoring Statistics

O Northampton Saints — by Situation / by Half

O Gloucester Rugby — by Situation / by Half

Northampton Saints:
- TC: 21
- T: 0
- P: 0
- DG: 0
- first: 33%
- second: 67%

Gloucester Rugby:
- TC: 14
- T: 0
- P: 6
- DG: 0
- first: 35%
- second: 65%

Newcastle Falcons 13
Northampton Saints 32

Premiership Away Record vs Newcastle Falcons					
Played	Won	Drawn	Lost	For	Against
9	**3**	**0**	**6**	**215**	**230**

Saints' form in 2006 had meant that eyes were gradually shifting towards the top of the league table rather than the bottom.

Northampton were quick off the mark. Bruce Reihana took a poor kick from Matt Burke before David Quinlan and Sean Lamont worked the ball to Cohen to score in the third minute.

Cohen's touchdown though was cancelled out when Owen Finegan went over from a lineout after penalties had enabled the Falcons to get into an attacking position. Spencer then hacked a knock on from James Grindal to run in from the halfway line. Prop Pat Barnard benefited from jinking runs by Reihana and Spencer to score his try as the break approached, and Saints had a healthy 8-20 lead.

▶ Did you know?

This match marked Bruce Reihana's 100th game for the club, Pat Barnard's first Saints try and a move away from the relegation zone.

Poor kicking was a thorn in the side of the Falcons, and Reihana collected another loose punt – this time from Dave Walder – to send Clarke in for the bonus-point-winning score. Darren Fox's knock-on was collected by Joe Shaw who found Anthony Elliot in support. The winger dived over and some consolation was gained with ten minutes to go.

It was not the last act of the game, however. The forwards, buoyed by Mark Easter's promotion from the Academy, helped Darren Fox to redeem himself as he went over for the fifth try. The match ended a very satisfactory 13-32 and the threat of relegation was finally over.

Venue:	Kingston Park	Referee:	Tony Spreadbury - Season 05/06	**Newcastle Falcons**
Attendance:	7,364	Matches:	9	**Northampton Saints**
Capacity:	10,000	Yellow Cards:	7	
Occupancy:	74%	Red Cards:	2	

Starting Line-Ups

Newcastle Falcons ○		Northampton Saints ○
Burke (c)	15	Reihana (c)
Elliott	14	Lamont
May	13	Clarke
Flood	12	Quinlan
Phillips	11	Cohen
Walder	10	Spencer
Grindal	9	Robinson
Ward	1	Smith
Long	2	Thompson (c)
Morris	3	Barnard
Perry	4	Dm Browne
Parling	5	Gerard
Finegan	6	Tupai
Woods	7	Harding
Buist	8	Easter

Replacements

Shaw	22	Rudd
Charlton	21	Kydd
Mayerhofler	20	Howard
Grimes	19	Fox
McCarthy	18	Lord
Thompson	17	Emms
Williams	16	Richmond

Match Stats

Tackles	117	133
Missed Tackles	33	13
Ball Carries	147	145
Metres	481	644
Defenders Beaten	13	33
Passes	153	111
Clean Breaks	12	21
Pens Conceded	5	12
Turnovers	16	7
Breakdowns Won	97	92
% Scrums Won	100%	89%
% Line-Outs Won	96%	67%

Event Line

TC	Try Converted		P	Penalty
T	Try		DG	Drop Goal

Min	Score Progress		Event	Players
3	0	5	T	○ Cohen
10	5	5	T	○ Finegan
16	5	10	T	○ Spencer
21	5	13	P	○ Reihana
30	8	13	P	○ Walder
34	8	20	TC	○ Barnard / Reihana

Half time 8-20

41	8	20	⇄	○ Mayerhofler > Flood
41	8	20	⇄	○ Williams > Ward
49	8	20	⇄	○ McCarthy > Finegan
49	8	20	⇄	○ Grimes > Parling
51	8	20	⇄	○ Lord > Gerard
51	8	20	⇄	○ Fox > Tupai
54	8	20	⇄	○ Ward > Morris
54	8	20	⇄	○ Emms > Barnard
54	8	20	⇄	○ Shaw > Phillips
54	8	25	T	○ Clarke
60	8	25	⇄	○ Richmond > Thompson
62	8	25	⇄	○ Charlton > Grindal
63	8	25	⇄	○ Thompson > Long
68	8	25	⇄	○ Kydd > Spencer
70	13	25	T	○ Elliott
75	13	25	⇄	○ Barnard > Smith
80	13	32	TC	○ Fox / Reihana

Full time 13-32

Scoring Statistics

○ Newcastle Falcons		
by Situation		by Half
▶ TC:	0	▶ first: 62%
▶ T:	10	▶ second: 38%
▶ P:	3	
▶ DG:	0	

○ Northampton Saints		
by Situation		by Half
▶ TC:	14	▶ first: 63%
▶ T:	15	▶ second: 38%
▶ P:	3	
▶ DG:	0	

Premiership Table

Team	P	W	D	L	F	A	BP	Pts
5 Gloucester Rugby	18	9	1	8	378	307	9	47
6 Northampton Saints	18	8	1	9	368	391	7	41
7 Worcester Warriors	18	8	1	9	368	403	5	39

Northampton Saints 25
Worcester Warriors 34

Worcester and Northampton had been evenly matched in all of their three previous matches in the season, and for sixty minutes this match, this game was no different. In the end though, it was clinical finishing from the visitors that told and Saints missed out on a place in the European Challenge Cup semi-finals.

▶ Did you know?

This game was Worcester's third victory at Franklin's Gardens since being promoted to the Premiership at the start of the 2004/05 season.

The lead changed hand six times in the first half. Carlos Spencer helped open the scoring with a jinking run. Sean Lamont drove on and then fed Paul Tupai to score. With Saints in the lead, Worcester took control of the game. Thomas Lombard scored by taking advantage of a drive by Pat Sanderson. Shane Drahm kicked the goal to give Warriors the lead. Northampton did not trail for long and a Bruce Reihana penalty nudged them back ahead. Worcester came straight back and from the kick-off when the ball was spun to Aisea Havili to dot down in the corner. The see-saw match continued with a try from Reihana and a second from Havili. The visitors again went ahead with a try from Gary Trueman and their two-point advantage was how the half ended.

The match was no different for the beginning of the second half, with Tupai grabbing a second score to put Saints ahead once more. Still the yo-yoing went on. Shane Drahm caused havoc with a grubber kick which fell to Dale Rasmussen. The Australian touched down to create a four-point gap, which was increased to seven with a penalty. The match was finally calmed when Havili finished off an astounding 95-metre counter-attack. Mike MacDonald was the engineer of the beautifully achieved try. Saints managed a consolation through Darren Fox but it was not enough and the home side were out of Europe.

Venue:	Franklin's Gardens	Referee:	George Clancy

Attendance: 9,531
Capacity: 13,591
Occupancy: 70%

Northampton Saints
Worcester Warriors

Starting Line-Ups

O Northampton Saints		Worcester Warriors O
Reihana (c)	15	Delport
Lamont	14	Havili
Clarke	13	Rasmussen
Quinlan	12	Lombard
Cohen	11	Trueman
Spencer	10	Drahm
Robinson	9	Powell
Smith	1	Windo
Thompson (c)	2	Van Niekerk
Barnard	3	Taumoepeau
Dm Browne	4	Murphy
Gerard	5	Gillies
Tupai	6	Vaili
Harding	7	Sanderson (c)
Soden	8	Horstmann

Replacements

Rudd	22	Whatling
Kydd	21	Gomarsall
Howard	20	Tu'amoheloa
Fox	19	Blaze
Lord	18	L Fortey
Budgen	17	C Fortey
Richmond	16	MacDonald

Event Line

TC	Try Converted		P	Penalty
T	Try		DG	Drop Goal

Min	Score Progress		Event	Players
14	5	0	T	O Tupai
28	5	7	TC	O Lombard / Lombard
32	8	7	P	O Reihana
33	8	12	T	O Havili
35	15	12	TC	O Reihana / Reihana
39	15	17	T	O Havili
Half time 15-17				
41	15	17	⇄	O Budgen > Barnard
41	15	17	⇄	O Fortey > Van Niekerk
48	15	17	▣	O Fortey
48	20	17	T	O Tupai
53	20	24	TC	O Rasmussen / Drahm
54	20	24	⇄	O Fox > Harding
55	20	24	⇄	O Fortey > Vaili
56	20	24	⇄	O Lord > Gerard
60	20	24	⇄	O Vaili > Fortey
61	20	24	⇄	O MacDonald > Windo
66	20	27	P	O Drahm
73	20	27	⇄	O Barnard > Smith
74	20	27	⇄	O Tu'amoheloa > Vaili
74	20	27	⇄	O Blaze > Murphy
77	20	34	TC	O Havili / Drahm
78	20	34	⇄	O Rudd > Cohen
78	20	34	⇄	O Kydd > Soden
80	25	34	T	O Fox
86	25	34	▣	O Tu'amoheloa
Full time 25-34				

Scoring Statistics

O Northampton Saints				O Worcester Warriors			
by Situation		by Half		by Situation		by Half	

Northampton Saints				Worcester Warriors			
TC:	7	first:	60%	TC:	21	first:	50%
T:	15	second:	40%	T:	10	second:	50%
P:	3			P:	3		
DG:	0			DG:	0		

Northampton Saints 24
Bath Rugby 21

Premiership Home Record vs Bath Rugby					
Played	Won	Drawn	Lost	For	Against
9	**8**	**0**	**1**	**212**	**113**

It was another see-saw affair for Saints following their loss to Worcester the previous week. This time it was the home side that prevailed.

Even though the first quarter was scoreless, the match was riveting entertainment and the ball went from end-to-end. Ben Cohen was the hero when he launched Andy Higgins into touch in goal in the fourth minute, but Jon Clarke knocked on in an attacking position in the 12th. Bath worked the phases when a penalty put them deep in Saints' half, and even though Pieter Dixon looked to have wasted the chance, Salesi Finau was on hand to draw first blood in the corner in the 19th minute.

Saints' Kiwi contingent came into play. Carlos Spencer once again left the defence perplexed and a blind pass to Bruce Reihana sent the co-captain over the line. The scoreline was doubled six minutes later when Cohen rounded off a simple backline move. A missed kick from Chris Malone meant Saints held a 14-5 half-time lead.

Bath blitzed the first 10 minutes of the second half. They cut the deficit to six points with a penalty, before a quick tap from Andy Williams gave Joe Maddock an easy score. Suddenly Saints were a point behind. The lead went from one side to the other for the next 10 minutes, with Olly Barkley eradicating a Reihana try with his kicking prowess.

The game went down to the wire, and on 75 minutes Mark Easter had the last say after Mark Robinson, Spencer, Ben Lewitt and Chris Budgen had all made ground.

▶ Did you know?

The lead changed hands five times during this close encounter.

Venue:	Franklin's Gardens		Referee:	David Rose - Season 05/06		**Northampton Saints**
Attendance:	13,454		Matches:	10		**Bath Rugby**
Capacity:	13,591		Yellow Cards:	16		
Occupancy:	99%		Red Cards:	0		

Starting Line-Ups

Northampton Saints ○			Bath Rugby ○
Reihana (c)	**15**		Maddock
Lamont	**14**		Finau
Clarke	**13**		Crockett
Quinlan	**12**		Barkley
Cohen	**11**		Higgins
Spencer	**10**		Malone
Robinson	**9**		Williams
Smith	**1**		Flatman
Thompson (c)	**2**		Dixon
Barnard	**3**		Filise
Dm Browne	**4**		Borthwick (c)
Lord	**5**		Grewcock
Tupai	**6**		Short
Harding	**7**		Lipman
Dn Browne	**8**		Delve

Replacements

Kydd	**22**		Abendanon
Howard	**21**		Fuimaono-Sapolu
Easter	**20**		Fulton
Lewitt	**19**		Feau'nati
Gerard	**18**		Fidler
Budgen	**17**		Bell
Richmond	**16**		Mears

Event Line

TC	Try Converted			P	Penalty
T	Try			DG	Drop Goal

Min	Score Progress		Event	Players
18	0	5	T	○ Finau
26	7	5	TC	○ Reihana / Reihana
32	14	5	TC	○ Cohen / Reihana
Half time 14-5				
41	14	5	⇄	○ Fuimaono-Sapolu > Malone
43	14	8	P	○ Barkley
46	14	15	TC	○ Maddock / Barkley
49	14	15	⇄	○ Bell > Flatman
53	19	15	T	○ Reihana
54	19	18	P	○ Barkley
59	19	18	⇄	○ Budgen > Barnard
59	19	18	⇄	○ Lewitt > Tupai
59	19	18	⇄	○ Mears > Dixon
60	19	21	P	○ Barkley
68	19	21	⇄	○ Feau'nati > Lipman
68	19	21	⇄	○ Easter > Browne
68	19	21	⇄	○ Richmond > Thompson
71	19	21	⇄	○ Abendanon > Maddock
74	24	21	T	○ Easter
77	24	21	⇄	○ Fidler > Borthwick
Full time 24-21				

Match Stats

Tackles	115	108
Missed Tackles	23	25
Ball Carries	134	149
Metres	736	653
Defenders Beaten	25	22
Passes	114	142
Clean Breaks	26	23
Pens Conceded	10	7
Turnovers	10	7
Breakdowns Won	73	81
% Scrums Won	90%	100%
% Line-Outs Won	91%	100%

Scoring Statistics

○ Northampton Saints

	by Situation	by Half
TC:	14	first: 58%
T:	10	second: 42%
P:	0	
DG:	0	

○ Bath Rugby

	by Situation	by Half
TC:	7	first: 24%
T:	5	second: 76%
P:	9	
DG:	0	

Premiership Table

Team	P	W	D	L	F	A	BP	Pts
5 Gloucester Rugby	19	9	1	9	393	325	10	48
6 Northampton Saints	19	9	1	9	392	412	8	46
7 Saracens	19	7	1	11	390	428	11	41

Northampton Saints 19
Leicester Tigers 24

Premiership Home Record vs Leicester Tigers					
Played	Won	Drawn	Lost	For	Against
9	**4**	**0**	**5**	**168**	**136**

Saints' win at home to Bath had propelled them into an unlikely possibility of a GUINNESS PREMIERSHIP play-off semi-final.

Saints contributed to probably the most exciting game of rugby played this term. Right from the off, both teams looked to spin the ball, which bore fruit in the third minute for Tom Varndell. Alex Tuilagi had made the score, catching a loose Carlos Spencer kick and returning it with interest. He bounced off Jon Clarke to storm down the left wing. Varndell to touched down from the resulting ruck.

▶ Did you know?

Matt Hampson attended this match and his sister Amy collected a cheque for more than £18,000 for the young injured prop's charity fund.

Both teams were reduced to 14 men for 10 minutes when Spencer retaliated to a Graham Rowntree punch, but Saints coped better with the loss by kicking two penalties reducing the deficit to just one point. Both sides looked dangerous, but Northampton managed to take the lead with mazy running from both Clarke and Bruce Reihana creating space and Daniel Browne went over unopposed. Then Leicester's Tuilagi collected and raced in from 60 metres. The conversion gave Leicester the lead, and the half ended a scintillating 13-14.

The second half picked up where the first left off. Deep runs were coming in all over the pitch and Saints were rewarded with two penalties, giving them a five-point lead. Leicester scored their third try in controversial fashion after Andy Goode 'helped' Sam Vesty break the line to put Varndell over for his second and Tigers' third. Goode added the conversion and a penalty, and despite constant Saints pressure in the dying moments, the match ended 19-24 to the visitors.

Venue:	Franklin's Gardens	Referee:	Tony Spreadbury - Season 05/06	**Northampton Saints**
Attendance:	13,493	Matches:	11	**Leicester Tigers**
Capacity:	13,591	Yellow Cards:	7	
Occupancy:	99%	Red Cards:	2	

Starting Line-Ups

○ Northampton Saints		Leicester Tigers ○
Reihana (c)	15	Murphy
Lamont	14	Tuilagi
Clarke	13	Hipkiss
Quinlan	12	Vesty
Cohen	11	Varndell
Spencer	10	Healey
Robinson	9	Bemand
Smith	1	Rowntree
Thompson (c)	2	Chuter
Barnard	3	White
Dm Browne	4	Cullen
Lord	5	Kay
Tupai	6	Deacon
Fox	7	Moody
Dn Browne	8	Corry (c)

Replacements

Kydd	22	Goode
Howard	21	Gibson
Harding	20	Smith
Lewitt	19	Jennings
Gerard	18	Hamilton
Budgen	17	Holford
Richmond	16	Buckland

Match Stats

Tackles	74	139
Missed Tackles	16	20
Ball Carries	113	69
Metres	710	563
Defenders Beaten	20	14
Passes	154	120
Clean Breaks	7	8
Pens Conceded	7	10
Turnovers	16	12
Breakdowns Won	92	53
% Scrums Won	100%	57%
% Line-Outs Won	80%	90%

Premiership Table

Team	P	W	D	L	F	A	BP	Pts
5 Gloucester Rugby	19	9	1	9	393	325	10	48
6 Northampton Saints	20	9	1	10	411	436	9	47
7 Saracens	19	7	1	11	390	428	11	41

Event Line

TC	Try Converted		P	Penalty
T	Try		DG	Drop Goal

Min	Score Progress		Event	Players
3	0	7	TC	○ Varndell / Vesty
7	0	7		○ Spencer
7	0	7		○ Rowntree
10	0	7	⇄	○ Holford > Deacon
12	3	7	P	○ Reihana
17	6	7	P	○ Reihana
18	6	7	⇄	○ Deacon > Holford
29	13	7	TC	○ Browne / Reihana
35	13	14	TC	○ Tuilagi / Vesty
Half time 13-14				
41	13	14	⇄	○ Holford > Rowntree
41	13	14	⇄	○ Smith > Murphy
41	13	14	⇄	○ Buckland > Chuter
46	16	14	P	○ Reihana
51	16	14	⇄	○ Gibson > Hipkiss
51	19	14	P	○ Reihana
54	19	17	P	○ Vesty
55	19	17	⇄	○ Goode > Healey
58	19	17	⇄	○ Harding > Fox
58	19	17	⇄	○ Lewitt > Tupai
62	19	17	⇄	○ Jennings > Moody
62	19	17	⇄	○ Budgen > Barnard
63	19	24	TC	○ Varndell / Goode
66	19	24	⇄	○ Hamilton > Kay
68	19	24	⇄	○ Gerard > Lord
78	19	24		○ Holford
Full time 19-24				

Scoring Statistics

○ Northampton Saints			
by Situation		by Half	
▶ TC:	7	▶ first:	68%
▶ T:	0	second:	32%
▶ P:	12		
DG:	0		

○ Leicester Tigers			
by Situation		by Half	
▶ TC:	21	▶ first:	58%
▶ T:	0	second:	42%
▶ P:	3		
DG:	0		

67

Bristol Rugby 16
Northampton Saints 19

Premiership Away Record vs Bristol Rugby

Played	Won	Drawn	Lost	For	Against
6	4	0	2	152	158

A win would guarantee Saints Heineken Cup rugby for the 2006/07 season, but the visitors were not going to make life easy for themselves.

In fact they let Bristol build up a 16 point to nil lead until the 70th minute when replacement hooker Steve Thompson thought he would wander over for a try when Saints should have been struggling due to Sam Harding's absence in the sin-bin.

Thompson's efforts reminded Saints what they had come for and Sean Lamont was the next to go over to bring the men in black, green and gold within reach. And just as Ben Cohen had saved the day against London Irish back in October, he was the body over the line to steal Saints a win. The Bristol crowd was understandably stunned, especially as they had begun to chant: "Easy, easy, easy," but it was the travelling Saints support who were cheering the loudest at the end.

▶ **Did you know?**

This was the latest comeback victory ever recorded in the Premiership, starting with the time Saints' first try was scored.

But even then the dressing room was not certain of the Heineken Cup spot until the Premiership's statistics service confirmed that even if Saints lost to Sale the following week and seventh placed Saracens equalled their points haul with a five-point win, Saints would still retain sixth place having won more games.

Head coach Paul Grayson had to return to the dressing room after the press conference to relay the news to the players having previously scolded them for their lacklustre performance ahead of the 70-minute mark. It was happy faces all round.

Venue:	Memorial Stadium	Referee:	Wayne Barnes - Season 05/06		**Bristol Rugby**
Attendance:	9,862	Matches:	10		**Northampton Saints**
Capacity:	12,000	Yellow Cards:	15		
Occupancy:	82%	Red Cards:	3		

Starting Line-Ups

Bristol Rugby		Northampton Saints
Stortoni	15	Reihana (c)
Robinson	14	Lamont
Higgitt	13	Clarke
Cox	12	Quinlan
Stanojevic	11	Cohen
Strange	10	Spencer
Perry	9	Robinson
Hilton	1	Smith
Regan	2	Richmond
Crompton	3	Barnard
Sambucetti	4	Dm Browne
Winters	5	Lord
Salter (c)	6	Tupai
Short	7	Harding
Lewis	8	Dn Browne

Replacements

Lima	22	Rudd
Gray	21	Kydd
Ward-Smith	20	Howard
Morgan	19	Fox
Clark	18	Gerard
Clarke	17	Budgen
Irish	16	Thompson

Match Stats

Tackles	117	96
Missed Tackles	28	10
Ball Carries	88	141
Metres	334	680
Defenders Beaten	9	27
Passes	98	152
Clean Breaks	1	19
Pens Conceded	10	12
Turnovers	13	21
Breakdowns Won	76	91
% Scrums Won	80%	92%
% Line-Outs Won	82%	77%

Event Line

TC	Try Converted		P	Penalty
T	Try		DG	Drop Goal

Min	Score Progress		Event	Players
9	3	0	P	Strange
26	6	0	P	Strange
33	13	0	TC	Stanojevic / Strange
Half time 13-0				
41	13	0	⇄	Budgen > Barnard
41	13	0	⇄	Thompson > Richmond
44	16	0	P	Strange
54	16	0	⇄	Fox > Tupai
55	16	0	⇄	Clarke > Hilton
57	16	0	⇄	Howard > Robinson
57	16	0	⇄	Ward-Smith > Lewis
59	16	0	⇄	Rudd > Clarke
59	16	0	⇄	Lima > Higgitt
61	16	0	⇄	Irish > Crompton
63	16	0	▪	Harding
63	16	0	⇄	Gerard > Browne
66	16	0	⇄	Clark > Regan
69	16	0	▪	Clark
70	16	5	T	Thompson
72	16	12	TC	Lamont / Reihana
73	16	12	⇄	Gray > Perry
73	16	12	⇄	Morgan > Salter
74	16	12	⇄	Regan > Short
77	16	19	TC	Cohen / Reihana
79	16	19	⇄	Short > Regan
Full time 16-19				

Scoring Statistics

○ Bristol Rugby		
by Situation		by Half

▶ TC:	7	▶ first:	81%
▶ T:	0	second:	19%
▶ P:	9		
DG:	0		

○ Northampton Saints		
by Situation		by Half

▶ TC:	14	▶ first:	0%
▶ T:	5	second:	100%
▶ P:	0		
DG:	0		

Premiership Table

Team	P	W	D	L	F	A	BP	Pts
5 Gloucester Rugby	21	11	1	9	451	348	11	57
6 Northampton Saints	21	10	1	10	430	452	9	51
7 Saracens	21	8	1	12	415	453	12	46

Northampton Saints 34
Sale Sharks 36

Premiership Home Record vs Sale Sharks					
Played	Won	Drawn	Lost	For	Against
9	**6**	**0**	**3**	**256**	**172**

This game was a micro-mirror of Saints' season: a very slow start with an exciting second half only for the final kick not to quite reach its target.

Sale arrived with a full squad – no chance of these boys being rested ahead of the GUINNESS PREMIERSHIP semi-final despite their top spot being guaranteed. And they put those players to good use by piling on a 16-point lead by half-time. When Valentin Courrent crossed for Sale's fourth try early in the second half, it looked like Saints were doomed to a disappointing end to their season.

But always expect the unexpected with Saints as they scored three tries in six minutes to come straight back into the game starting with a Carlos Spencer special followed by a Bruce Reihana classic and Daniel Browne's third try of the season.

Saints took the lead for the first time that afternoon with centre David Quinlan scoring his debut try for the club which made the stadium rock. But former Saintsman Oriol Ripol had something to add with a typical jinking run that gave his new team the lead once more.

However, Ben Cohen had yet to get his name on the scoresheet and he went over for Saints' fifth to take his try-scoring tally up to 15 for the season.

Saints were still two points down though and when Reihana missed the last kick of the game, the home side had to be content with a narrow but entertaining loss.

▶ Did you know?

This match marked Saints 11th sell-out in 12 GUINNESS PREMIERSHIP games.

Venue:	Franklin's Gardens	Referee:	Martin Fox - Season 05/06	**Northampton Saints**
Attendance:	13,577	Matches:	10	**Sale Sharks**
Capacity:	13,591	Yellow Cards:	10	
Occupancy:	100%	Red Cards:	0	

Starting Line-Ups

○ Northampton Saints		Sale Sharks ○
Reihana (c)	15	Robinson (c)
Rudd	14	Ripol Fortuny
Clarke	13	Cueto
Quinlan	12	Mayor
Cohen	11	Hanley
Spencer	10	Hodgson
Howard	9	Foden
Smith	1	Faure
Thompson (c)	2	Titterrell
Emms	3	Stewart
Dm Browne	4	Fernandez Lobbe
Lord	5	Day
Tupai	6	White (c)
Harding	7	Jones
Dn Browne	8	Chabal

Replacements

Lamont	22	Riley
Kydd	21	Courrent
Robinson	20	Wigglesworth
Fox	19	Hills
Gerard	18	Lloyd
Sturgess	17	Roberts
Grove	16	Jones

Match Stats

Tackles	53	114
Missed Tackles	31	32
Ball Carries	148	86
Metres	791	560
Defenders Beaten	32	30
Passes	138	96
Clean Breaks	31	22
Pens Conceded	10	8
Turnovers	14	9
Breakdowns Won	80	46
% Scrums Won	87%	100%
% Line-Outs Won	70%	100%

Premiership Table

Team	P	W	D	L	F	A	BP	Pts
5 Gloucester Rugby	22	11	1	10	483	385	13	59
6 Northampton Saints	22	10	1	11	464	488	11	53
7 Newcastle Falcons	22	9	1	12	416	433	9	47

Event Line

TC	Try Converted		P	Penalty
T	Try		DG	Drop Goal

Min	Score Progress		Event	Players
13	0	0	⇄	○ Jones > Titterrell
14	3	0	P	○ Reihana
22	3	0	⇄	○ Titterrell > Jones
22	3	7	TC	○ Fernandez Lobbe / Hodgson
27	3	12	T	○ Foden
32	3	19	TC	○ Hanley / Hodgson
36	3	19	⇄	○ Gerard > Browne

Half time 3-19

41	3	19	⇄	○ Browne > Gerard
41	3	19	⇄	○ Jones > Titterrell
41	3	19	⇄	○ Hills > White
41	3	19	⇄	○ Courrent > Hodgson
48	3	26	TC	○ Courrent / Courrent
49	3	26	⇄	○ Robinson > Howard
51	3	26	⇄	○ Fox > Tupai
52	3	26	⇄	○ Gerard > Lord
52	3	26	⇄	○ Lloyd > Jones
52	3	26	⇄	○ Roberts > Faure
52	10	26	TC	○ Spencer / Reihana
55	10	26	◾	○ Robinson
55	17	26	TC	○ Reihana / Reihana
56	17	26	⇄	○ Lamont > Rudd
56	17	26	⇄	○ Riley > Mayor
58	22	26	T	○ Browne
68	27	26	T	○ Quinlan
73	27	29	P	○ Courrent
74	27	29	⇄	○ Wigglesworth > Stewart
75	27	29	⇄	○ Grove > Emms
76	27	36	TC	○ Ripol Fortuny / Courrent
78	34	36	TC	○ Cohen / Reihana
79	34	36	⇄	○ Sturgess > Smith

Full time 34-36

Scoring Statistics

○ **Northampton Saints**

by Situation   by Half

▶ TC:	21	▶ first:	9%
▶ T:	10	second:	91%
▶ P:	3		
DG:	0		

○ **Sale Sharks**

by Situation   by Half

▶ TC:	28	▶ first:	53%
▶ T:	5	second:	47%
▶ P:	3		
DG:	0		

Profiles

Budge Pountney
Director of rugby

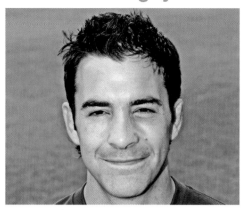

Budge took over as director of rugby at the start of last season having been swiftly made head coach the previous November in the wake of Alan Solomons' departure. A reshuffle in the summer months, gave Budge the official title of DoR so he could concentrate on the paperwork and legwork required, including the harnessing of new signings. Budge produced Carlos Spencer, Pat Barnard, Sam Harding, David Gerard and Paul Tupai, to name but a few, last season and had already signed up the services of massive prop Soane Tonga'uiha, Connacht lock Christian Short, Cambridge Blue David Akinluyi, former Academy player Ian Vass and new forwards coach Peter Sloane ahead of this season.

Paul Grayson
Head coach

After working under the rather complicated title of tactical coach in the 2004/05 season, Paul was officially named as head coach at the start of Saints' last campaign. Not a new boy to coaching, as Paul had assisted with the coaching of England A and U21s, Saints' record points-scorer met the challenge head on and eased the team from relegation threat before Christmas to sixth place in the GUINNESS PREMIERSHIP and a Heineken Cup qualification place for this season. The team's performances against Bristol, Worcester and Leeds in January earned him the title of GUINNESS PREMIERSHIP coach of the month.

Paul Larkin
Assistant coach

Paul has been a coach at Franklin's Gardens for 11 seasons now and has adapted to new-look coaching teams as they have come along, as well as changes in technology. The former Saints fly-half has carved out a niche for himself in terms of operating the player analysis systems now required by coaches and is generally the man with all the stats.

Frank Ponissi
Assistant coach

Frank arrived at Franklin's Gardens two seasons ago from Clermont Avergne after former Saints head coach Alan Solomons had sought out a favourable reference from Corne Krige. Frank had worked as a defence consultant with the South African team during the 2003 Rugby World Cup after a spell with the Australia Kangaroos. Having battled through a difficult 2004/05 season, Frank really enjoyed last season and agreed to sign a new two-year deal to keep him at Franklin's Gardens.

Steve Williams
Assistant coach

Former player Steve Williams returned to Franklin's Gardens at the start of last season to help coach the forwards. A former lock, Steve is an expert in the lineout area and had already honed his coaching skills as head coach of Division One's Coventry RFC. He completed his year-long contract with Saints having taken the forwards to a new level.

Tom Smith
Assistant coach

Tom valiantly lent his services to Budge and Grase in the initial days that followed former head coach Alan Solomons' departure. Still a player, Tom continued to provide support to Paul, Steve and Frank last season leading to rumours that he would be retiring from the game. Not so, Tom still has a year left on his contract and will be actively using it in 2006/07.

Peter Sloane
New for 2006/07
Forwards coach

Peter arrives at Franklin's Gardens with a wealth of coaching knowledge. As a former All Blacks and Crusaders assistant coach, Peter worked alongside ex-Saints coach Wayne Smith back in New Zealand. Peter went on to collect Super 12 honours with the Auckland Blues before stepping down last year. Paul Grayson was looking for an experienced head to work alongside him and to glean ideas and support from, and Peter came with the approval of Smithy. Peter also embodies much of the work ethos that the coaching team has being trying to instil at Franklin's Gardens and fully believes in family values – another sought after quality in a Saints coach.

Geoff Appleford
Centre

Date of Birth: 26.09.77
Place of Birth: Dundee, South Africa
Nationality: English
Height: 6'3"
Weight: 14st 13lbs

Geoff did not have the easiest of first seasons with Northampton Saints after a shoulder injury picked up during an England sevens game in France last summer ruled him out for the entire season. The South African-born England international has undergone two bouts of surgery for the injury with the latest operation involving the transfer of a nerve from his forearm to the damaged area.

The ex-London Irish centre has put his time to good use though by assisting Frank Ponissi with some aspects of the coaching timetable and developing his skills in computer programming, including on that will assist Saints coaches next season. It is hoped Geoff may return to action at the start of 2007 and see out the rest of his three-year contract in a more active fashion.

Pat Barnard
Prop

Date of Birth: 03.07.1981
Place of Birth: Port Elizabeth
Nationality: South African
Height: 6'
Weight: 17st 8lb

Having played rugby non-stop since January 2005, Pat has fared very well. He arrived in England following Western Province's last game in the 2005 Currie Cup and made his debut as a replacement against Saracens in November and racked up 13 appearances last season. He would have made more though had he been able to register for the pool stages of the European Challenge Cup and had not been thwarted by a calf injury which struck him down against Sale on Boxing Day against Bristol during the penultimate game of the season.

The earlier enforced rest seemed to do Pat a power of good though as he came back fitter, stronger and more determined for the game against Gloucester in which the Saints forwards exerted a great deal of pressure over the infamous Cherry & White pack. He followed this performance up with his debut try, albeit much to do with Carlos Spencer's hard work, at Newcastle.

Season Review 05/06

Northampton Saints fought off offers from London Wasps, Saracens, Gloucester and Worcester Warriors to nail this man after Pat made a casual comment to a South African newspaper that he fancied the idea of playing rugby in England. Saints' director of rugby Budge Pountney was the first on the telephone to the tighthead prop and Franklin's Gardens was enough of a draw to seal the deal.

Interest has definitely grown in Pat this season in that rugby writers have been wondering whether this former IRB U21s Player of the Year for South Africa may soon run out in England colours thanks to his mother's Reading heritage.

Prem. Career History

Premiership Career Milestones

Club Debut:	First Try Scored for the Club:
vs Saracens (A), L, 22-28	vs Newcastle (A), W, 32-13
▶ **05.11.05**	▶ **26.03.06**
Time Spent at the Club:	Full International:
▶ **1 Season**	▶ **—**

Premiership Totals

97–06	
Appearances	10
Points	5
Tries	1
Yellow Cards	0
Red Cards	0

Clubs

Year	Club	Apps	Pts
05-06	Northampton	10	5

Ross Beattie
Back Row/Lock

Date of Birth: 15.11.1977
Place of Birth: Sittingbourne
Nationality: Scottish
Height: 6'5"
Weight: 17st 8lb

Season Review 05/06

Ross arrived midway through last season when Saints were amid an injury crisis. He made his debut against Bedford Blues in the Powergen Cup and went on to make another eight appearances for Saints, but could only manage one replacement appearance in 2005/06. Competition in the back-row has intensified this season following the arrival of Daniel Browne, Paul Tupai, Sam Harding and Ben Lewitt, and the swift development of No 8s Mark Easter and Mark Hopley. Ross left the club at the end of the season..

Prem. Career History

Premiership Career Milestones

Club Debut:
vs L Irish (A), W, 22-21

▶ 27.12.04

Time Spent at the Club:

▶ 1 Season

First Try Scored for the Club:
—

▶ —

Full International:

▶ Scotland

Premiership Totals

97–06

Appearances	59
Points	20
Tries	4
Yellow Cards	2
Red Cards	0

Clubs

Year	Club	Apps	Pts
04-05	Northampton	7	0
02-03	Bristol Rugby	10	0
98-01	Newcastle	42	20

Selborne Boome
Lock

Date of Birth: 16.04.1975
Place of Birth: Somerset West, SA
Nationality: South African
Height: 6'3"
Weight: 17st

Season Review 05/06

When former head coach Alan Solomons arrived in 2004, he brought three big South African names with him: Corne Krige, Robbie Kempson and Selborne. The latter was the sole survivor from that season after Krige retired from rugby and Kempson left the club after he failed to recover from a neck injury. He wanted the opportunity to show the Northampton faithful the full range of his talent after knee and back injuries cut into his game-time last season.

The 2005/06 season started well with Boomer fit but injury befell him once again. During his fifth game Selborne stepped back into a lineout and his Achilles tendon gave way. He spent the rest of the season successfully rehabilitating the injury before leaving the club to concentrate on the arrival of his first child.

Prem. Career History

Premiership Career Milestones

Club Debut:
vs Bath (H), W, 29-14

▶ 04.09.04

Time Spent at the Club:

▶ 2 Seasons

First Try Scored for the Club:
—

▶ —

Full International:

▶ South Africa

Premiership Totals

97–06

Appearances	16
Points	0
Tries	0
Yellow Cards	0
Red Cards	0

Clubs

Year	Club	Apps	Pts
04-06	Northampton	16	0

Damien Browne
Lock

Date of Birth: 17.05.1980
Place of Birth: Galway
Nationality: Irish
Height: 6'6"
Weight: 20st 6lb

Season Review 05/06

The 2005/06 season has been a massive one for Damien. Injuries to Selborne Boome and new lock James Percival gave him a challenge which he met manfully. Damien started every game for Saints last season bar one and has taken over the responsibility for calling the lineouts. The coaching team handed him the honour of the captaincy in the absence of both Steve Thompson and Bruce Reihana.

He also scored his debut try for the club last season during Saints game against Gloucester at Kingsholm. He has been rewarded with a new two-year contract and who knows how much more Damien will develop in that time under the guidance of former All Blacks assistant coach Peter Sloane. He also came second to Carlos Spencer in the Saints Player of the Year award.

Player Performance 05/06

Premiership Performance

Percentage of total possible time player was on pitch   ⊙ position in league table at end of month

Month:	Sep	Oct	Nov	Dec	Jan	Feb	Mar	Apr	May	Total
	100%	100%	95%	88%	100%	96%	100%	93%	94%	97%
	11	9	11	11	10	8	6	6	6	
League Pts:	6/20	4/5	3/20	0/5	12/15	7/15	9/10	10/15	2/5	53/110
Points F:	50	25	81	14	65	80	53	62	34	464
Points A:	85	23	99	34	51	66	33	61	36	488
Try Bonus:	0	0	0	0	0	1	1	1	1	4
Lose Bonus:	2	0	3	0	0	0	0	1	1	7
Total mins:	320	80	304	70	240	230	160	223	75	1,702
Starts (sub):	4	1	4	1	3	3	2	3	1	22
Points:	5	0	0	0	0	0	0	0	0	5
Tries:	1	0	0	0	0	0	0	0	0	1
Ball Carries:	19	7	21	4	25	15	16	22	9	138
Metres:	79	20	48	7	59	48	40	68	30	399
Tackles:	26	3	23	1	15	18	12	16	1	115

Prem. Performance Totals

Tries
- Browne: 1
- Team-mates: 51
- **Total: 52**
- Penalty Tries: 1

Points
- Browne: 5
- Team-mates: 454
- **Total: 459**
- Penalty Tries: 5

Cards
- Browne: 1
- Team-mates: 14
- **Total: 15**

Cup Games

	Apps	Pts
Euro Challenge Cup	5	0
Powergen Cup	3	0
Total	8	0

Prem. Career History

Premiership Career Milestones

Club Debut:
vs Bath (H), W, 29-14

▶ 04.09.04

Time Spent at the Club:

▶ 2 Seasons

First Try Scored for the Club:
vs Gloucester (A), L, 24-28

▶ 24.09.05

Full International:

▶ —

Premiership Totals

97–06

Appearances	43
Points	5
Tries	1
Yellow Cards	2
Red Cards	0

Clubs

Year	Club	Apps	Pts
04-06	Northampton	43	5

Off the Pitch

Age:
- Browne: 26 years
- Team: 26 years, 4 months
- League: 26 years, 10 months

Height:
- Browne: 6'6"
- Team: 6'1"
- League: 6'1"

Weight:
- Browne: 20st 6lb
- Team: 15st 13lb
- League: 15st 10lb

Dan Browne
No8

Date of Birth:	13.04.1979
Place of Birth:	Auckland, NZ
Nationality:	New Zealander
Height:	6'5"
Weight:	16st 3lb

Season Review 05/06

Daniel arrived at Franklin's Gardens following three years at the French club Grenoble where he benefited from the expert No 8 tutelage of former England and Lions international Dean Richards. It was time for a change however and Daniel answered Saints' call for an out and out No 8.

Ireland-qualified Daniel fitted in well to Saints' new-look squad and started every game last season when he has been fit to do so. His pace and handling skills added extra impetus to Saints' attacking style of rugby and he was rewarded with his first three club tries against Narbonne, Leicester and Sale, on the last day of the season.

Player Performance 05/06

Premiership Performance

Percentage of total possible time player was on pitch · position in league table at end of month

Month:	Sep	Oct	Nov	Dec	Jan	Feb	Mar	Apr	May	Total
	41%		97%	100%	82%	76%		95%	100%	69%
League Pts:	6/20	4/5	3/20	0/5	12/15	7/15	9/10	10/15	2/5	53/110
Points F:	50	25	81	14	65	80	53	62	34	464
Points A:	85	23	99	34	51	66	33	61	36	488
Try Bonus:	0	0	0	0	0	1	1	1	1	4
Lose Bonus:	2	0	3	0	0	0	0	1	1	7
Total mins:	130	0	311	80	197	183	0	228	80	1,209
Starts (sub):	2	0	4	1	3	3	0	3	1	17
Points:	0	0	0	0	0	0	0	5	5	10
Tries:	0	0	0	0	0	0	0	1	1	2
Ball Carries:	6	0	37	10	31	22	0	32	14	152
Metres:	43	0	132	40	91	31	0	189	82	608
Tackles:	9	0	22	5	22	11	0	23	4	96

League position line: 11, 9, 0%, 11, 11, 10, 8, 6, 6, 6, 0%

Prem. Performance Totals

Tries
- Browne: 2
- Team-mates: 50
- **Total: 52**
- Penalty Tries: 1

Points
- Browne: 10
- Team-mates: 449
- **Total: 459**
- Penalty Tries: 5

Cards
- Browne: 1
- Team-mates: 14
- **Total: 15**

Cup Games

	Apps	Pts
Euro Challenge Cup	5	5
Powergen Cup	1	0
Total	**6**	**5**

Prem. Career History

Premiership Career Milestones

Club Debut:
vs Leicester (A), L, 0-32
03.09.05

First Try Scored for the Club:
vs Leicester (H), L, 19-24
14.04.06

Time Spent at the Club:
1 Season

Full International:
—

Premiership Totals

97–06	
Appearances	17
Points	10
Tries	2
Yellow Cards	1
Red Cards	0

Clubs

Year	Club	Apps	Pts
05-06	Northampton	17	10

Off the Pitch

Age:
- Browne: 27 years, 1 month
- Team: 26 years, 4 months
- League: 26 years, 10 months

Height:
- Browne: 6'5"
- Team: 6'1"
- League: 6'1"

Weight:
- Browne: 16st 3lb
- Team: 15st 13lb
- League: 15st 10lb

Chris Budgen
Prop

Date of Birth: 21.01.1973
Place of Birth: Hamilton, NZ
Nationality: New Zealander
Height: 5'8"
Weight: 17st 10lb

Season Review 05/06

Chris just seems to get better and better with each season he remains at Franklin's Gardens and the club more than relied on him while Pat Barnard was out injured at the start of 2006. Still "Chicken" to his mates, and still serving the Army when needed, Chris played in 26 games last season and passed the 100-game milestone as Saints racked up eight tries against Saracens. Chris also scored one of his own this year against Bristol.

Chris covers both sides of the scrum and hooker, which makes him ideal cover on the bench. However, the 33-year-old made more starts than replacements appearances in 2005/06 to prove he is a worthy member of the squad.

Player Performance 05/06

Premiership Performance

Percentage of total possible time player was on pitch   ⊕ position in league table at end of month

Month:	Sep	Oct	Nov	Dec	Jan	Feb	Mar	Apr	May	Total
	45%	88%	61%	96%	94%	86%	25%	33%	0%	59%
	11	9	11	11	10	8	6	6	6	
League Pts:	6/20	4/5	3/20	0/5	12/15	7/15	9/10	10/15	2/5	53/110
Points F:	50	25	81	14	65	80	53	62	34	464
Points A:	85	23	99	34	51	66	33	61	36	488
Try Bonus:	0	0	0	0	0	1	1	1	1	4
Lose Bonus:	2	0	3	0	0	0	0	1	1	7
Total mins:	144	70	194	77	226	207	40	79	0	1,037
Starts (sub):	1 (3)	1	3	0 (1)	3	3	0 (1)	0 (3)	0	11 (8)
Points:	0	0	0	0	5	0	0	0	0	5
Tries:	0	0	0	0	1	0	0	0	0	1
Ball Carries:	9	9	15	7	27	20	5	13	0	105
Metres:	29	42	46	16	84	53	15	41	0	326
Tackles:	2	0	8	7	15	18	3	6	0	59

Prem. Performance Totals

Tries
- Budgen: 1
- Team-mates: 51
- **Total: 52**
- Penalty Tries: 1

Points
- Budgen: 5
- Team-mates: 454
- **Total: 459**
- Penalty Tries: 5

Cards
- Budgen: 0
- Team-mates: 15
- **Total: 15**

Cup Games

	Apps	Pts
Euro Challenge Cup	6	0
Powergen Cup	3	0
Total	**9**	**0**

Prem. Career History

Premiership Career Milestones

Club Debut:
vs Gloucester (A), L, 9-22
▶ **01.09.01**

Time Spent at the Club:
▶ **5 Seasons**

First Try Scored for the Club:
vs Gloucester (H), W, 30-17
▶ **01.11.03**

Full International:
▶ —

Premiership Totals

97–06

Appearances	69
Points	15
Tries	3
Yellow Cards	3
Red Cards	0

Clubs

Year	Club	Apps	Pts
01-06	Northampton	69	15

Off the Pitch

Age:
- Budgen: 33 years, 4 months
- Team: 26 years, 4 months
- League: 26 years, 10 months

Height:
- Budgen: 5'8"
- Team: 6'1"
- League: 6'1"

Weight:
- Budgen: 17st 10lb
- Team: 15st 13lb
- League: 15st 10lb

Jon Clarke
Centre

Date of Birth: 22.10.1983
Place of Birth: Sheffield
Nationality: English
Height: 6'3"
Weight: 14st 1lb

Season Review 05/06

If this is the Year of the Dog in Chinese terms, then this season surely has to be the Year of the JC in Saints terms. The 22-year-old has literally gone from zero to hero care of a decision by head coach Paul Grayson. Jon was out of the running in the 2004/05 season due to a groin injury but was catapulted back into the limelight when Grayson handed him the No 13 shirt in the absence of injured Geoff Appleford.

Ahead of the 2005/06 season, Jon had either played at full-back or on the wing… and was successful at both. He was at full-back when he started all the games for the England U21s squad that won the Grand Slam in 2004, and was rewarded with the Saints Young Player of the Year prize at the end of 2003/04 season for his efforts on the wing. JC has slotted in

very well at outside centre and started every game last season – bar one – and scored eight tries. He also recorded his 50th game for the club, and picked up his cap for doing so at the end of season dinner, on the last day of the season.

But last season also saw the return of Jon to the England set-up. He played in both of England A's games against Italy and Ireland but was also invited to the full England training sessions at Pennyhill Park Hotel during the Six Nations to get him used to the international environment. Sadly, a hernia operation prevented him from furthering his international career during the summer but he was nominated for both the PRA and GUINNESS PREMIERSHIP Young Player of the Year awards.

Player Performance 05/06

Premiership Performance

Percentage of total possible time player was on pitch   ⊖ position in league table at end of month

Month:	Sep	Oct	Nov	Dec	Jan	Feb	Mar	Apr	May	Total
	100%	100%	96%	100%	100%	95%	100%	91%	100%	97%
League Pts:	6/20	4/5	3/20	0/5	12/15	7/15	9/10	10/15	2/5	53/110
Points F:	50	25	81	14	65	80	53	62	34	464
Points A:	85	23	99	34	51	66	33	61	36	488
Try Bonus:	0	0	0	0	0	1	1	1	1	4
Lose Bonus:	2	0	3	0	0	0	0	1	1	7
Total mins:	320	80	307	80	240	229	160	219	80	1,715
Starts (sub):	4	1	4	1	3	3	2	3	1	22
Points:	5	0	0	0	10	5	10	0	0	30
Tries:	1	0	0	0	2	1	2	0	0	6
Ball Carries:	9	8	25	3	25	21	15	24	8	138
Metres:	112	120	175	9	231	203	121	150	74	1195
Tackles:	32	1	21	6	24	15	19	22	7	147

Prem. Performance Totals

Tries

- ▶ Clarke: 6
- Team-mates: 46
- **Total: 52**
- ▶ Penalty Tries: 1

Points

- ▶ Clarke: 30
- Team-mates: 429
- **Total: 459**
- ▶ Penalty Tries: 5

Cards

- ▶ Clarke: 0
- Team-mates: 15
- **Total: 15**

Cup Games

	Apps	Pts
Euro Challenge Cup	6	5
Powergen Cup	2	5
Total	**8**	**10**

Prem. Career History

Premiership Career Milestones

Club Debut:
vs Wasps (H), W, 27-17
 **27.09.03**

Time Spent at the Club:
▶ **3 Seasons**

First Try Scored for the Club:
vs Wasps (H), W, 27-17
▶ **27.09.03**

Full International:
▶ —

Premiership Totals

97–06

Appearances	37
Points	45
Tries	9
Yellow Cards	0
Red Cards	0

Clubs

Year	Club	Apps	Pts
03-06	Northampton	37	45

Off the Pitch

Age:

- ▶ Clarke: 22 years, 7 months
- Team: 26 years, 4 months
- League: 26 years, 10 months

Height:

- ▶ Clarke: 6'3"
- Team: 6'1"
- League: 6'1"

Weight:

- ▶ Clarke: 14st 1lb
- Team: 15st 13lb
- League: 15st 10lb

Ben Cohen
Wing

Date of Birth: 14.09.1978
Place of Birth: Northampton,
Nationality: English
Height: 6'2"
Weight: 15st 10lb

Season Review 05/06

The 2005/06 season was an excellent one for Big Ben following a turbulent time the season before which almost saw him leave the Gardens. After a summer off from rugby, Ben turned up to pre-season training fresher than he had been for years. He also seemed to relish the restructured coaching regime now officially under the guidance of former England team mate Paul Grayson.

Ben appeared in 23 games last season and scored the most tries for Saints with 15. He passed the 200-game milestone in 2005/06 and was given the honour of leading the team out against Gloucester at Kingsholm to mark the event.

He also played himself back into the good books of England's head coach Andy Robinson with his sterling efforts for Saints and was rewarded with not only a recall to the squad but a starting place in two of England's autumn internationals and all five of their Six Nations tests.

Ben also notched up a first for rugby by wearing a partial face mask that protected a site of a shattered cheekbone. He wore it for the first time against Worcester and proved he was unfazed by the whole experience by scoring Saints' only try of the afternoon.

However, his best try of the season was arguably the final-minute score against London Irish – only Ben can score tries like that. And coupled with Bruce Reihana's touchline conversion, it provided a winning end to another close GUINNESS PREMIERSHIP game.

Player Performance 05/06

Premiership Performance

Percentage of total possible time player was on pitch   ⊙ position in league table at end of month

Month:	Sep	Oct	Nov	Dec	Jan	Feb	Mar	Apr	May	Total
	100%	100%	25%	0%	50%	25%	50%	100%	100%	60%
	11	9	11	11	10	8	6	6	6	
League Pts:	6/20	4/5	3/20	0/5	12/15	7/15	9/10	10/15	2/5	53/110
Points F:	50	25	81	14	65	80	53	62	34	464
Points A:	85	23	99	34	51	66	33	61	36	488
Try Bonus:	0	0	0	0	0	1	1	1	1	4
Lose Bonus:	2	0	3	0	0	0	0	1	1	7
Total mins:	320	80	80	0	120	59	80	240	80	1,059
Starts (sub):	4	1	1	0	1 (1)	1	1	3	1	13 (1)
Points:	0	5	0	0	5	5	5	10	5	35
Tries:	0	1	0	0	1	1	1	2	1	7
Ball Carries:	33	14	9	0	15	13	13	41	12	150
Metres:	212	101	83	0	64	114	81	301	73	1029
Tackles:	14	2	6	0	8	5	3	10	1	49

Prem. Performance Totals

Tries

- Cohen: 7
- Team-mates: 45
- **Total: 52**
- Penalty Tries: 1

Points

- Cohen: 35
- Team-mates: 424
- **Total: 459**
- Penalty Tries: 5

Cards

- Cohen: 0
- Team-mates: 15
- **Total: 15**

Cup Games

	Apps	Pts
Euro Challenge Cup	6	30
Powergen Cup	3	10
Total	**9**	**40**

Prem. Career History

Premiership Career Milestones

Club Debut:
vs Newcastle (A), L, 12-37

Time Spent at the Club:

▶▶ **9 Seasons**

First Try Scored for the Club:
vs Newcastle (H), W, 57-16

Full International:

▶▶ **England**

Premiership Totals

97–06

Appearances	132
Points	225
Tries	45
Yellow Cards	4
Red Cards	0

Clubs

Year	Club	Apps	Pts
97-06	Northampton	132	225

Off the Pitch

Age:

- Cohen: 27 years, 8 months
- Team: 26 years, 4 months
- League: 26 years, 10 months

Height:

- Cohen: 6'2"
- Team: 6'1"
- League: 6'1"

Weight:

- Cohen: 15st 10lb
- Team: 15st 13lb
- League: 15st 10lb

Rhodri Davies
Centre

Date of Birth: 11.01.1983
Place of Birth: Caerfyrddin
Nationality: Welsh
Height: 5'9"
Weight: 14st

Season Review 05/06

Last season was Rhodri's second chance of making it as a Saints player and he embraced the opportunity. Injuries to Seamus Mallon and David Quinlan opened up opportunities for the 23-year-old and he settled in well to a centre partnership with fellow Academy product Jon Clarke. Rhodri's turn of pace and strength in a contact situation caught some opposing teams on the hop and he managed to rack up three tries in his 12 appearances for the first team as well as a new two-year contract.

He also may well have played for Wales sevens team in the Commonwealth Games had a groin injury not brought his season to a halt. He has already started running again and will be back for next season.

Prem. Career History

Premiership Career Milestones

Club Debut:	First Try Scored for the Club:
vs Leicester (A), L, 0-32	vs Wasps (H), L, 13-21
▶ 03.09.05	▶ 12.11.05
Time Spent at the Club:	Full International:
▶ 1 Season	▶ —

Premiership Totals
97–06

Appearances	7
Points	10
Tries	2
Yellow Cards	0
Red Cards	0

Clubs

Year	Club	Apps	Pts
05-06	Northampton	7	10

Simon Emms
Prop

Date of Birth: 27.01.1975
Place of Birth: Carmarthen
Nationality: Welsh
Height: 5'11"
Weight: 17st 8lb

Season Review 05/06

Simon was another player who joined Saints midway through the previous season when the club simply ran out of props. Saints offered Emms a way back into the sport after he had pretty much given up on the idea of making his living from rugby following a serious of raw deals with other clubs.

Saints, however, made the Welshman feel welcome and he played 13 games for the first team in the 2004/05 season but was thwarted from building on that tally at the start of last season when he ruptured a bicep. The injury was originally supposed to be the end of Emms's contribution to 2005/06 but he came back earlier than expected and played in eight games, including his first start for the year on the last day of the season, to complete the first year of his two-year contract.

Prem. Career History

Premiership Career Milestones

Club Debut:	First Try Scored for the Club:
vs L Irish (A), W, 22-21	—
▶ 27.12.04	▶ —
Time Spent at the Club:	Full International:
▶ 2 Seasons	▶ —

Premiership Totals
97–06

Appearances	58
Points	0
Tries	0
Yellow Cards	4
Red Cards	0

Clubs

Year	Club	Apps	Pts
04-06	Northampton	18	0
04-05	Gloucester	1	0
00-03	Bath Rugby	39	0

Darren Fox
Flanker

Date of Birth: 20.01.1981
Place of Birth: Peterborough
Nationality: English
Height: 6'
Weight: 15st 10lb

Season Review 05/06

Darren had a difficult start to his Saints career following two big operations on a knee injury when he was supposed to be spending time being nurtured by the Academy. He made his debut in the 2002/03 season and has not looked back since.

However, competition for places in the back-row seriously intensified last season with potentially three players battling it out for a start in the No 7 shirt. Sam Harding and Ben Lewitt's arrival created the competition, but Fox continued to work hard to prove his worth. He started 14 games last season and also came on as a replacement 11 times and scored three tries for 2005/06. Darren has also signed a new two-year contract with Saints last season, so there will much more to come from this home-grown player.

Prem. Career History

Premiership Career Milestones

Club Debut:
vs Leicester (H), L, 3-16

First Try Scored for the Club:
vs Bristol (H), W, 43-13

09.11.02

16.04.03

Time Spent at the Club:

Full International:

4 Seasons

—

Premiership Totals

97–06	
Appearances	68
Points	40
Tries	8
Yellow Cards	2
Red Cards	0

Clubs

Year	Club	Apps	Pts
02-06	Northampton	68	40

David Gerard
Lock

Date of Birth: 26.11.1977
Place of Birth: Toulon, France
Nationality: French
Height: 6'6"
Weight: 19st

Season Review 05/06

David arrived at Franklin's Gardens midway through last season when Selborne Boome ruptured his Achilles tendon. Selborne's problem added to Saints' injury concerns in the second row following James Percival's neck fracture, so reinforcements were called for!

David joined Saints from triple Heineken Cup champions Toulouse in the hope of securing more appearances amid a starting XV. The amiable Frenchman battled with Matt Lord for the No 5 shirt for the majority of last season and came away with 11 starts and 14 replacement appearances. He has another year left on his current contract so more will follow from this impressive 28-year-old.

Prem. Career History

Premiership Career Milestones

Club Debut:
vs L Irish (H), W, 25-23

First Try Scored for the Club:
—

15.10.05

—

Time Spent at the Club:

Full International:

1 Season

France

Premiership Totals

97–06	
Appearances	16
Points	0
Tries	0
Yellow Cards	1
Red Cards	0

Clubs

Year	Club	Apps	Pts
05-06	Northampton	16	0

Luke Harbut
Prop

Date of Birth: 18.04.1980
Place of Birth: London
Nationality: English
Height: 5'10"
Weight: 17st 7lb

Season Review 05/06

Tighthead prop Luke joined Northampton Saints at the start of last season having spent three years out of professional rugby. Slightly disillusioned by the sport, Luke went travelling before taking up his trade of carpentry on a full-time basis. The lure of getting up early to work on a freezing cold building site was soon overshadowed when Saints offered him a trial at Franklin's Gardens.

Luke spent the early part of pre-season catching up with the level of physical fitness required of a Saints player and then began to make his mark in the Wanderers team, and then the first team. Luke made three first team appearances for Saints last season.

Prem. Career History

Premiership Career Milestones

Club Debut:	First Try Scored for the Club:
vs Wasps (H), L, 13-21	—
▶ 12.11.05	▶ —
Time Spent at the Club:	Full International:
▶ 1 Season	▶ —

Premiership Totals

97–06	
Appearances	26
Points	10
Tries	2
Yellow Cards	0
Red Cards	0

Clubs

Year	Club	Apps	Pts
05-06	Northampton	3	0
00-02	Saracens	23	10

Johnny Howard
Scrum Half

Date of Birth: 02.10.1980
Place of Birth: London
Nationality: English
Height: 5'9"
Weight: 12st 7lb

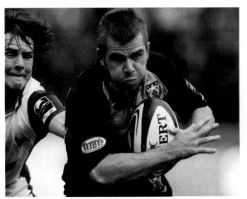

Season Review 05/06

At just 25, Johnny is one of Saints' longest serving current players having made his debut eight years ago. And it looks like he may reach that 10th season having signed a new two-year contract last year.

Johnny has been a constant feature of the Saints teamsheet for the last couple of seasons, either as cover for Mark Robinson or indeed in the starting No 9 shirt. However, he was called upon to cover the wing against Bristol in the European Challenge Cup, from where he scored a blistering try. Injuries meant he was also called up to start on the wing against Viadana the following weekend, but bad weather meant the game was called off and Johnny was one of the most disappointed to have missed out on a chance to show his pace!

Prem. Career History

Premiership Career Milestones

Club Debut:	First Try Scored for the Club:
vs Bristol (A), L, 16–46	vs Rotherham (A), W, 42-13
▶ 16.04.01	▶ 04.10.03
Time Spent at the Club:	Full International:
▶ 6 Seasons	▶ —

Premiership Totals

97–06	
Appearances	53
Points	20
Tries	4
Yellow Cards	0
Red Cards	0

Clubs

Year	Club	Apps	Pts
00-06	Northampton	53	20

Sam Harding
Flanker

Date of Birth: 01.12.1980
Place of Birth: Subiaco, NZ
Nationality: New Zealander
Height: 6'1"
Weight: 16st 4lb

Season Review 05/06

Sam literally burst onto the scene when he scored his first Saints try with his first touch of the ball on his debut against Worcester Warriors in the Powergen Cup last season. And from then on, the former All Black began making his name as an attacking line-breaker giving the coaching staff a headache as to which skilful player should start in the No 7 shirt.

A latecomer to the squad care of his duties to Canterbury during the NPC season, Sam edged the battle with Darren Fox and Ben Lewitt with 17 starts and nine replacement appearances. He was also the highest scoring forward with six and his debut try was among the shortlist for the Saints Try of the Season.

Player Performance 05/06

Premiership Performance

Percentage of total possible time player was on pitch   ⊙ position in league table at end of month

Month:	Sep	Oct	Nov	Dec	Jan	Feb	Mar	Apr	May	Total
	0%	100%	60%	26%	16%	71%	100%	72%	100%	52%
League Pts:	6/20	4/5	3/20	0/5	12/15	7/15	9/10	10/15	2/5	53/110
	11	9	11	11	10	8	6	6	6	
Points F:	50	25	81	14	65	80	53	62	34	464
Points A:	85	23	99	34	51	66	33	61	36	488
Try Bonus:	0	0	0	0	0	1	1	1	1	4
Lose Bonus:	2	0	3	0	0	0	0	1	1	7
Total mins:	0	80	193	21	39	171	160	172	80	916
Starts (sub):	0	1	2 (2)	0 (1)	0 (2)	2 (1)	2	2 (1)	1	10 (7)
Points:	0	0	0	0	0	5	0	0	0	5
Tries:	0	0	0	0	0	1	0	0	0	1
Ball Carries:	0	11	22	3	4	20	20	15	3	98
Metres:	0	38	67	7	11	73	56	67	10	329
Tackles:	0	5	23	2	5	21	17	27	7	107

Prem. Performance Totals

Tries
- ■ Harding: 1
- ■ Team-mates: 51
- **Total:** 52
- ▶ Penalty Tries: 1

Points
- ■ Harding: 5
- ■ Team-mates: 454
- **Total:** 459
- ▶ Penalty Tries: 5

Cards
- ■ Harding: 1
- ■ Team-mates: 14
- **Total:** 15

Cup Games

	Apps	Pts
Euro Challenge Cup	6	20
Powergen Cup	3	5
Total	**9**	**25**

Prem. Career History

Career Milestones

Club Debut:
vs L Irish (H), W, 25-23

▶ 15.10.05
Time Spent at the Club:
▶ 1 Season

First Try Scored for the Club:
vs Saracens (H), W, 58-17

▶ 18.02.06
Full International:
▶ New Zealand

Premiership Totals

97–06

Appearances	17
Points	5
Tries	1
Yellow Cards	1
Red Cards	0

Clubs

Year	Club	Apps	Pts
05-06	Northampton	17	5

Off the Pitch

Age:
- ▶ Harding: 25 years, 5 months
- ■ Team: 26 years, 4 months
- | League: 26 years, 10 months

Height:
- ▶ Harding: 6'1"
- ■ Team: 6'1"
- | League: 6'1"

Weight:
- ▶ Harding: 16st 4lb
- ■ Team: 15st 13lb
- | League: 15st 10lb

Ben Jones
Scrum Half

Date of Birth: 21.02.1983
Place of Birth: Plymouth
Nationality: English
Height: 5'5"
Weight: 13st

Season Review 05/06

After the elation of winning the club's Young Player of the Year award at the end of the 2004/05 season, Ben set about trying to impress the Saints coaching staff during last season. A shoulder injury blighted his progress however, but he did cement his position as a key element of the Wanderers side.

Prem. Career History

Premiership Career Milestones	
Club Debut:	First Try Scored for the Club:
vs Gloucester (H), L, 12-18	—
▶▶ **18.09.04**	▶▶ **—**
Time Spent at the Club:	Full International:
▶▶ **1 Season**	▶▶ **—**

Premiership Totals	
97–06	
Appearances	6
Points	0
Tries	0
Yellow Cards	0
Red Cards	0

Clubs			
Year	Club	Apps	Pts
04-05	Northampton	6	0

Robbie Kydd
Centre/Fly Half

Date of Birth: 19.01.1982
Place of Birth: Auckland, NZ
Nationality: New Zealander
Height: 5'11"
Weight: 14st 3lb

Season Review 05/06

If nothing else, Robbie got his timing down to a tee last season. As Saints lurched towards a backline injury crisis in January, the Scotland-qualified Kiwi went from zero to hero by being called up to his first Saints start for a vital Guinness Premiership game against Worcester. He had not played any rugby for nine months after he suffered a serious knee injury in training with Saracens and, as a result, Saints had had to pull out of his contract. He did however remain under the care of the Franklin's Gardens medical team and he bounced back to action, at inside centre, to help Saints to a memorable win at Sixways. Robbie has made six appearances since then and is a useful man to have around as he covers fly-half, centre and full-back and has a mean goal-kicking boot on him too.

Prem. Career History

Premiership Career Milestones	
Club Debut:	First Try Scored for the Club:
vs Worcester (A), W, 15-11	—
▶▶ **07.01.06**	▶▶ **—**
Time Spent at the Club:	Full International:
▶▶ **1 Season**	▶▶ **—**

Premiership Totals	
97–06	
Appearances	33
Points	63
Tries	5
Yellow Cards	0
Red Cards	0

Clubs			
Year	Club	Apps	Pts
05-06	Northampton	6	0
03-05	Saracens	19	58
03-04	Bath Rugby	8	5

Sean Lamont
Wing

Date of Birth:	15.01.1981
Place of Birth:	Perth, Scotland
Nationality:	Scottish
Height:	6'2"
Weight:	15st

Season Review 05/06

Sean is the only Saints player to have scored four tries in one match in the Premiership era. That match was in February when Saints ran riot over a struggling Saracens. Having scored so many tries for his previous club Glasgow, it helped end a frustrating try-less run. Monty was also among the top six contenders for Saints Player of the Year and won the Saints Try of the Year with the fourth of those tries against Saracens.

Sean's impressive form was not just in evidence for his club though as he more than helped Scotland on to a classic win over the French with his two tries in front of an ecstatic Murrayfield. The much-hyped meeting between him and his team mate Ben Cohen of England was also another win for the Scots.

Player Performance 05/06

Premiership Performance

Percentage of total possible time player was on pitch   ⊕ position in league table at end of month

Month:	Sep	Oct	Nov	Dec	Jan	Feb	Mar	Apr	May	Total
	78%	100%	25%	0%	67%	33%	50%	100%	30%	56%
position	11	9	11	11	10	8	6	6	6	
League Pts:	6/20	4/5	3/20	0/5	12/15	7/15	9/10	10/15	2/5	53/110
Points F:	50	25	81	14	65	80	53	62	34	464
Points A:	85	23	99	34	51	66	33	61	36	488
Try Bonus:	0	0	0	0	0	1	1	1	1	4
Lose Bonus:	2	0	3	0	0	0	0	1	1	7
Total mins:	248	80	80	0	160	80	80	240	24	992
Starts (sub):	3 (1)	1	1	0	2	1	1	3	0 (1)	12 (2)
Points:	0	0	0	0	5	20	0	5	0	30
Tries:	0	0	0	0	1	4	0	1	0	6
Ball Carries:	25	9	9	0	10	12	9	33	9	116
Metres:	210	59	60	0	29	244	59	269	86	1016
Tackles:	14	1	4	0	9	3	4	10	1	46

Prem. Performance Totals

Tries

- Lamont: 6
- Team-mates: 46
- **Total: 52**
- Penalty Tries: 1

Points

- Lamont: 30
- Team-mates: 429
- **Total: 459**
- Penalty Tries: 5

Cards

- Lamont: 0
- Team-mates: 15
- **Total: 15**

Cup Games

	Apps	Pts
Euro Challenge Cup	4	0
Powergen Cup	3	5
Total	7	5

Prem. Career History

Premiership Career Milestones

Club Debut:
vs Leicester (A), L, 0-32
▶ **03.09.05**
Time Spent at the Club:
▶ **1 Season**

First Try Scored for the Club:
vs Leeds (H), W, 21-18
▶ **28.01.06**
Full International:
▶ **Scotland**

Premiership Totals

97–06

Appearances	14
Points	30
Tries	6
Yellow Cards	0
Red Cards	0

Clubs

Year	Club	Apps	Pts
05-06	Northampton	14	30

Off the Pitch

Age:
- Lamont: 25 years, 4 months
- Team: 26 years, 4 months
- League: 26 years, 10 months

Height:
- Lamont: 6'2"
- Team: 6'1"
- League: 6'1"

Weight:
- Lamont: 15st
- Team: 15st 13lb
- League: 15st 10lb

Ben Lewitt
Flanker

Date of Birth: 23.10.1978
Place of Birth: Leamington Spa
Nationality: English
Height: 6'3"
Weight: 15st

Season Review 05/06

Ben has done the rounds of the East Midlands clubs with Leicester, Coventry and Bedford Blues already under his belt, but seems set on staying with Saints after he signed a new two-year deal at the end of last season. Ben fitted in well to life at Franklin's Gardens and played at both blindside and openside flanker for the team.

However, his season was interrupted when he was called up to England's Commonwealth Games sevens squad in Melbourne. He did not make the final 10 however, but still enjoyed the Games experience. Ben played in 17 games for Saints in 2005/06 before resting for part of the summer following a toe operation.

Player Performance 05/06

Premiership Performance

Percentage of total possible time player was on pitch   position in league table at end of month

Month:	Sep	Oct	Nov	Dec	Jan	Feb	Mar	Apr	May	Total
	16%	0%	32%	93%	97%	24%	0%	18%	0%	32%
	11	9	11	11	10	8	6	6	6	
League Pts:	6/20	4/5	3/20	0/5	12/15	7/15	9/10	10/15	2/5	53/110
Points F:	50	25	81	14	65	80	53	62	34	464
Points A:	85	23	99	34	51	66	33	61	36	488
Try Bonus:	0	0	0	0	0	1	1	1	1	4
Lose Bonus:	2	0	3	0	0	0	0	1	1	7
Total mins:	52	0	102	74	233	57	0	43	0	561
Starts (sub):	0 (3)	0	1 (2)	1	3	1	0	0 (2)	0	6 (7)
Points:	0	0	0	0	0	0	0	0	0	0
Tries:	0	0	0	0	0	0	0	0	0	0
Ball Carries:	1	0	6	5	21	4	0	6	0	43
Metres:	0	0	24	15	69	6	0	22	0	136
Tackles:	12	0	7	6	31	6	0	6	0	68

Prem. Performance Totals

Tries
- Lewitt: 0
- Team-mates: 52
- **Total: 52**
- Penalty Tries: 1

Points
- Lewitt: 0
- Team-mates: 459
- **Total: 459**
- Penalty Tries: 5

Cards
- Lewitt: 0
- Team-mates: 15
- **Total: 15**

Cup Games

	Apps	Pts
Euro Challenge Cup	3	0
Powergen Cup	1	0
Total	**4**	**0**

Prem. Career History

Premiership Career Milestones

Club Debut:
vs Leicester (A), L, 0-32
▶ 03.09.05

Time Spent at the Club:
▶ 1 Season

First Try Scored for the Club:

▶ —

Full International:
▶ —

Premiership Totals
97–06
Appearances	14
Points	0
Tries	0
Yellow Cards	0
Red Cards	0

Clubs
Year	Club	Apps	Pts
05-06	Northampton	13	0
99-00	Leicester Tigers	1	0

Off the Pitch

Age:
- Lewitt: 27 years, 7 months
- Team: 26 years, 4 months
- League: 26 years, 10 months

Height:
- Lewitt: 6'3"
- Team: 6'1"
- League: 6'1"

Weight:
- Lewitt: 15st
- Team: 15st 13lb
- League: 15st 10lb

Matt Lord
Lock

Date of Birth:	07.01.1978
Place of Birth:	Taumarunui, NZ
Nationality:	New Zealander
Height:	6'4"
Weight:	17st 2lb

Season Review 05/06

The Player of the Year and the Players' Player of the Year of 2004/05 did not let anyone down last season either. The farmer's lad continued to work hard and to lead by example as the competition in the second row began to hot up. Injuries to Selborne Boome and James Percival cut out some of the contenders but the arrival of French lock David Gerard certainly upped the ante. And, indeed, the scrap for the No 5 shirt became a straight fight between Gerard and Matt while Damien Browne ran the show from No 4. Lord played 28 games for Saints last season to bring him three away from his 100th game.

Player Performance 05/06

Premiership Performance

Percentage of total possible time player was on pitch   ◯ position in league table at end of month

Month:	Sep	Oct	Nov	Dec	Jan	Feb	Mar	Apr	May	Total
	93%	24%	70%	93%	88%	83%	43%	95%	65%	78%
Position	11	9	11	11	10	8	6	6	6	
League Pts:	6/20	4/5	3/20	0/5	12/15	7/15	9/10	10/15	2/5	53/110
Points F:	50	25	81	14	65	80	53	62	34	464
Points A:	85	23	99	34	51	66	33	61	36	488
Try Bonus:	0	0	0	0	0	1	1	1	1	4
Lose Bonus:	2	0	3	0	0	0	0	1	1	7
Total mins:	296	19	225	74	212	199	69	228	52	1,374
Starts (sub):	4	0 (1)	2 (2)	1	3	3	0 (2)	3	1	17 (5)
Points:	0	0	0	0	0	0	0	0	0	0
Tries:	0	0	0	0	0	0	0	0	0	0
Ball Carries:	5	0	4	4	15	11	5	14	1	59
Metres:	14	0	6	6	59	34	3	50	7	179
Tackles:	29	1	24	9	20	21	6	22	2	134

Prem. Performance Totals

Tries
- Lord: 0
- Team-mates: 52
- **Total: 52**
- Penalty Tries: 1

Points
- Lord: 0
- Team-mates: 459
- **Total: 459**
- Penalty Tries: 5

Cards
- Lord: 1
- Team-mates: 14
- **Total: 15**

Cup Games

	Apps	Pts
Euro Challenge Cup	5	0
Powergen Cup	1	0
Total	**6**	**0**

Prem. Career History

Premiership Career Milestones

Club Debut:
vs Leeds (A), L, 19-26

▶ **17.11.02**

Time Spent at the Club:

▶ **4 Seasons**

First Try Scored for the Club:
vs Newcastle (A), L, 20-22

▶ **20.04.03**

Full International:

▶ —

Premiership Totals

97–06

Appearances	73
Points	5
Tries	1
Yellow Cards	2
Red Cards	0

Clubs

Year	Club	Apps	Pts
02-06	Northampton	73	5

Off the Pitch

Age:
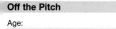
- Lord: 28 years, 4 months
- Team: 26 years, 4 months
- League: 26 years, 10 months

Height:
- Lord: 6'4"
- Team: 6'1"
- League: 6'1"

Weight:
- Lord: 17st 2lb
- Team: 15st 13lb
- League: 15st 10lb

Seamus Mallon
Centre

Date of Birth: 21.11.1980
Place of Birth: Ulster
Nationality: Irish
Height: 6'3"
Weight: 14st 11lb

Season Review 05/06

Seamus took the honour of scoring Saints' first try, amid a new-look back-line, of the 2005/06 season. At the press conference that followed the Bath game, former Ulsterman then set the newspapers alight with his tale of how he attracted director of rugby Budge Pountney's attention with a video of his greatest rugby moments. This is a well-used recruitment tool in rugby circles but it sent ripples of excitement through the media world!

The 25-year-old made eight appearances for Saints last season and scored two tries, but his progress was thwarted when he suffered a serious knee injury in training. He is due back to action this season.

Prem. Career History

Premiership Career Milestones

Club Debut:
vs Leicester (A), L, 0-32
▶ **03.09.05**

Time Spent at the Club:
▶ **1 Season**

First Try Scored for the Club:
vs Bath (A), W, 17-9
▶ **10.09.05**

Full International:
▶ **—**

Premiership Totals

97–06

Appearances	5
Points	10
Tries	2
Yellow Cards	1
Red Cards	0

Clubs

Year	Club	Apps	Pts
05-06	Northampton	5	10

Player Performance 05/06

Prem. Performance Totals

Tries
▶ Mallon: 2
▷ Team-mates: 50
Total: 52
▶ Penalty Tries: 1

Points
▶ Mallon: 10
▷ Team-mates: 449
Total: 459
▶ Penalty Tries: 5

Cards
▶ Mallon: 1
▷ Team-mates: 14
Total: 15

Cup Games

	Apps	Pts
Euro Challenge Cup	1	0
Powergen Cup	2	0
Total	3	0

Brett McNamee
Back-row

Date of Birth: 08.06.1984
Place of Birth: Northampton
Nationality: English
Height: 6'2"
Weight: 15st 13lbs

Season Review 05/06

Local lad Brett did not have the best start to last season in that he missed out on playing for Ireland in the U21s World Championship in Argentina with a knee injury. The injury also meant he missed out on action at the start of this season allowing other young players to make their mark for the first team. On returning to fitness, Brett played for Catania in Italy before going on loan to Coventry for the final months of the season.

Luke Myring
Fly Half

Date of Birth: 20.12.1983
Place of Birth: Leicester
Nationality: English
Height: 6'
Weight: 14st 3lb

Season Review 05/06

Luke always knew he would have big boots to fill when the time came that Carlos Spencer would not be available to play for Saints. That time emerged just before Christmas when Spencer broke a finger and Luke was called up to fill the breach. Luke took his opportunity against Narbonne in the European Challenge Cup and helped steer Saints to a healthy away win. He was then well and truly put under the spotlight when he started at fly-half against Sale Sharks in front of the Sky cameras on Boxing Day. Saints did not come away with a win that day but Luke did chalk up his debut try. He made a further two appearances for the first team last season before finally admitting defeat to a shoulder injury. An operation ruled him out of action for the rest of the season, but he will be raring to go in 2006/07.

Prem. Career History

Premiership Career Milestones

Club Debut:
vs Leicester (H), W, 26-11
▶ **26.02.05**

Time Spent at the Club:
▶ **2 Seasons**

First Try Scored for the Club:
vs Sale (A), L, 14-34
▶ **26.12.05**

Full International:
▶ —

Premiership Totals
97–06

Appearances	5
Points	8
Tries	1
Yellow Cards	0
Red Cards	0

Clubs

Year	Club	Apps	Pts
04-06	Northampton	2	5
03-04	Leicester Tigers	3	3

Colin Noon
Prop

Date of Birth: 24.10.1975
Place of Birth: Bridgend
Nationality: Welsh
Height: 5'11"
Weight: 18st 3lb

Season Review 05/06

Colin arrived at Saints under a cloud with "suspended" stamped on it. It is hard to believe the mild-mannered Welshman was the same player that allegedly stamped on another during a game for Rotherham, but that apparently was the case. The date September 26 was the date imprinted on Colin's brain and he made his return to rugby against his former club Leicester Tigers in a Wanderers game. His performance earned him a start against Worcester Warriors in the Powergen Cup but his Saints debut was cut short by a calf injury. Colin played in eight games for the first team – starting five – before moving to Biarritz at the end of the season in search a more regular place in the starting XV.

Prem. Career History

Premiership Career Milestones

Club Debut:
vs Saracens (A), L, 22-28
▶ **05.11.05**

Time Spent at the Club:
▶ **1 Season**

First Try Scored for the Club:
—
▶ —

Full International:
▶ —

Premiership Totals
97–06

Appearances	20
Points	5
Tries	1
Yellow Cards	3
Red Cards	0

Clubs

Year	Club	Apps	Pts
05-06	Northampton	3	0
04-05	Leicester Tigers	1	0
04-05	Worcester	3	0
03-04	Rotherham	13	5

James Percival
Lock

Date of Birth: 09.11.1983
Place of Birth: Wordsley
Nationality: English
Height: 6'5"
Weight: 17st 5lbs

Season Review 05/06

James had the worst possible start to his Saints career. During Saints' second warm-up game, against Munster, the young lock was hit in a ruck situation and he had to be stretchered off the field. At first, the injury did not appear to be too serious but then a second x-ray revealed he had in fact broken his neck. It obviously ruled him out of action, but not for good. James was in the rehab pool almost immediately and then, with the medical team's help, he slowly built up his strength to enable him to take part in contact training at the end of last season. Watch out, James is champing at the bit to get going in 2006/07.

James Pritchard
Full Back

Date of Birth: 21.07.1979
Place of Birth: Parks, NSW, Australia
Nationality: Canadian
Height: 5'9"
Weight: 13st 5lb

Season Review 05/06

James was the latest arrival to the squad last season to provide extra cover in the back three. The Australian-born Canadian international (work that one out) was plucked from French club Perpignan to do just that. A prolific kicker, especially during his time with Saints' rugby neighbours Bedford Blues, James helped steer Saints to a vital victory over Gloucester with a difficult conversion. He made two appearances for the first team in 2005/06.

Player Performance 05/06

Prem. Performance Totals

Tries

Pritchard:	0
Team-mates:	52
Total:	**52**
Penalty Tries:	1

Points

Pritchard:	4
Team-mates:	455
Total:	**459**
Penalty Tries:	5

Cards

Pritchard:	0
Team-mates:	15
Total:	**15**

Cup Games

	Apps	Pts
Euro Challenge Cup	0	0
Powergen Cup	0	0
Total	**0**	**0**

Prem. Career History

Premiership Career Milestones

Club Debut:
vs Wasps (A), D, 19-19

⯈ 12.02.06

Time Spent at the Club:

⯈ 1 Season

First Try Scored for the Club:
—

⯈ —

Full International:

⯈ Canada

Premiership Totals

97–06	
Appearances	2
Points	4
Tries	0
Yellow Cards	0
Red Cards	0

Clubs

Year	Club	Apps	Pts
05-06	Northampton	2	4

David Quinlan
Centre

Date of Birth: 04.01.1978
Place of Birth: Dublin, Ireland
Nationality: Irish
Height: 6'4"
Weight: 16st 2lb

Season Review 05/06

David had a frustrating start to last season when he picked up a rib injury in Saints' final pre-season game against his former club Leinster. It meant the Irish international missed out on the first three GUINNESS PREMIERSHIP games but was raring to go when he was finally unleashed against Gloucester at Kingsholm to play in what he described as "the kind of match he came to England to play in". David worked well with new centre Jon Clarke last season, but he had to be replaced by a raft of No 12s when he suffered a knee injury against Narbonne. His return in the early part of 2006 has coincided with a more settled-looking Northampton Saints and his hard work around the field has not gone unnoticed. David played in 21 games last season and scored his debut try on the last day of the league programme against Sale Sharks.

Player Performance 05/06

Premiership Performance
Percentage of total possible time player was on pitch   ⊖ position in league table at end of month

Month:	Sep	Oct	Nov	Dec	Jan	Feb	Mar	Apr	May	Total
	25%	91%	47%	0%	25%	95%	100%	100%	100%	61%
League Pts:	6/20	4/5	3/20	0/5	12/15	7/15	9/10	10/15	2/5	53/110
Points F:	50	25	81	14	65	80	53	62	34	464
Points A:	85	23	99	34	51	66	33	61	36	488
Try Bonus:	0	0	0	0	0	1	1	1	1	4
Lose Bonus:	2	0	3	0	0	0	0	1	1	7
Total mins:	80	73	149	0	59	227	160	240	80	1,068
Starts (sub):	1	1	2 (1)	0	1	3	2	3	1	14 (1)
Points:	0	0	0	0	0	0	0	0	5	5
Tries:	0	0	0	0	0	0	0	0	1	1
Ball Carries:	7	11	19	0	7	15	15	29	5	108
Metres:	16	52	70	0	29	24	56	122	21	390
Tackles:	5	2	13	0	11	16	27	31	9	114

Prem. Performance Totals

Tries

▶ Quinlan: 1
Team-mates: 51
Total: 52
▶ Penalty Tries: 1

Points

▶ Quinlan: 5
Team-mates: 454
Total: 459
▶ Penalty Tries: 5

Cards

▶ Quinlan: 0
Team-mates: 15
Total: 15

Cup Games

	Apps	Pts
Euro Challenge Cup	4	0
Powergen Cup	2	0
Total	**6**	**0**

Prem. Career History

Premiership Career Milestones

Club Debut:
vs Gloucester (A), L, 24-28
▶ **24.09.05**
Time Spent at the Club:
▶ **1 Season**

First Try Scored for the Club:
vs Sale (H), L, 34-36
▶ **06.05.06**
Full International:
▶ **Ireland**

Premiership Totals
97–06

Appearances	15
Points	5
Tries	1
Yellow Cards	0
Red Cards	0

Clubs

Year	Club	Apps	Pts
05-06	Northampton	15	5

Off the Pitch

Age:
▶ Quinlan: 28 years, 4 months
▷ Team: 26 years, 4 months
| League: 26 years, 10 months

Height:
▶ Quinlan: 6'4"
▷ Team: 6'1"
| League: 6'1"

Weight:
▶ Quinlan: 16st 2lb
▷ Team: 15st 13lb
| League: 15st 10lb

Bruce Reihana
Full Back

Date of Birth: 06.04.1976
Place of Birth: Thames, NZ
Nationality: New Zealander
Height: 6'
Weight: 13st 7lb

Season Review 05/06

The last time a player had a terrace chant of his own was back in the 90s when Harvey Thorneycroft was blessed with his own chime. The shouts of "Bruce, Bruce, Bruce," are now part and parcel of the Franklin's Gardens experience and befits a player who always gives his all when he pulls on a black, green and gold jersey.

In fact Bruce would not have missed a game all season had he not been called home following the sad passing of his elder brother. His brief absence meant his missed out on celebrating his 100th game with a home win against Gloucester, but he did mark it with a victory against Newcastle Falcons at Kingston Park. And for the majority of his 30 games, Bruce took over the mantle of the captaincy or shared the responsibility with club captain Steve Thompson. He also took over the kicking duties following the retirement of Paul Grayson and departure of Shane Drahm.

Bruce also scored a few tries, as you would expect, and ended the rugby year with nine, leaving him in second place, six behind scoring king Ben Cohen. He also consistently made the most metres in the Premiership week in week out to prove Bruce is still one of the slipperiest customers in the Saints backline and was therefore deservedly came in third place in Saints' Player of the Year awards.

Player Performance 05/06

Premiership Performance

Percentage of total possible time player was on pitch ⟶ position in league table at end of month

Month:	Sep	Oct	Nov	Dec	Jan	Feb	Mar	Apr	May	Total
	100%	100%	100%	100%	100%	67%	100%	100%	100%	95%
	11	9	11	11	10	8	6	6	6	
League Pts:	6/20	4/5	3/20	0/5	12/15	7/15	9/10	10/15	2/5	53/110
Points F:	50	25	81	14	65	80	53	62	34	464
Points A:	85	23	99	34	51	66	33	61	36	488
Try Bonus:	0	0	0	0	0	1	1	1	1	4
Lose Bonus:	2	0	3	0	0	0	0	1	1	7
Total mins:	320	80	320	80	240	160	160	240	80	1,680
Starts (sub):	4	1	4	1	3	2	2	3	1	21
Points:	30	20	33	9	27	32	9	32	14	206
Tries:	0	2	0	0	0	0	0	2	1	5
Ball Carries:	33	11	37	9	23	8	23	38	20	202
Metres:	325	49	334	123	173	55	146	378	129	1712
Tackles:	9	1	3	2	9	6	4	6	0	40

Prem. Performance Totals

Tries

- Reihana: 5
- Team-mates: 47
- **Total: 52**
- Penalty Tries: 1

Points

- Reihana: 206
- Team-mates: 253
- **Total: 459**
- Penalty Tries: 5

Cards

- Reihana: 0
- Team-mates: 15
- **Total: 15**

Cup Games

	Apps	Pts
Euro Challenge Cup	6	74
Powergen Cup	3	30
Total	**9**	**104**

Prem. Career History

Premiership Career Milestones

Club Debut:
vs Leicester (H), L, 3-16
 09.11.02

First Try Scored for the Club:
vs Harlequins (H), W, 35-7
 **23.11.02**

Time Spent at the Club:
4 Seasons

Full International:
New Zealand

Premiership Totals

97–06

Appearances	78
Points	344
Tries	21
Yellow Cards	0
Red Cards	0

Clubs

Year	Club	Apps	Pts
02-06	Northampton	78	344

Off the Pitch

Age:
- Reihana: 30 years, 1 month
- Team: 26 years, 4 months
- League: 26 years, 10 months

Height:
- Reihana: 6'
- Team: 6'1"
- League: 6'1"

Weight:
- Reihana: 13st 7lb
- Team: 15st 13lb
- League: 15st 10lb

Dan Richmond
Hooker

Date of Birth:	12.02.1979
Place of Birth:	Bath
Nationality:	English
Height:	5'11"
Weight:	15st 6lb

Season Review 05/06

Dan again contributed fully to another season at Saints – his eighth since he signed up to Saints Academy in 1998 – with 20 appearances. He also racked up his 100th game for Saints last season to join fellow century celebrators Bruce Reihana and Tom Smith. Dan had to battle with young up-and-coming hooker Dylan Hartley to nail a place in the 22 as well as continuing his age-old battle with another Academy product England and Lions hooker Steve Thompson.

Player Performance 05/06

Premiership Performance

Percentage of total possible time player was on pitch   position in league table at end of month

Month:	Sep	Oct	Nov	Dec	Jan	Feb	Mar	Apr	May	Total
% on pitch	8%	70%	93%	70%	0%	54%	63%	22%	0%	41%
Position	11	9	11	11	10	8	6	6	6	
League Pts:	6/20	4/5	3/20	0/5	12/15	7/15	9/10	10/15	2/5	53/110
Points F:	50	25	81	14	65	80	53	62	34	464
Points A:	85	23	99	34	51	66	33	61	36	488
Try Bonus:	0	0	0	0	0	1	1	1	1	4
Lose Bonus:	2	0	3	0	0	0	0	1	1	7
Total mins:	25	56	298	56	0	130	100	52	0	717
Starts (sub):	0 (2)	1	4	1	0	2	1 (1)	1 (1)	0	10 (4)
Points:	0	0	0	0	0	0	0	0	0	0
Tries:	0	0	0	0	0	0	0	0	0	0
Ball Carries:	2	8	16	0	0	9	5	3	0	43
Metres:	14	20	29	0	0	23	12	9	0	107
Tackles:	2	0	6	8	0	8	5	5	0	34

Prem. Performance Totals

Tries
- Richmond: 0
- Team-mates: 52
- **Total: 52**
- Penalty Tries: 1

Points
- Richmond: 0
- Team-mates: 459
- **Total: 459**
- Penalty Tries: 5

Cards
- Richmond: 1
- Team-mates: 14
- **Total: 15**

Cup Games

	Apps	Pts
Euro Challenge Cup	4	0
Powergen Cup	2	0
Total	**6**	**0**

Prem. Career History

Premiership Career Milestones

Club Debut:
vs Sale (A), L, 23-34
09.09.00

First Try Scored for the Club:
vs LEED (H), W, 34-14
16.03.02

Time Spent at the Club:
6 Seasons

Full International:
—

Premiership Totals
97–06

Appearances	78
Points	20
Tries	4
Yellow Cards	1
Red Cards	0

Clubs

Year	Club	Apps	Pts
00-06	Northampton	78	20

Off the Pitch

Age:
- Richmond: 27 years, 3 months
- Team: 26 years, 4 months
- League: 26 years, 10 months

Height:
- Richmond: 5'11"
- Team: 6'1"
- League: 6'1"

Weight:
- Richmond: 15st 6lb
- Team: 15st 13lb
- League: 15st 10lb

Mark Robinson
Scrum Half

Date of Birth: 21.08.1975
Place of Birth: Palmerston North, NZ
Nationality: New Zealander
Height: 5'10"
Weight: 13st 8lb

Season Review 05/06

With much of the hype surrounding Mark's half-back partner Carlos Spencer last season, some folk may have forgotten the talents of this scrum-half. The former All Black was a near constant on the Saints team-sheet this season and as such he made 29 appearances. He also scored a few decent tries too with two coming against Saracens at Vicarage Road and a peach of a score marking a good win over the Newport-Gwent Dragons in the Powergen Cup. He scored five tries last season and helped nurture his former Blues team-mate into his new life at Franklin's Gardens. The Robinson-Spencer partnership looks set to get better and better.

Player Performance 05/06

Premiership Performance

Percentage of total possible time player was on pitch   ○ position in league table at end of month

Month:	Sep	Oct	Nov	Dec	Jan	Feb	Mar	Apr	May	Total
	97%	70%	71%		80%	93%	100%	90%		82%
				20%					39%	
	11	9	11	11	10	8	6	6	6	
League Pts:	6/20	4/5	3/20	0/5	12/15	7/15	9/10	10/15	2/5	53/110
Points F:	50	25	81	14	65	80	53	62	34	464
Points A:	85	23	99	34	51	66	33	61	36	488
Try Bonus:	0	0	0	0	0	1	1	1	1	4
Lose Bonus:	2	0	3	0	0	0	0	1	1	7
Total mins:	311	56	228	16	193	223	160	217	31	1,435
Starts (sub):	4	1	3 (1)	0 (1)	2 (1)	3	2	3	0 (1)	18 (4)
Points:	0	0	10	0	0	0	0	0	0	10
Tries:	0	0	2	0	0	0	0	0	0	2
Ball Carries:	22	6	25	3	17	29	29	24	4	159
Metres:	71	12	126	10	26	132	62	83	28	550
Tackles:	22	1	17	1	10	21	14	21	1	108

Prem. Performance Totals

Tries
- ▶ Robinson: 2
- ▷ Team-mates: 50
- **Total: 52**
- ▶ Penalty Tries: 1

Points
- ▶ Robinson: 10
- ▷ Team-mates: 449
- **Total: 459**
- ▶ Penalty Tries: 5

Cards
- ▶ Robinson: 0
- ▷ Team-mates: 15
- **Total: 15**

Cup Games

	Apps	Pts
Euro Challenge Cup	4	5
Powergen Cup	3	10
Total	**7**	**15**

Prem. Career History

Premiership Career Milestones

Club Debut:
vs Sale (A), D, 37-37
▶ **12.09.03**

Time Spent at the Club:
▶ **3 Seasons**

First Try Scored for the Club:
vs L Irish (H), L, 24-30
▶ **11.10.03**

Full International:
▶ **New Zealand**

Premiership Totals

97–06
Appearances	53
Points	30
Tries	6
Yellow Cards	1
Red Cards	1

Clubs

Year	Club	Apps	Pts
03-06	Northampton	53	30

Off the Pitch

Age:
- ▶ Robinson: 30 years, 9 months
- ▷ Team: 26 years, 4 months
- | League: 26 years, 10 months

Height:
- ▶ Robinson: 5'10"
- ▷ Team: 6'1"
- | League: 6'1"

Weight:
- ▶ Robinson: 13st 8lb
- ▷ Team: 15st 13lb
- | League: 15st 10lb

John Rudd
Wing

Date of Birth: 26.05.1981
Place of Birth: London
Nationality: English
Height: 6'2"
Weight: 17st

Season Review 05/06

John ended the 2006/07 season with 21 appearances under his belt to take him to 48 for his Saints career. He also scored five tries during last season, including one among the eight-try performance against Saracens. He scored 10 tries during his two-year tenure with Saints. The big winger will be playing his rugby for Newcastle Falcons at Kingston Park next season but will also be a welcome visitor whenever he returns to Franklin's Gardens.

Player Performance 05/06

Premiership Performance — Percentage of total possible time player was on pitch — Ⓖ position in league table at end of month

Month:	Sep	Oct	Nov	Dec	Jan	Feb	Mar	Apr	May	Total
	23%	1%	68%	100%	50%	75%	50%		70%	47%
	11	9	11	11	10	8	6	6	6	
								9%		
League Pts:	6/20	4/5	3/20	0/5	12/15	7/15	9/10	10/15	2/5	53/110
Points F:	50	25	81	14	65	80	53	62	34	464
Points A:	85	23	99	34	51	66	33	61	36	488
Try Bonus:	0	0	0	0	0	1	1	1	1	4
Lose Bonus:	2	0	3	0	0	0	0	1	1	7
Total mins:	72	1	216	80	120	181	80	21	56	827
Starts (sub):	1	0 (1)	3	1	2 (1)	2 (1)	1	0 (1)	1	11 (4)
Points:	0	0	0	0	0	5	0	0	0	5
Tries:	0	0	0	0	0	1	0	0	0	1
Ball Carries:	3	1	24	6	18	19	7	3	11	92
Metres:	26	2	263	50	125	179	31	50	45	771
Tackles:	3	0	6	2	4	5	5	1	4	30

Prem. Performance Totals

Tries
- Rudd: 1
- Team-mates: 51
- Total: 52
- Penalty Tries: 1

Points
- Rudd: 5
- Team-mates: 454
- Total: 459
- Penalty Tries: 5

Cards
- Rudd: 0
- Team-mates: 15
- Total: 15

Cup Games

	Apps	Pts
Euro Challenge Cup	5	15
Powergen Cup	1	5
Total	6	20

Prem. Career History

Premiership Career Milestones

Club Debut:
vs Bath (H), W, 29-14
▶ **04.09.04**
Time Spent at the Club:
▶ **2 Seasons**

First Try Scored for the Club:
vs Bath (H), W, 29-14
▶ **04.09.04**
Full International:
▶ —

Premiership Totals
97–06

Appearances	64
Points	45
Tries	9
Yellow Cards	1
Red Cards	0

Clubs

Year	Club	Apps	Pts
04-06	Northampton	33	20
01-04	London Wasps	30	25
99-00	Harlequins	1	0

Off the Pitch

Age:
- Rudd: 25 years
- Team: 26 years, 4 months
- League: 26 years, 10 months

Height:
- Rudd: 6'2"
- Team: 6'1"
- League: 6'1"

Weight:
- Rudd: 17st
- Team: 15st 13lb
- League: 15st 10lb

Grant Seely
Back Row/Lock

Date of Birth: 17.01.1974
Place of Birth: Aylesbury
Nationality: English
Height: 6'4"
Weight: 17st

Season Review 05/06

The 2005/06 season was Grant Seely's last as a professional rugby player and among the four games he played in, he racked up his 250th appearance for the club. He also celebrated his testimonial year with the club as the longest serving player of the 2005/06 squad and was announced as one of the new Junior Academy coaches. He will work alongside former Saints fly-half Ali Hepher, who also retired from the game at the end of last season.

Prem. Career History

Premiership Career Milestones

Club Debut:
vs Harlequins (H), L, 23-26
▶ 23.08.97

First Try Scored for the Club:
vs Gloucester (A), L, 15-20
▶ 14.02.98

Time Spent at the Club:
▶ 9 Seasons

Full International:
▶ —

Premiership Totals
97–06

Appearances	133
Points	75
Tries	15
Yellow Cards	1
Red Cards	0

Clubs

Year	Club	Apps	Pts
97-06	Northampton	133	75

Mark Soden
Back Row

Date of Birth: 10.04.1981
Place of Birth: Leicester
Nationality: English
Height: 6'2"
Weight: 16st 4lb

Season Review 05/06

Competition in the back-row intensified last season with arrival of Paul Tupai, Daniel Browne, Ben Lewitt and Sam Harding, so games were hard to come by for Mark. He did, however, make nine appearances for Saints, including five starts, as well as regularly competing for the Wanderers too.

Mark also undertook the task of climbing to base camp of Mount Everest in June to raise awareness and extra funds for Show Racism The Red Card and the Anthony Nolan Bone Marrow Trust to follow in the footsteps of Academy coach Rob Hunter and former operations director John Steele.

Prem. Career History

Premiership Career Milestones

Club Debut:
vs Newcastle (H), W, 26-18
▶ 18.11.00

First Try Scored for the Club:
vs Bristol (H), L, 20-23
▶ 25.11.01

Time Spent at the Club:
▶ 6 Seasons

Full International:
▶ —

Premiership Totals
97–06

Appearances	63
Points	20
Tries	4
Yellow Cards	1
Red Cards	0

Clubs

Year	Club	Apps	Pts
00-06	Northampton	63	20

Carlos Spencer
Fly Half

Date of Birth: 14.10.1975
Place of Birth: Levin, NZ
Nationality: New Zealander
Height: 6'1"
Weight: 15st

Season Review 05/06

Carlos is probably the biggest overseas signing ever seen in the Premiership and he has not disappointed thus far. Although, when Saints were beaten 32-0 on the first day of last season by Leicester Tigers, there did not seem too many sparks of Spencer magic on show. But since that rude awakening, Carlos slowly but surely put his mark on the new-look Saints team and together the squad began to produce some truly exciting rugby.

The pinnacle of that excitement was reached when Saints beat Saracens with eight tries in February with one of the best performances ever seen at Franklin's Gardens. The former All Black did not get over the whitewash himself but he made sure five members of his team did as well as providing the moment of the day when, with his back to the Saracens defenders, he mastered a chip kick over his own head to swiftly spin round and collect the ball to pass it out to Ben Cohen for a near try chance. Fortunately, the Sky cameras were there that day too, 104

so the television rugby fans could witness the kind of rugby that was beginning to evolve at Saints.

Carlos has scored a few of his own tries too with his first coming in the European Challenge Cup against Bristol at the Memorial Stadium and one of his most important coming in a crucial away win at Newcastle when Saints dragged themselves out of relegation contention for good. Carlos also fought back from a dead-leg injury suffered in that game to turn out a week later against Worcester Warriors to prove there is a lot more to this Kiwi than a box of tricks. He played in 29 games last season and scored seven tries.

Carlos won the Saints' Player of the Year award by a landslide margin after just one season at the club, as well as the Saints Supporters' Club Player of the Year. He was also nominated for the PRA Players' Player of the Year and the GUINNESS PREMIERSHIP Player of the Year awards.

Player Performance 05/06

Premiership Performance

Percentage of total possible time player was on pitch   ⊖ position in league table at end of month

Month:	Sep	Oct	Nov	Dec	Jan	Feb	Mar	Apr	May	Total
	100%	100%	97%	0%	100%	96%	93%	95%	100%	93%
	11	9	11	11	10	8	6	6	6	
League Pts:	6/20	4/5	3/20	0/5	12/15	7/15	9/10	10/15	2/5	53/110
Points F:	50	25	81	14	65	80	53	62	34	464
Points A:	85	23	99	34	51	66	33	61	36	488
Try Bonus:	0	0	0	0	0	1	1	1	1	4
Lose Bonus:	2	0	3	0	0	0	0	1	1	7
Total mins:	320	80	310	0	240	230	148	229	80	1,637
Starts (sub):	4	1	4	0	3	3	2	3	1	21
Points:	0	0	13	0	8	3	5	0	5	34
Tries:	0	0	2	0	0	0	1	0	1	4
Ball Carries:	21	12	31	0	22	26	19	30	24	185
Metres:	245	32	285	0	51	226	117	137	143	1236
Tackles:	14	2	10	0	12	18	9	17	3	85

Prem. Performance Totals

Tries

- Spencer: 4
- Team-mates: 48
- **Total: 52**
- ▶ Penalty Tries: 1

Points

- Spencer: 34
- Team-mates: 425
- **Total: 459**
- ▶ Penalty Tries: 5

Cards

- Spencer: 3
- Team-mates: 12
- **Total: 15**

Cup Games

	Apps	Pts
Euro Challenge Cup	5	15
Powergen Cup	3	0
Total	**8**	**15**

Prem. Career History

Premiership Career Milestones

Club Debut:
vs Leicester (A), L, 0-32
 **03.09.05**

Time Spent at the Club:
▶ **1 Season**

First Try Scored for the Club:
vs Saracens (A), L, 22-28
 **05.11.05**

Full International:
▶ **New Zealand**

Premiership Totals

97–06

Appearances	21
Points	34
Tries	4
Yellow Cards	3
Red Cards	0

Clubs

Year	Club	Apps	Pts
05-06	Northampton	21	34

Off the Pitch

Age:

- Spencer: 30 years, 7 months
- Team: 26 years, 4 months
- League: 26 years, 10 months

Height:

- Spencer: 6'1"
- Team: 6'1"
- League: 6'1"

Weight:

- Spencer: 15st
- Team: 15st 13lb
- League: 15st 10lb

Tom Smith
Prop

Date of Birth:	31.10.1971
Place of Birth:	London
Nationality:	Scottish
Height:	5'10"
Weight:	16st 3lb

Season Review 05/06

Tom was another player to go through the century mark for appearances made for his club last season. He would have got there earlier had he not spent so much time serving Scotland but after he announced his retirement from international rugby in the 2004/05 season, Tom was left free to concentrate on Northampton Saints and as such made 27 appearances for the club – the most he has ever made in a year.

Tom also took on a part-time coaching role with the club last season to help out with the forwards. No doubt he will still have some contribution this season, although most of the work will fall to new forwards coach Peter Sloane. And despite rumours of retirement, Tom still has a year left on his current contract and is not intending to hang up his boots just yet!

Player Performance 05/06

Premiership Performance
Percentage of total possible time player was on pitch · position in league table at end of month

Month:	Sep	Oct	Nov	Dec	Jan	Feb	Mar	Apr	May	Total
	84%	100%	13%	100%	88%	83%	83%	100%	99%	76%
	11	9	11	11	10	8	6	6	6	
League Pts:	6/20	4/5	3/20	0/5	12/15	7/15	9/10	10/15	2/5	53/110
Points F:	50	25	81	14	65	80	53	62	34	464
Points A:	85	23	99	34	51	66	33	61	36	488
Try Bonus:	0	0	0	0	0	1	1	1	1	4
Lose Bonus:	2	0	3	0	0	0	0	1	1	7
Total mins:	269	80	40	80	212	198	132	240	79	1,330
Starts (sub):	4	1	1	1	3	3	2	3	1	19
Points:	0	0	0	0	0	0	0	0	0	0
Tries:	0	0	0	0	0	0	0	0	0	0
Ball Carries:	11	9	2	4	20	9	13	9	4	81
Metres:	48	28	4	14	34	20	20	23	7	198
Tackles:	11	2	0	4	7	14	8	12	2	60

Prem. Performance Totals

Tries
- Smith: 0
- Team-mates: 52
- Total: 52
- Penalty Tries: 1

Points
- Smith: 0
- Team-mates: 459
- Total: 459
- Penalty Tries: 5

Cards
- Smith: 2
- Team-mates: 13
- Total: 15

Cup Games

	Apps	Pts
Euro Challenge Cup	6	0
Powergen Cup	2	0
Total	8	0

Prem. Career History

Premiership Career Milestones

Club Debut:
vs Gloucester (A), L, 9-22

 **01.09.01**

Time Spent at the Club:
5 Seasons

First Try Scored for the Club:
vs Harlequins (A), W, 24-16

26.01.02

Full International:
Scotland

Premiership Totals
97–06

Appearances	73
Points	20
Tries	4
Yellow Cards	2
Red Cards	0

Clubs

Year	Club	Apps	Pts
01-06	Northampton	73	20

Off the Pitch

Age:
- Smith: 34 years, 7 months
- Team: 26 years, 4 months
- League: 26 years, 10 months

Height:
- Smith: 5'10"
- Team: 6'1"
- League: 6'1"

Weight:
- Smith: 16st 3lb
- Team: 15st 13lb
- League: 15st 10lb

Neil Starling
Centre

Date of Birth: 08.06.1982
Place of Birth: Kingston
Nationality: English
Height: 6'5"
Weight: 15st

Season Review 05/06

Neil had shot into the spotlight in the 2004/05 season when he signed to Saints from Rotherham and started making himself useful in a No 13 shirt. He also played for the England sevens team that season until a niggling knee pain turned into something much more serious. The knee required surgery and it meant he would miss out on most of last season's action. Neil did return, however, and turned out for the Wanderers before the end of the season.

Brett Sturgess
Prop

Date of Birth: 16.11.1981
Place of Birth: Kettering
Nationality: English
Height: 6'1"
Weight: 17st 10lb

Season Review 05/06

Brett began last season well with a series of starts in a black, green and gold jersey, but as with several other positions within the squad, the competition intensified following the arrival of former IRB U21s Player of the Year Pat Barnard and the return to fitness of Simon Emms. Still, Brett made eight appearances for Saints last season as well as turning out regularly for the Wanderers.

Player Performance 05/06

Prem. Performance Totals

Tries

Sturgess:	0
Team-mates:	52
Total:	**52**
Penalty Tries:	1

Points

Sturgess:	0
Team-mates:	459
Total:	**459**
Penalty Tries:	5

Cards

Sturgess:	0
Team-mates:	15
Total:	**15**

Cup Games

	Apps	Pts
Euro Challenge Cup	1	0
Powergen Cup	1	0
Total	**2**	**0**

Prem. Career History

Premiership Career Milestones

Club Debut:
vs Harlequins (H), D, 13-13
09.11.01

Time Spent at the Club:
5 Seasons

First Try Scored for the Club:
vs Harlequins (H), W, 35-7
23.11.02

Full International:
—

Premiership Totals

97–06

Appearances	33
Points	10
Tries	2
Yellow Cards	0
Red Cards	0

Clubs

Year	Club	Apps	Pts
01-06	Northampton	33	10

Steve Thompson
Hooker

Date of Birth: 15.07.1978
Place of Birth: Hemel Hempstead
Nationality: English
Height: 6'2"
Weight: 18st 2lb

Season Review 05/06

Steve had to wait a little before making his mark for Saints last season due to the rest for England's Lions players honoured by the club. When he came back, it was at flanker, not a popular decision among rugby's written press. Steve, however, loved the run around that helped ease him back into club life. It is also gave him the freedom to pop up for a try at Kingsholm in front of a none too impressed Gloucester crowd.

England coach Andy Robinson selected him for the autumn internationals and the Six Nations squads. Steve played in 22 games for Saints this season, on top of his international commitments and scored three Saints tries. He also opted to rest for England's two-game tour to Australia to recharge his batteries for this season.

Player Performance 05/06

Premiership Performance

Percentage of total possible time player was on pitch   ⊕ position in league table at end of month

Month:	Sep	Oct	Nov	Dec	Jan	Feb	Mar	Apr	May	Total
% on pitch	46%	30%	0%	0%	100%	25%	38%	6%/78%	100%/6%	45%
position	11	9	11	11	10	8	6	6	6	
League Pts:	6/20	4/5	3/20	0/5	12/15	7/15	9/10	10/15	2/5	53/110
Points F:	50	25	81	14	65	80	53	62	34	464
Points A:	85	23	99	34	51	66	33	61	36	488
Try Bonus:	0	0	0	0	0	1	1	1	1	4
Lose Bonus:	2	0	3	0	0	0	0	1	1	7
Total mins:	148	24	0	0	240	59	60	188	80	799
Starts (sub):	1 (2)	0 (1)	0	0	3	1	1	2 (1)	1	9 (4)
Points:	5	0	0	0	5	0	0	5	0	15
Tries:	1	0	0	0	1	0	0	1	0	3
Ball Carries:	7	1	0	0	23	3	4	16	3	57
Metres:	52	0	0	0	76	19	23	42	15	227
Tackles:	14	1	0	0	18	2	5	11	1	52

Prem. Performance Totals

Tries
- Thompson: 3
- Team-mates: 49
- **Total:** 52
- Penalty Tries: 1

Points
- Thompson: 15
- Team-mates: 444
- **Total:** 459
- Penalty Tries: 5

Cards
- Thompson: 1
- Team-mates: 14
- **Total:** 15

Cup Games

	Apps	Pts
Euro Challenge Cup	6	0
Powergen Cup	3	0
Total	**9**	**0**

Prem. Career History

Premiership Career Milestones

Club Debut:
vs Leicester (A), L, 25-35

⮞ **19.09.98**

Time Spent at the Club:

⮞ **8 Seasons**

First Try Scored for the Club:
vs L Irish (H), W, 24-19

⮞ **13.11.99**

Full International:

⮞ **England**

Premiership Totals

97–06

Appearances	115
Points	70
Tries	14
Yellow Cards	3
Red Cards	0

Clubs

Year	Club	Apps	Pts
98-06	Northampton	115	70

Age:
- Thompson: 27 years, 10 months
- Team: 26 years, 4 months
- | League: 26 years, 10 months

Height:
- Thompson: 6'2"
- Team: 6'1"
- | League: 6'1"

Weight:
- Thompson: 18st 2lb
- Team: 15st 13lb
- | League: 15st 10lb

Paul Tupai
Back Row

Date of Birth: 16.09.1974
Place of Birth: Rotorua, NZ
Nationality: Samoan
Height: 6'4"
Weight: 17st 10lb

Season Review 05/06

Paul was a late arrival from the sunshine of the Bay of Plenty to the snow of Northampton just after Christmas last season. The Samoan international had fulfilled all his ambitions in New Zealand by playing for his father's country, playing against the Lions, winning the Ranfurly Shield and playing in his 100th game for the Bay, so when a Saints call went out for an out and out six, he was the perfect candidate.

Paul made an instant impact on the Saints pack with his no-nonsense physical approach and amiable disregard for anyone who fancies a tussle with him. He gave extra impetus to the forwards and has scored a few tries along the way. Paul played in 13 games for Saints last season and started 12. He scored three tries.

Prem. Career History

Premiership Career Milestones

Club Debut:	First Try Scored for the Club:
vs Bristol (H), W, 29-22	vs Saracens (H), W, 58-17
▶ 01.01.06	▶ 18.02.06
Time Spent at the Club:	Full International:
▶ 1 Season	▶ W Samoa

Premiership Totals

97–06	
Appearances	12
Points	5
Tries	1
Yellow Cards	0
Red Cards	0

Clubs

Year	Club	Apps	Pts
05-06	Northampton	12	5

Andy Vilk
Centre

Date of Birth: 11.06.1981
Place of Birth: London
Nationality: English
Height: 5'11"
Weight: 15st 6lb

Season Review 05/06

Andy was absent for the majority of last season but with good cause as he was serving his time as a core member of the England sevens squad. After the disappointment of missing out on being a part of the final 10 that played in the Sevens Rugby World Cup the season before, Andy made up for it with wins in Los Angeles, Dubai and Hong Kong, as well as a silver medal in the Commonwealth Games in Melbourne.

When Andy was back at home, he did manage a few games for Saints – seven to be precise – and a try against Leeds Tykes at Headingley. He requested a release from his contract at the end of last season to go in search of regular first XV rugby at another club.

Prem. Career History

Premiership Career Milestones

Club Debut:	First Try Scored for the Club:
vs Rotherham (H), W, 18-8	vs Leeds (A), L, 25-28
▶ 07.02.04	▶ 20.11.05
Time Spent at the Club:	Full International:
▶ 3 Seasons	▶ —

Premiership Totals

97–06	
Appearances	21
Points	5
Tries	1
Yellow Cards	0
Red Cards	0

Clubs

Year	Club	Apps	Pts
03-06	Northampton	21	5

The Academy
Profiles 2005/06

Adam Barnard
Dob 03.07.87
Birthplace Hemel Hempstead
Height 6'1"/1.85m
Weight 14st/89kg
Position Centre
School Northampton School
for boys
Prev Club Old Scouts
Honours England U18s

Charlie Beech
Dob 21.07.87
Birthplace Stevenage
Height 6'1"/1.85m
Weight 18st 2lbs/115kg
Position Prop
School Oakham School
Prev Club Biggleswade RFC
Honours England U19s

Julian Bishop
Dob 21.10.86
Birthplace Torquay
Height 5'7"/1.70m
Weight 11st 5lbs/72kg
Position Scrum-Half
School Millfield School
Prev Club -
Honours Wales U18s

Paul Diggin
Dob 23.01.85
Birthplace Northampton
Height 5'8"/1.73m
Weight 13st 3lbs/84kg
Position Wing/Centre
Prev Club BBOB
School Northampton School
for boys
Honours England U21s

Matt Grove
Dob 16.11.82
Birthplace Exeter
Height 6'3"/1.90m
Weight 17st 5lbs/110kg
Position Hooker
School Clyst Vale Community
College
Prev Club Exeter Chiefs
Honours South West U18s

Will Harries
Dob 30.03.87
Birthplace Cardiff

Height 5'8"/1.73m
Weight 12st/76kg
Position Full-back/Wing
School Millfield School
Prev Club Newport Gwent Dragons
Honours Wales U18s

Dylan Hartley
Dob 24.03.86
Birthplace Rotorua
Height 6'1"/1.85m
Weight 17st 11lbs/113kg
Position Hooker
School Rotorua Boys
High School
Prev Club Worcester
Honours England U21s

Mark Hopley
Dob 01.05.84
Birthplace Crewe
Height 6'3"/1.91m
Weight 17st/108kg
Position No 8
School Bishop Heber
High School
Prev Club Worcester Warriors
Honours England U21s

Tom Laws
Dob 19.07.87
Birthplace Swindon
Height 6'/1.82m
Weight 17st 9lbs/112kg
Position Prop
School Stowe School
Prev Club -
Honours England U18s

Ashley Maggs
Dob 15.05.86
Birthplace Bristol
Height 6'4"/1.93m
Weight 15st/95kg
Position Centre
School Colston's School
Prev Club Canterbury
Honours England U18s
Schoolboys

Ben Patston
Dob 18.06.85
Birthplace Norwich
Height 5'11"/1.80m
Weight 13st 8lbs//86kg
Position Fly-half/Full-back

Prev Club Wymondham
School Wymondham College
Honours -

Simon Pitfield
Dob 25.02.87
Birthplace Milton Keynes
Height 6'4"/1.93
Weight 14st 7lbs/92kg
Position Lock
School Bedford School
Prev Club Biggleswade
Honours England U18s

Tom Powell
Dob 11.10.85
Birthplace Rotherham
Height 6'5"/1.96m
Weight 16st 1lb/102kg
Position Flanker
School Millfield School
Prev Club NEC Harlequins
Honours -

Alex Rae
Dob 02.02.86
Birthplace Coventry
Height 6'5"/1.96m
Weight 15st 8lbs/99kg
Position Lock
School Counden Court School
Prev Club Worcester
Honours England U21s

Jamie Supple
Dob 22.10.86
Birthplace Northampton
Height 5'11"/1.80m
Weight 12st 13lbs/82kg
Position Flanker
School Oundle School
Prev Club Towcestrians RFC
Honours East Midlands

New for 2006/07 season
Joe Ansbro   centre
John Brake   centre
Matthew Burke   flanker
Philip Hoy   lock
Dan Lavery   fly-half
Ross McMillan   hooker
Danny Pointon   scrum-half
David Smith   wing

Academy Coaches

James Sinclair
Academy director

James arrived at Franklin's Gardens from Bracknell RFC in the 2003/04 season to assist Wayne Smith and his coaching team with the statistical side to running a Premiership team. James became Bracknell's assistant chief executive after two years as director of rugby at Norwich RFC. Before Norwich, he was head of rugby development at North Walsham RFC at the heart of the eastern counties where James grew up.

The former centre, who played his rugby for Saracens and Rotherham, took up the position of Academy director at the end of his first season at Franklin's Gardens.

Rob Hunter
Academy coach

Rob gave up his professional playing career to take up his post with the Northampton Saints RFU Academy. His background as a Royal Engineer and community officer has served him well in this coaching role.

Rob coaches the full-time Academy players who work with the professional squad and play in the GUINNESS A League, as well as the part-time members who train at the Elite Player Development Centres. He also gives advice and support to club and school coaches in the region through the coach development programme.

New for 2006/07

Two new coaches will join the Saints Academy this season – both former players. Ali Hepher has left his job as player-coach at Bedford Blues to take up his new role with the Junior Academy and will join Grant Seely, who retired from playing professional rugby at the end of last season.

▶ Grant Seely – new role at the Junior Academy

David Akinluyi
Wing

Date of Birth: 10.02.1984
Place of Birth: Ilesha, Nigeria
Nationality: Nigerian
Height: 6'1"
Weight: 15st 7lbs

Profile

Cambridge Blue David Akinluyi has signed a two-year contract to join Northampton Saints at the start of the 2006/07 season. Nigerian-born winger David, who scored one of the five tries in Cambridge's Varsity Match 31-16 win over Oxford in December, is currently studying engineering at Christ's College.

Devout Christian David was educated at St Olave's Grammar School in Orpington and played for Kent and London & SE at U18s Schools level. The 22-year-old is the second Cambridge Blue to join Saints in recent years as centre David Quinlan also played in the Varsity Match in 2000.

Christian Short
Lock

Date of Birth: 15.11.1979
Place of Birth: —
Nationality: English/Irish
Height: 6'7"
Weight: 16st 5lbs

Profile

Northampton Saints have signed lock Christian Short from Irish province Connacht to start work with the club this summer. Christian is the second lock to move to Franklin's Gardens from Connacht after Damien Browne flew over the Irish Sea at the start of last season. Short, aged 26, is 6ft 7ins tall and weighs in at 16st 5lbs. He has played for Connacht for the last two seasons after making his debut in the last game of the 2003/04 season against the Celtic Warriors. He played in 27 of Connacht's 28 games last season.

Christian, who grew up in Newcastle and played for Bracknell RFC while he attended St Mary's College in London, has a dual nationality and can play for either England or Ireland.

Soane Tonga'uiha
Prop

Date of Birth: 21.02.1982
Place of Birth: St Germans
Nationality: Tongan
Height: 6'5"
Weight: 20st 7lbs

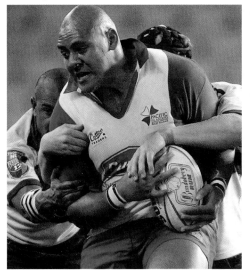

Profile

Northampton Saints have signed the massive prop Soane Tonga'uiha from their rugby neighbours Bedford Blues on a two-year deal. The Tongan international stands at 6ft 5ins tall and weighs in at 20st 7lbs making him the heaviest player in the Saints squad by at more than a stone. Lock Damien Browne is 19st 5lbs.

Soane won two caps for Tonga against France and Italy in 2005, and three for the Pacific Islanders against South Africa, Australia and New Zealand in 2004. The 23-year-old loosehead has been playing for Bedford for the past two seasons. He will begin training with Saints in the summer ahead of the 2006/07 season.

Soane is the second player in as many years that Saints have signed from the Blues. Flanker Ben Lewitt crossed over the county border last season.

Ian Vass
Scrum-half/Fly-half

Date of Birth: 17.08.1981
Place of Birth: Northampton
Nationality: English
Height: 5'11"
Weight: 15st 5lbs

Profile

Scrum-half Ian Vass will return to his home club ahead of next season after signing a new two-year deal. The Northampton-born Academy product left the club at the end of the 2002/03 season to join French club side Stade Francais for one year. He then spent a season at Bedford Blues before joining Harlequins at the start of 2005/06.

Ian, who will also cover fly-half, will begin training with the Saints squad in July. He has already made 26 appearances for Saints, following his Heineken Cup debut against Neath in 1999, and scored five tries.

Plus Academy graduates

Paul Diggin

Mark Easter

Dylan Hartley

Mark Hopley

RUGBY PREMIERSHIP
KICK OFF
2006/07

Premiership Roll of Honour

Season	Champions	Relegated	Promoted
2005/06 Premiership	**Sale Sharks**	Leeds Tykes	NEC Harlequins
2004/05 Premiership	**London Wasps**	NEC Harlequins	Bristol Rugby
2003/04 Premiership	**London Wasps**	Rotherham Titans	Worcester Warriors
2002/03 Premiership	**London Wasps**	Bristol Rugby	Rotherham Titans
2001/02 Premiership	**Leicester Tigers**	N/A	N/A
2000/01 Premiership	**Leicester Tigers**	Rotherham Titans	Leeds Tykes
1999/00 Premiership	**Leicester Tigers**	Bedford Blues	Rotherham Titans
1998/99 Premiership	**Leicester Tigers**	West Hartlepool	Bristol Rugby
1997/98 Premiership	**Newcastle Falcons**	Bristol Rugby	Bedford
			West Hartlepool
			London Scottish

RUGBY PREMIERSHIP
KICK OFF
2006/07

SIDAN PRESS
Passionate about sport

Season Statistics 2005/06

Final Premiership Table 2005/06

Team	W	D	L	TB	LB	Tot	T	C	PG	DG	For	T	C	PG	DG	Agst	PD
				POINTS			**ATTACK**					**DEFENCE**					
1 **Sale Sharks (C)**	16	1	5	6	2	74	52	38	73	6	573	42	27	56	4	444	129
2 Leicester Tigers	14	3	5	5	1	68	51	34	64	1	518	24	20	78	7	415	103
3 London Irish	14	0	8	6	4	66	54	32	47	6	493	44	30	56	2	454	39
4 London Wasps	12	3	7	7	3	64	53	41	58	2	527	42	30	57	2	447	80
5 Gloucester Rugby	11	1	10	4	9	59	46	32	61	2	483	33	26	53	3	385	98
6 Northampton Saints	10	1	11	4	7	53	53	35	41	2	464	50	32	54	4	488	-24
7 Newcastle Falcons	9	1	12	3	6	47	42	25	45	7	416	44	30	50	1	433	-17
8 Worcester Warriors	9	1	12	3	6	47	40	28	61	4	451	56	32	48	2	494	-43
9 Bath Rugby	9	1	12	3	5	46	38	25	61	6	441	49	33	58	3	494	-53
10 Saracens	8	1	13	5	7	46	42	32	51	2	433	48	30	56	5	483	-50
11 Bristol Rugby	8	1	13	0	7	41	28	23	69	0	393	41	30	55	5	445	-52
12 Leeds Tykes (R)	5	0	17	1	7	28	36	24	42	3	363	62	49	52	3	573	-210

■ = Premiership Semi-Finalists   ■ = Qualified for European Cup   ■ = Relegated

Premiership Play-Off SF

14 May 2006   **Sale Sharks   22-12   London Wasps**   **Edgeley Park**

Scoring sequence: 1' Hodgson (PG) 3-0, 5' Van Gisbergen (PG) 3-3, 16' Hodgson (PG) 6-3, 20' Hodgson (PG) 9-3, 31' Robinson (T) 14-3, Hodgson (C) 16-3, 43' Van Gisbergen (PG) 16-6, 45' Hodgson (PG) 19-6, 51' Van Gisbergen (PG) 19-9, 65' Van Gisbergen (PG) 19-12, 78' Hodgson (PG) 22-12.

Referee: Chris White (England)

Attendance: 10,641

Premiership Play-Off SF

14 May 2006   **Leicester Tigers   40-8   London Irish**   **Welford Road**

Scoring sequence: 7' Goode (PG) 3-0, 15' Alesana Tuilagi (T) 8-0, Goode (C) 10-0, 25' Magne (T) 10-5, 32' Ellis (T) 15-5, Goode (C) 17-5, 40' Goode (PG) 20-5, 51' Catt (PG) 20-8, 56' Goode (PG) 23-8, 60' Lloyd (T) 28-8, 67' Murphy (T) 33-8, Goode (C) 35-8, 73' Lloyd (T) 40-8.

Referee: Dave Pearson (England)

Attendance: 14,069

Premiership Play-Off Final

27 May 2006   **Sale Sharks   45-20   Leicester Tigers**   **Twickenham**

Scoring sequence: 3' Hodgson (PG) 3-0, 8' Cueto (T) 8-0, 9' Moody (T) 8-5, Goode (C) 8-7, 17' Lund (T) 13-7, 31' Hodgson (PG) 16-7, 36' Goode (PG) 16-10, 40' Ripol (T) 21-10, Hodgson (C) 23-10, 43' Goode (PG) 23-13, 45' Hodgson (PG) 26-13, 48' Hodgson (PG) 29-13, 63' Hodgson (PG) 32-13, 70' Hodgson (DG) 35-13, 74' Hamilton (T) 35-18, Goode (C) 35-20, 78' Hodgson (PG) 38-20, 80' Mayor (T) 43-20, Courrent (C) 45-20.

Referee: Dave Pearson (England)

Attendance: 58,000

Tries and Points

[includes play-off data]

Top Try Scorer

	Player	Team	Tries
1	**Tom Varndell**	**Leicester Tigers**	**14**
2	Tom Voyce	London Wasps	10
3	Delon Armitage	London Irish	8
4	Tom Biggs	Leeds Tykes	8
5	Matthew Burke	Newcastle Falcons	8
6	Anthony Elliott	Newcastle Falcons	8
7	David Lemi	Bristol Rugby	8
8	Paul Sackey	London Wasps	8

Top Points Scorer

	Player	Team	Points
1	**Charlie Hodgson**	**Sale Sharks**	**248**
2	Jason Strange	Bristol Rugby	244
3	Glen Jackson	Saracens	238
4	Shane Drahm	Worcester Warriors	233
5	Andy Goode	Leicester Tigers	225
6	Ludovic Mercier	Gloucester Rugby	213
7	Mark Van Gisbergen	London Wasps	211
8	Bruce Reihana	Northampton Saints	206

Statistics

Premiership Records

Individual Game Records

	All Time	Best in 2005/06
Most points	32 – Niall Woods (Irish v Harlequins, 25 Apr 98) 32 – Dave Walder (Falcons v Saracens, 26 Nov 00) 32 – Tim Stimpson (Tigers v Falcons, 21 Sep 02)	27 – Andy Goode (Tigers v Sharks, 28 Jan)
Most tries	6 – Ryan Constable (Saracens at Bedford, 16 Apr 00)	4 – Sean Lamont (Saints v Saracens, 18 Feb)
Most conversions	13 – Richie Butland (Richmond at Bedford, 16 May 99)	6 – Valentin Courrent (Sharks at Warriors, 11 Feb) 6 – Bruce Reihana (Saints v Saracens, 18 Feb) 6 – Jonny Wilkinson (Falcons v Tykes, 6 May)
Most penalty goals	9 – Simon Mannix (Gloucester v Quins, 23 Sep 00) 9 – Luke Smith (Saracens v Gloucester, 8 Sep 01) 9 – Braam van Straaten (Tykes v Irish, 8 Sep 02) 9 – Alex King (Wasps v Falcons, 11 Nov 01)	8 – Andy Goode (Tigers v Sharks, 28 Jan)
Most drop goals	3 – Ludovic Mercier (Gloucester at Sharks, 22 Sep 01) 3 – Mark Mapletoft (Irish vs Saints, 27 Dec 04)	2 – Shane Drahm (Warriors at Irish, 11 Sep) 2 – Dave Walder (Falcons at Saints, 17 Sep) 2 – Barry Everitt (Irish v Tigers, 8 Jan)
Fastest try	9.63 secs – Tom Voyce (Wasps v Harlequins, 5 Nov 04)	28 secs – Tom Varndell (Tigers v Bath, 17 Sep)
Quickest bonus point try	14 mins – Mike Worsley (Quins v Saracens, 12 Nov 04)	20 mins – Sailosi Tagicakibau (Irish at Wasps, 30 Apr)

Team Records

	All Time	Best in 2005/06
Most points in a home game	77-19 – Bath v Harlequins (The Rec, 29 Apr 00)	58-17 – Saints v Saracens (Franklin's Gardens, 18 Feb)
Most points in an away game	106-12 – Richmond at Bedford (Goldington Road, 16 May 99)	56-37 – Irish at Wasps (Causeway Stadium, 30 Apr)
Highest aggregate of points in game	118pts – Bedford 12, Richmond 106 (Goldington Road, 16 May 99)	93pts – Wasps 37, Irish 56 (Causeway Stadium, 30 Apr)
Biggest home win	76pts – Sale 76, Bristol 0 (Heywood Road, 9 Nov 97)	41pts – Saints 58, Saracens 17 (Franklin's Gardens, 18 Feb)
Biggest away win	94pts – Bedford 12, Richmond 106 (Goldington Road, 16 May 99)	32pts – Bristol 9, Gloucester 41 (Memorial Stadium, 18 Sep)
Highest attendance (non-Twickenham)	20,840 – Irish v Bath (Madejski Stadium, 21 Mar 04)	19,884 – Irish v Sharks (Madejski Stadium, 25 Mar)

119

Bath Rugby

Season Summary 2005/06

Position	Won	Drawn	Lost	For	Against	Bonus Points	Total Points
9	**9**	**1**	**12**	**441**	**494**	**8**	**46**

Despite pre-season optimism, this was another disappointing Premiership campaign for the West Country side. Three consecutive defeats in the opening games left John Connolly's side playing catch up. Connolly's departure opened the way for the return of Rec favourite Brian Ashton and performances improved. However, despite reaching the semi-finals of both the Heineken and Powergen Cups, ninth in the league was ultimately disappointing for a club that sets such high standards. The season ended with the club looking to appoint a new coaching set-up following the summer departures of Ashton, Michael Foley and Richard Graham.

Forwards Coach: Mark Bakewell
Backs Coach: Steve Meehan

Club Honours
Courage League / Zurich Premiership: 1988-89, 1990-91, 1991-92, 1992-93, 1993-94, 1995-96, 2003-04 (lost play-offs)

John Player Cup / Pilkington Cup: 1984, 1985, 1986, 1987 1989, 1990, 1992, 1994, 1995, 1996
Heineken Cup: 1997-1998

Season Squad

Stats 2005-06

Position	Player	Height	Weight	Apps	Rep	Tries	Points	Position	Player	Height	Weight	Apps	Rep	Tries	Points
FB/W	N.Abendanon	5'10"	13st 0lb	1	3	-	-	P	D.Flatman	6'1"	18st 12lb	6	3	-	-
FH/C	O.Barkley	5'10"	14st 6lb	12	-	-	118	FH	E.Fuimaono-Sapolu	6'1"	16st 0lb	3	1	1	5
P	D.Barnes	6'0"	17st 10lb	11	1	-	-	BR	C.Goodman	6'2"	16st 5lb	1	1	-	-
SH	M.Baxter	5'10"	13st 10lb	-	1	-	-	L	D.Grewcock	6'6"	18st 10lb	14	-	-	-
BR	A.Beattie	6'5"	18st 8lb	20	-	2	10	H	R.Hawkins	6'0"	16st 4lb	-	3	-	-
P	D.Bell	6'2"	19st 8lb	17	4	1	5	C	A.Higgins	5'11"	13st 12lb	15	2	1	5
FB/W	L.Best	6'3"	15st 2lb	4	2	1	5	L	J.Hudson	6'7"	17st 10lb	6	-	2	10
L	S.Borthwick	6'6"	17st 5lb	13	-	-	-	BR	M.Lipman	6'1"	15st 7lb	11	2	2	10
W	D.Bory	5'11"	14st 9lb	14	-	2	10	P	C.Loader	5'10"	18st 6lb	-	3	-	-
C	T.Cheeseman	6'0"	14st 2lb	2	1	-	-	FB/W	J.Maddock	5'8"	13st 5lb	16	1	3	15
C	A.Crockett	5'11"	14st 9lb	14	-	2	10	FH	C.Malone	6'0"	14st 9lb	17	-	4	130
C	S.Davey	6'1"	15st 2lb	-	1	-	-	H	L.Mears	5'9"	15st 8lb	14	1	2	10
FB/FH/C	R.Davis	5'6"	13st 12lb	1	7	-	-	FB	M.Perry	6'1"	13st 12lb	7	-	-	-
BR	G.Delve	6'3"	18st 0lb	7	10	3	15	BR	J.Scaysbrook	6'3"	15st 6lb	8	4	1	5
H	P.Dixon	5'11"	16st 7lb	8	5	-	-	BR/L	P.Short	6'5"	18st 8lb	8	5	-	-
FH	A.Dunne	5'8"	12st 8lb	4	1	-	20	W	M.Stephenson	6'0"	13st 0lb	9	4	1	8
L	J.Fa'amatuainu	6'4"	16st 4lb	1	1	-	-	P	M.Stevens	6'0"	19st 0lb	6	3	1	5
8	Z.Feau'nati	6'2"	18st 8lb	17	3	3	15	SH	N.Walshe	5'10"	13st 6lb	11	2	-	-
L	R.Fidler	6'5"	18st 4lb	4	7	-	-	W/C	F.Welsh	6'1"	15st 6lb	7	1	2	10
P	T.Filise	6'2"	19st 7lb	4	3	1	5	SH	A.Williams	5'11"	13st 12lb	6	8	-	-
W	S.Finau	6'0"	16st 0lb	6	2	2	10	SH	M.Wood	5'10"	14st 11lb	5	-	1	5

Bath Rugby

Last Season Form 2005/06

Season Progression

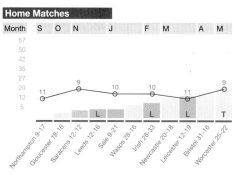

Home Matches

Away Matches

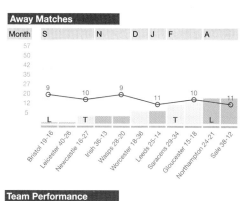

Premiership Statistics

	Home	Away
Tries		
38	15	23
Coversions		
25	9	16
Penalty goals		
61	35	26
Drop goals		
6	2	4
Kick %		
67%	69%	66%
Yellow/Red cards		
16/1	10/1	6/0
Powerplay tries	Powerplay tries are scored when your side is playing with a man or more advantage due to yellow or red cards.	
4	1	3
Shorthand tries	Shorthand tries are scored when your side are playing with a man or more fewer due to yellow or red cards.	
1	1	0

Team Performance

Position	Team	% total points won	% won at home	% won away
1	Sale			
2	Leicester	4%	7%	0%
3	Irish			
4	Wasps			
5	Gloucester	24%	26%	20%
6	Northampton			
7	Newcastle			
8	Worcester	49%	44%	55%
9	**Bath**			
10	Saracens			
11	Bristol	23%	23%	25%
12	Leeds			

Bath Rugby

Top Scorer

Points Facts

Total points	% team points	Home	Away
▶130	▶29	▶73	▶57

Points by Time Period

7	21	23	21	16	15	9	18	-
0	10	20	30	40	50	60	70	80 Inj.

Team Tries and Points

Tries by Time Period

- scored
- conceded

3	5	3	8	6	5	3	4	1
0	10min	20min	30min	40min	50min	60min	70min	80 Injury time
5	1	5	7	4	8	5	14	0

Tries by Halves

- scored
- conceded

38	**19**	**19**	**50%**	**50%**
Total	1st half	2nd half	1st half %	2nd half %
49	**18**	**31**	**37%**	**63%**

How Points were Scored

- tries: 190
- conversions: 50
- pen goals: 183
- drop goals: 18

How Points were Conceded

- tries: 245
- conversions: 66
- pen goals: 174
- drop goals: 9

Tries Scored by Player

- backs: 20
- forwards: 18

Tries Conceded by Player

- backs: 36
- forwards: 10

Bath Rugby

Eight-Season Form 1998-2006

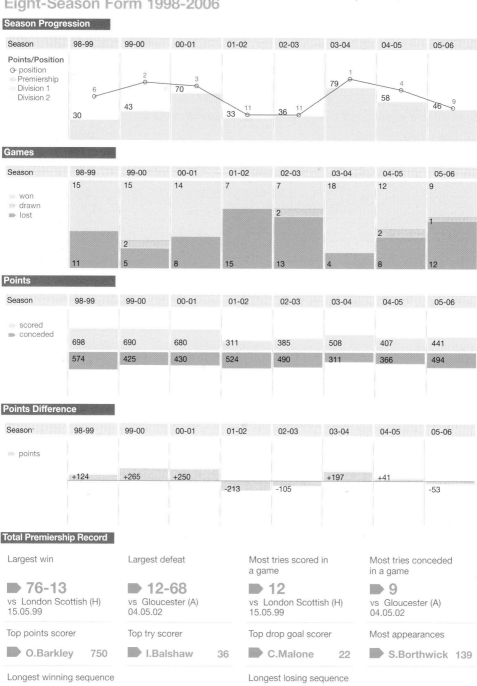

Season Progression

Season	98-99	99-00	00-01	01-02	02-03	03-04	04-05	05-06
Points/Position								

- position
- Premiership
- Division 1
- Division 2

Position: 6, 2, 3, 11, 11, 1, 4, 9
Points: 30, 43, 70, 33, 36, 79, 58, 46

Games

Season	98-99	99-00	00-01	01-02	02-03	03-04	04-05	05-06
won	15	15	14	7	7	18	12	9
drawn		2			2		2	1
lost	11	5	8	15	13	4	8	12

Points

Season	98-99	99-00	00-01	01-02	02-03	03-04	04-05	05-06
scored	698	690	680	311	385	508	407	441
conceded	574	425	430	524	490	311	366	494

Points Difference

Season	98-99	99-00	00-01	01-02	02-03	03-04	04-05	05-06
points	+124	+265	+250	-213	-105	+197	+41	-53

Total Premiership Record

Largest win
76-13
vs London Scottish (H)
15.05.99

Largest defeat
12-68
vs Gloucester (A)
04.05.02

Most tries scored in a game
12
vs London Scottish (H)
15.05.99

Most tries conceded in a game
9
vs Gloucester (A)
04.05.02

Top points scorer
O.Barkley   750

Top try scorer
I.Balshaw   36

Top drop goal scorer
C.Malone   22

Most appearances
S.Borthwick   139

Longest winning sequence
10 wins from 22.01.00 to 06.05.00

Longest losing sequence
6 defeats from 31.10.98 to 02.01.99

Bath Rugby `EFL`

ENHANCED FIXTURE LIST
[does not include play-off data]

Guinness Premiership 2006-07 | **Premiership History**

Date	Team	H/A	05-06	Played	98-99	99-00	00-01	01-02	02-03	03-04	04-05	05-06	Total Points F	A	Outcome after a half-time lead No.	W	D	L	Close games No.	W
02.09.06	Gloucester	A	15-18	9									164	230	6	3	-	3	4	3
09.09.06	Leicester	H	12-19	9									125	135	5	3	-	2	2	-
16.09.06	Northampton	A	24-21	9									113	212	2	1	-	1	3	1
23.09.06	Worcester	H	25-22	2									43	32	1	1	-	-	1	1
15.10.06	Saracens	A	29-34	9									202	229	5	5	-	-	1	1
04.11.06	Irish	H	28-33	9									239	163	7	6	1	-	5	3
12.11.06	Wasps	A	28-20	9									167	202	3	3	-	-	3	2
17.11.06	Bristol	H	31-16	6									167	99	4	4	-	-	2	2
25.11.06	Newcastle	H	20-18	9									199	137	5	5	-	-	2	2
22.12.06	Sale	H	9-21	9									212	151	7	6	-	1	4	4
27.12.06	Bristol	A	19-16	6									115	143	3	1	1	1	3	1
01.01.07	Wasps	H	28-16	9									221	179	4	4	-	-	5	1
06.01.07	Harlequins	A	N/A	8									167	165	3	1	-	2	2	-
27.01.07	Harlequins	H	N/A	8									241	116	8	6	-	2	2	-
17.02.07	Irish	A	36-13	9									287	239	3	3	-	-	3	3
24.02.07	Saracens	H	12-12	9									178	172	5	3	-	2	1	-
03.03.07	Worcester	A	18-36	2									62	40	1	1	-	-	1	1
10.03.07	Northampton	H	9-17	9									188	135	4	4	-	-	1	-
17.03.07	Leicester	A	40-26	9									163	277	5	1	1	3	3	1
07.04.07	Gloucester	H	18-16	9									272	122	7	7	-	-	4	3
13.04.07	Sale	A	38-12	9									167	224	3	1	-	2	6	3
28.04.07	Newcastle	A	16-27	9									161	175	3	2	-	1	7	3

Legend: ▥ won ▦ drawn ▨ lost ☐ not played

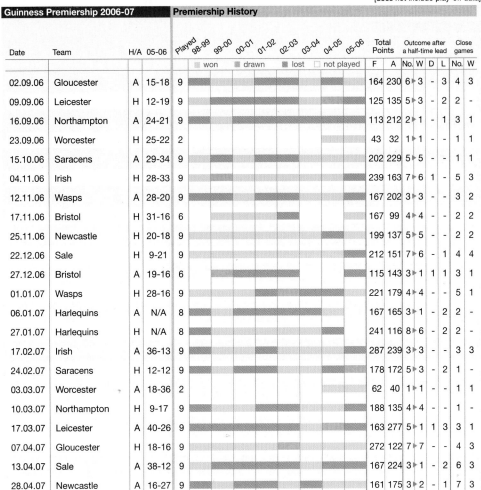

Club Information

Useful Information

Founded
1865
Address
The Recreation Ground
Bath
BA2 6PW
Capacity
10,600 (5,740 seated)
Main switchboard
01225 325200
Website
www.bathrugby.com

Travel Information

Car
(Lambridge Park & Ride):
Leave the M4 at Junction 18 and follow the A46 to Bath. Follow the signs for the town centre. The Park & Ride is at Bath Rugby's training ground on your left after the first set of traffic lights.
The Park & Ride is open for all 1st XV weekend fixtures. To go direct to the stadium, carry on past the training ground until you reach the junction on London Road with Bathwick Street. Turn left and then right down Sydney Place. Go straight on at the roundabout then turn left down North Parade. The ground is on your right.

Train
Bath has direct links to London, Bristol, Cardiff, Salisbury and Southampton. From Birmingham and the Midlands, there are con-necting services at Bristol Temple Meads. National Rail enquiries: 08457 48 49 50.

Coach
National Express services operate between most major towns and cities in Britain.
For further information contact Bath Bus Station on 01225 464446 or National Express direct on 08705 80 80 80 or visit www.nationalexpress.com

Bath Rugby

Maps

Area Map

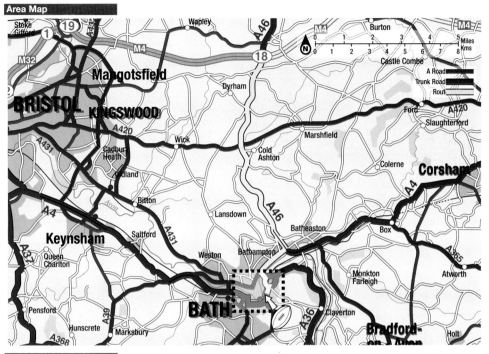

Local Map

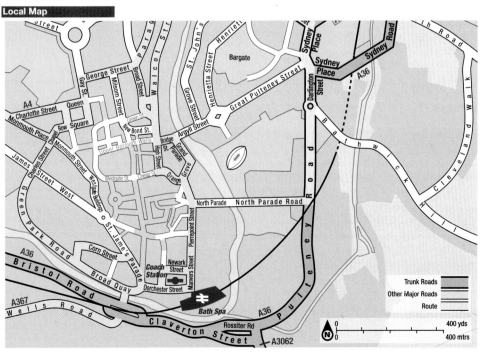

Bristol Rugby

Season Summary 2005/06

Position	Won	Drawn	Lost	For	Against	Bonus Points	Total Points
11	8	1	13	393	445	7	41

As with Worcester the previous year, there are few that would have wanted to see Bristol fall at the first hurdle. Head coach Richard Hill made a series of shrewd signings to ensure his side was no easy proposition and they proved to be a hard team to beat, enjoying victories against Tigers, Sale and Saracens. Fly half Jason Strange formed a successful pairing with newcomer Shaun Perry, with Strange finishing the season as the Premiership's top points scorer. The West Country side finished the season in 11th place with 41 points.

Head Coach: Richard Hill

Club Honours
John Player Cup: 1983

Season Squad

Stats 2005-06

Position	Player	Height	Weight	Apps	Rep	Tries	Points	Position	Player	Height	Weight	Apps	Rep	Tries	Points
BR	N.Budgett	6'5"	17st 0lb	8	-	-	-	L	G.Llewellyn	6'6"	17st 7lb	19	-	-	-
H	N.Clark	5'11"	16st 0lb	-	6	-	-	BR	R.Martin-Redman	6'3"	17st 0lb	-	1	-	-
P	A.Clarke	5'11"	17st 0lb	-	8	-	-	FL	C.Morgan	6'2"	16st 4lb	-	2	-	-
C	M.Contepomi	6'2"	14st 2lb	4	2	-	-	H	S.Nelson	5'10"	14st 9lb	4	4	-	-
C	S.Cox	6'0"	13st 10lb	16	-	1	5	SH	G.Nicholls	5'8"	12st 0lb	1	1	-	-
P	D.Crompton	6'2"	18st 0lb	22	-	1	5	SH	S.Perry	5'10"	15st 0lb	19	-	4	20
C	M.Denney	6'0"	17st 4lb	-	5	-	-	SH	J.Rauluni	5'11"	14st 6lb	2	2	-	-
FL	J.El Abd	6'2"	16st 0lb	14	-	2	10	H	M.Regan	5'10"	15st 2lb	18	-	1	5
FB	V.Going	5'11"	14st 2lb	14	1	-	-	W	L.Robinson	6'2"	17st 1lb	17	-	3	15
FH	D.Gray	5'10"	13st 0lb	-	5	-	-	BR	M.Salter	6'4"	16st 4lb	21	-	-	-
FH	T.Hayes	6'0"	14st 4lb	1	5	1	19	L	M.Sambucetti	6'5"	17st 1lb	6	6	-	-
C	R.Higgitt	6'2"	14st 7lb	17	1	-	-	BR	C.Short	6'2"	16st 0lb	8	1	-	-
P	D.Hilton	5'11"	16st 10lb	21	-	-	-	W	M.Stanojevic	5'11"	12st 7lb	5	1	2	10
L	O.Hodge	6'8"	16st 10lb	-	1	-	-	FB	B.Stortoni	6'1"	14st 4lb	14	-	-	-
P	M.Irish	6'0"	16st 0lb	1	4	-	-	FH	J.Strange	5'10"	13st 3lb	21	1	1	244
W	D.Lemi	5'9"	11st 11lb	12	-	8	40	8	D.Ward-Smith	6'4"	17st 8lb	10	8	-	-
BR	G.Lewis	6'3"	15st 8lb	13	6	1	5	L	R.Winters	6'4"	17st 10lb	11	5	1	5
W	B.Lima	6'0"	15st 4lb	11	2	2	10								

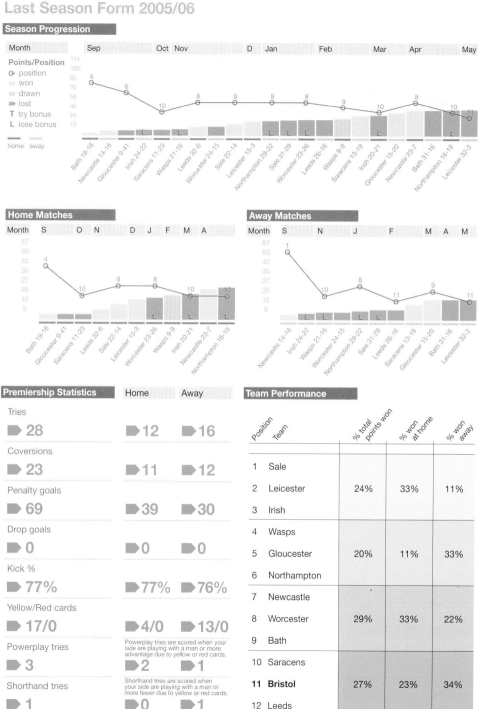

Bristol Rugby

Top Scorer

Jason Strange

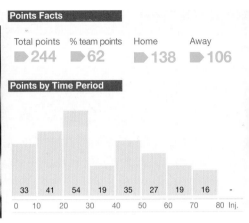

Points Facts

Total points	% team points	Home	Away
▶ 244	▶ 62	▶ 138	▶ 106

Points by Time Period

33	41	54	19	35	27	19	16	-
0	10	20	30	40	50	60	70	80 Inj.

Team Tries and Points

Tries by Time Period

- scored
- conceded

7	3	4	4	6	0
	0	2	2		

0	10min	20min	30min	40min	50min	60min	70min	80 Injury time

3	8	2	7	1
3	7	6	4	

Tries by Halves

- scored
- conceded

▶ 28	▶ 12	▶ 16	▶ 43%	▶ 57%
Total	1st half	2nd half	1st half %	2nd half %
▶ 41	▶ 21	▶ 20	▶ 51%	▶ 49%

How Points were Scored

- tries: 140
- conversions: 46
- pen goals: 207
- drop goals: 0

How Points were Conceded

- tries: 205
- conversions: 60
- pen goals: 165
- drop goals: 15

Tries Scored by Player

- backs: 22
- forwards: 6

Tries Conceded by Player

- backs: 25
- forwards: 16

Bristol Rugby

Eight-Season Form 1998-2006

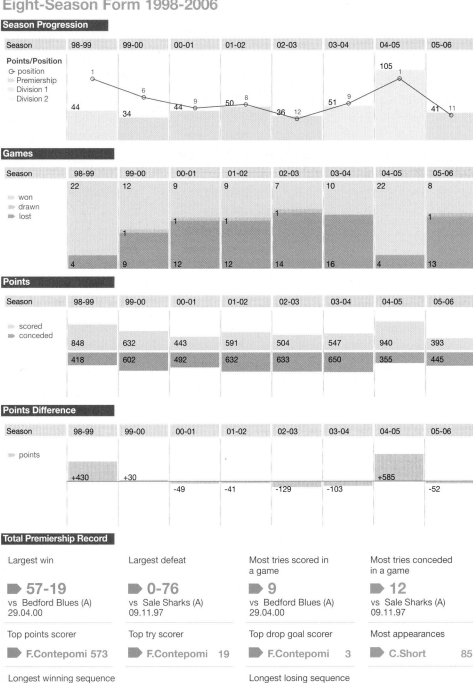

Season Progression

Season	98-99	99-00	00-01	01-02	02-03	03-04	04-05	05-06
Points/Position								

- position
- Premiership
- Division 1
- Division 2

	1	6	9	8	12	9	1	11
	44	34	44	50	36	51	105	41

Games

Season	98-99	99-00	00-01	01-02	02-03	03-04	04-05	05-06
won	22	12	9	9	7	10	22	8
drawn		1	1	1	1			1
lost	4	9	12	12	14	16	4	13

Points

Season	98-99	99-00	00-01	01-02	02-03	03-04	04-05	05-06
scored	848	632	443	591	504	547	940	393
conceded	418	602	492	632	633	650	355	445

Points Difference

Season	98-99	99-00	00-01	01-02	02-03	03-04	04-05	05-06
points	+430	+30	-49	-41	-129	-103	+585	-52

Total Premiership Record

Largest win	Largest defeat	Most tries scored in a game	Most tries conceded in a game
57-19	**0-76**	**9**	**12**
vs Bedford Blues (A) 29.04.00	vs Sale Sharks (A) 09.11.97	vs Bedford Blues (A) 29.04.00	vs Sale Sharks (A) 09.11.97

Top points scorer	Top try scorer	Top drop goal scorer	Most appearances
F.Contepomi 573	F.Contepomi 19	F.Contepomi 3	C.Short 85

Longest winning sequence	Longest losing sequence
4 wins from 19.04.00 to 10.05.00	**13 defeats** from 18.01.98 to 10.05.98

Bristol Rugby EFL

ENHANCED FIXTURE LIST
[does not include play-off data]

Guinness Premiership 2006-07 | Premiership History

Legend: ■ won ■ drawn ■ lost □ not played

Date	Team	H/A	05-06	Played	98-99	99-00	00-01	01-02	02-03	03-04	04-05	05-06	Total Points F	A	Outcome after a half-time lead No.	W	D	L	Close games No.	W
02.09.06	Worcester	A	24-15	1									15	24	-	▶-	-	-	-	-
10.09.06	Saracens	H	11-23	6									151	186	2	▶-	-	2	1	-
16.09.06	Irish	A	24-22	6									126	188	-	▶-	-	-	2	-
24.09.06	Wasps	H	9-9	6									124	140	3	▶2	-	1	1	-
15.10.06	Harlequins	H	N/A	5									165	142	5	▶4	-	1	2	2
03.11.06	Newcastle	A	14-16	6									126	161	3	▶3	-	-	2	2
10.11.06	Sale	H	22-14	6									128	132	3	▶3	-	-	-	-
17.11.06	Bath	A	31-16	6									99	167	1	▶1	-	-	2	-
24.11.06	Gloucester	H	9-41	6									126	181	1	▶-	-	1	2	-
22.12.06	Leicester	A	32-3	6									82	185	1	▶-	-	1	-	-
27.12.06	Bath	H	19-16	6									143	115	2	▶2	-	-	3	1
01.01.07	Sale	A	31-29	6									156	228	1	▶1	-	-	3	1
07.01.07	Northampton	H	16-19	6									158	152	2	▶-	-	2	1	-
27.01.07	Northampton	A	29-22	6									99	170	2	▶1	-	1	2	2
18.02.07	Newcastle	H	23-7	6									159	109	5	▶5	-	-	-	-
24.02.07	Harlequins	A	N/A	5									140	163	2	▶1	-	1	3	2
04.03.07	Wasps	A	21-16	6									133	173	3	▶1	-	2	4	1
10.03.07	Irish	H	20-21	6									130	145	2	▶-	-	2	5	1
18.03.07	Saracens	A	13-19	6									95	148	1	▶1	-	-	3	2
08.04.07	Worcester	H	23-26	1									23	26	-	▶-	-	-	1	-
15.04.07	Leicester	H	15-3	6									149	121	4	▶4	-	-	3	2
28.04.07	Gloucester	A	15-20	6									107	213	3	▶-	-	3	2	1

Club Information

Useful Information

Founded
1888
Address
The Memorial Stadium
Filton Avenue
Horfield
Bristol
BS7 0AQ
Stadium capacity
12,000 (3,000 seated)
Main switchboard
0117 952 0500
Website
www.bristolrugby.co.uk

Travel Information

Car
From the M4: Exit at junction 19 and follow signs onto the M32. Leave the M32 at junction 2 and at the roundabout turn right towards Horfield and the B4469. Continue for 1.4 miles, then after passing the bus garage (on your right) turn left at the second set of traffic lights into Filton Avenue. Take the first left into the club car park.

From the M5: Exit at junction 16 and join the A38 towards Bristol City Centre. After 5 miles turn left at traffic lights onto B4469. Turn right at the next traffic lights into Filton Avenue and then first left into car park.

Train
Nearest mainline rail stations are Bristol Parkway or Bristol Temple Meads.

Bristol Rugby

Maps

Area Map

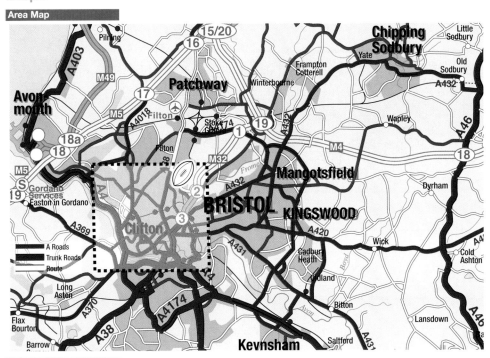

Local Map

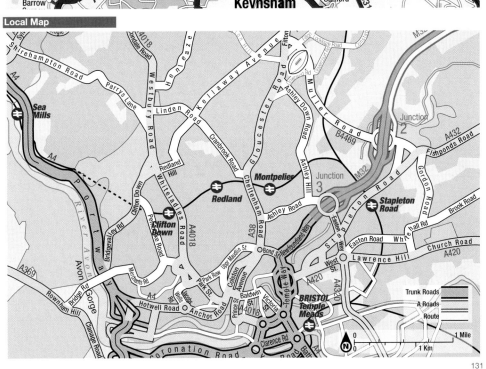

Gloucester Rugby

Season Summary 2005/06

Position	Won	Drawn	Lost	For	Against	Bonus Points	Total Points
5	**11**	**1**	**10**	**483**	**385**	**13**	**59**

The Kingsholm faithful had high expectations at the start of the season and welcomed new boy Mike Tindall from Bath. However, it was the young fly half Ryan Lamb who really stole the show throughout the season, especially for his performance against Worcester in the semi-final of the European Challenge Cup. Despite a positive start to their league campaign – winning four out of their first six matches – Dean Ryan's side failed to display that kind of consistency throughout the season. They did enjoy success in the European Challenge Cup, beating London Irish in the final thanks to a moment of inspirational attacking instinct from James Forrester to score what proved to be the winning try.

Head Coach: Dean Ryan

Club Honours
Zurich Premiership: 2002-03 (playoffs won by Wasps)
John Player Cup: 1972, 1978, 1982, 2003
European Challenge Cup: 2006

Season Squad

Stats 2005-06

Position	Player	Height	Weight	Apps	Rep	Tries	Points	Position	Player	Height	Weight	Apps	Rep	Tries	Points
C	J.Adams	6'0"	16st 5lb	-	2	-	-	FB	J.Goodridge	6'1"	13st 8lb	9	1	1	5
C	A.Allen	5'11"	14st 2lb	8	1	4	20	FL	A.Hazell	6'0"	14st 9lb	17	1	1	5
FH/SH	S.Amor	5'7"	12st 0lb	1	3	-	-	C	R.Keil	6'1"	13st 5lb	3	1	-	-
H	O.Azam	6'0"	18st 0lb	3	3	1	5	FH	R.Lamb	5'10"	12st 10lb	4	1	1	49
W	J.Bailey	5'11"	13st 0lb	10	2	5	25	FH/FB	D.McRae	5'7"	12st 10lb	-	2	-	-
8	A.Balding	6'2"	17st 7lb	8	5	-	-	FH	L.Mercier	5'10"	14st 2lb	18	4	2	213
FL	J.Boer	6'1"	16st 8lb	9	3	1	5	FL	J.Merriman	6'0"	14st 7lb	1	-	-	-
L	A.Brown	6'7"	17st 5lb	18	-	-	-	FB	O.Morgan	6'2"	14st 0lb	12	-	1	5
BR	P.Buxton	6'3"	17st 9lb	16	3	-	-	BR	L.Narraway	6'3"	15st 10lb	2	8	-	-
P	P.Collazo	6'1"	17st 4lb	19	-	-	-	H	J.Parkes	5'10"	15st 6lb	2	4	-	-
L	M.Cornwell	6'7"	18st 2lb	1	2	-	-	C	H.Paul	5'11"	14st 10lb	5	-	-	-
L	Q.Davids	6'6"	19st 4lb	2	1	-	-	L	J.Pendlebury	6'7"	16st 5lb	8	3	-	-
FH	B.Davies	5'9"	14st 1lb	1	4	-	-	P	G.Powell	6'0"	17st 9lb	7	5	-	-
H	M.Davies	5'10"	15st 0lb	13	3	-	-	SH	P.Richards	5'9"	14st 10lb	14	4	6	30
H	R.Elloway	6'0"	15st 6lb	4	2	-	-	P	T.Sigley	6'2"	19st 4lb	3	8	-	-
L	A.Eustace	6'4"	17st 0lb	14	8	-	-	W/C	J.Simpson-Daniel	6'0"	12st 7lb	16	-	6	30
C	T.Fanolua	6'0"	14st 10lb	5	5	1	5	W	R.Thirlby	6'1"	14st 0lb	7	3	1	5
8	J.Forrester	6'5"	15st 9lb	14	2	3	15	SH	H.Thomas	5'8"	12st 4lb	7	7	1	5
P	J.Forster	6'1"	17st 11lb	4	3	-	-	C	M.Tindall	6'2"	16st 8lb	13	1	1	11
W	M.Foster	6'0"	14st 4lb	19	-	5	25	P	P.Vickery	6'3"	18st 4lb	8	-	-	-
W	M.Garvey	5'8"	13st 7lb	2	1	-	-	P	N.Wood	6'1"	17st 0lb	3	4	-	-

Gloucester Rugby

Last Season Form 2005/06

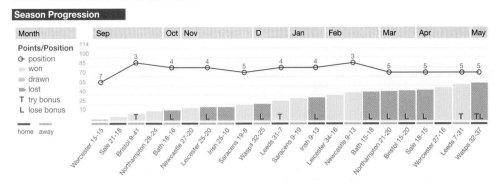

Season Progression

Home Matches

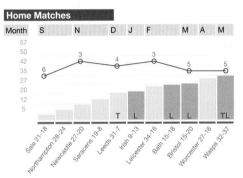

Away Matches

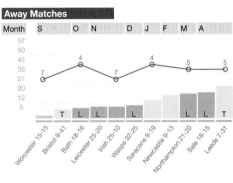

Premiership Statistics

	Home	Away
Tries		
46	27	19
Coversions		
32	15	17
Penalty goals		
61	30	31
Drop goals		
2	1	1
Kick %		
70%	63%	77%
Yellow/Red cards		
15/1	4/1	11/0
Powerplay tries		
11	7	4
Shorthand tries		
3	3	0

Powerplay tries are scored when your side is playing with a man or more advantage due to yellow or red cards.

Shorthand tries are scored when your side is playing with a man or more fewer due to yellow or red cards.

Team Performance

Position	Team	% total points won	% won at home	% won away
1	Sale			
2	Leicester	17%	24%	8%
3	Irish			
4	Wasps			
5	**Gloucester**	19%	24%	12%
6	Northampton			
7	Newcastle			
8	Worcester	25%	24%	27%
9	Bath			
10	Saracens			
11	Bristol	39%	28%	53%
12	Leeds			

Gloucester Rugby

Top Scorer

Ludovic Mercier

Points Facts

Total points	% team points	Home	Away
▶213	▶47	▶104	▶109

Points by Time Period

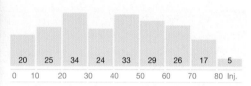

20	25	34	24	33	29	26	17	5
0	10	20	30	40	50	60	70	80 Inj.

Team Tries and Points

Tries by Time Period

- scored
- conceded

2	5	7	5	4	9	4	9	1
0	10min	20min	30min	40min	50min	60min	70min	80 Injury time
3	4	4	8	3	2	5	4	0

Tries by Halves

- scored
- conceded

	Total	1st half	2nd half	1st half %	2nd half %
scored	▶46	▶19	▶27	▶41%	▶59%
conceded	▶33	▶19	▶14	▶58%	▶42%

How Points were Scored

- tries: 230
- conversions: 64
- pen goals: 183
- drop goals: 6

How Points were Conceded

- tries: 165
- conversions: 52
- pen goals: 159
- drop goals: 9

Tries Scored by Player

- backs: 35
- forwards: 6

Tries Conceded by Player

- backs: 14
- forwards: 18

Gloucester Rugby

Eight-Season Form 1998-2006

Season Progression

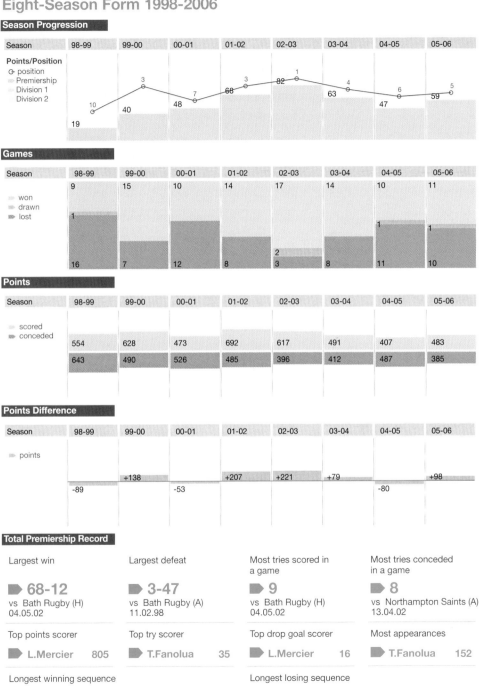

Season	98-99	99-00	00-01	01-02	02-03	03-04	04-05	05-06

Points/Position
- ○ position
- ▬ Premiership
- Division 1
- Division 2

Position: 10, 3, 7, 3, 1, 4, 6, 5

Points: 19, 40, 48, 68, 82, 63, 47, 59

Games

Season	98-99	99-00	00-01	01-02	02-03	03-04	04-05	05-06
won	9	15	10	14	17	14	10	11
drawn	1				2		1	1
lost	16	7	12	8	3	8	11	10

Points

Season	98-99	99-00	00-01	01-02	02-03	03-04	04-05	05-06
scored	554	628	473	692	617	491	407	483
conceded	643	490	526	485	396	412	487	385

Points Difference

Season	98-99	99-00	00-01	01-02	02-03	03-04	04-05	05-06
points	-89	+138	-53	+207	+221	+79	-80	+98

Total Premiership Record

Largest win
▶ **68-12**
vs Bath Rugby (H)
04.05.02

Largest defeat
▶ **3-47**
vs Bath Rugby (A)
11.02.98

Most tries scored in a game
▶ **9**
vs Bath Rugby (H)
04.05.02

Most tries conceded in a game
▶ **8**
vs Northampton Saints (A)
13.04.02

Top points scorer
▶ L.Mercier   805

Top try scorer
▶ T.Fanolua   35

Top drop goal scorer
▶ L.Mercier   16

Most appearances
▶ T.Fanolua   152

Longest winning sequence
▶ **8 wins**   from 24.11.02 to 12.04.03

Longest losing sequence
▶ **8 defeats**   from 23.01.99 to 07.05.99

Gloucester Rugby `EFL`

ENHANCED FIXTURE LIST
[does not include play-off data]

Guinness Premiership 2006-07 | **Premiership History**

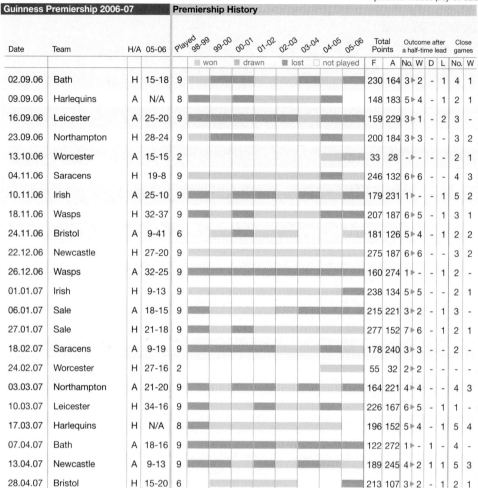

Date	Team	H/A	05-06	Played	98-99	99-00	00-01	01-02	02-03	03-04	04-05	05-06	Total Points F	A	Outcome after a half-time lead No.	W	D	L	Close games No.	W
02.09.06	Bath	H	15-18	9									230	164	3	2	-	1	4	1
09.09.06	Harlequins	A	N/A	8									148	183	5	4	-	1	2	1
16.09.06	Leicester	A	25-20	9									159	229	3	1	-	2	3	-
23.09.06	Northampton	H	28-24	9									200	184	3	3	-	-	3	2
13.10.06	Worcester	A	15-15	2									33	28	-	-	-	-	2	1
04.11.06	Saracens	H	19-8	9									246	132	6	6	-	-	4	3
10.11.06	Irish	A	25-10	9									179	231	1	-	-	1	5	2
18.11.06	Wasps	H	32-37	9									207	187	6	5	-	1	3	1
24.11.06	Bristol	A	9-41	6									181	126	5	4	-	1	2	2
22.12.06	Newcastle	H	27-20	9									275	187	6	6	-	-	3	2
26.12.06	Wasps	A	32-25	9									160	274	1	-	-	1	2	-
01.01.07	Irish	H	9-13	9									238	134	5	5	-	-	2	1
06.01.07	Sale	A	18-15	9									215	221	3	2	-	1	3	-
27.01.07	Sale	H	21-18	9									277	152	7	6	-	1	2	1
18.02.07	Saracens	A	9-19	9									178	240	3	3	-	-	2	-
24.02.07	Worcester	H	27-16	2									55	32	2	2	-	-	-	-
03.03.07	Northampton	A	21-20	9									164	221	4	4	-	-	4	3
10.03.07	Leicester	H	34-16	9									226	167	6	6	-	1	1	-
17.03.07	Harlequins	H	N/A	8									196	152	5	4	-	1	5	4
07.04.07	Bath	A	18-16	9									122	272	1	-	1	-	4	-
13.04.07	Newcastle	A	9-13	9									189	245	4	2	1	1	5	3
28.04.07	Bristol	H	15-20	6									213	107	3	2	-	1	2	1

Legend: ■ won ■ drawn ■ lost □ not played

Club Information

Useful Information

Founded
1873
Address
Kingsholm
Kingsholm Road
Gloucester
GL1 3AX
Capacity
13,000 (1,498 seated)
Main switchboard
01452 381087
Website
www.gloucesterrugbyclub.com

Travel Information

Car
From Midlands: From the M5 southbound, exit at junction 11 (Cheltenham south and Gloucester north). Follow A40 to Gloucester/ Ross and Northern Bypass. Turn left at Longford roundabout (where A40 crosses A38) towards the City Centre. Go straight over the Tewkesbury Road roundabout and the ground is on your right after a quarter of a mile.
From South: From the M4 westbound, exit at junction 15 (Swindon) and follow the A419/417 to Gloucester. At Zoons Court roundabout follow the signs A40 to Ross and continue along Northern Bypass until you reach Longford roundabout. The as route for Midlands.
From West Country: Exit the M5 northbound at junction 11A (Gloucester) until you reach Zoons Court round-about. Then as above.
Parking is available approx 5 minutes from the ground. Turn right at the Tewkesbury Road roundabout and follow the signs for the Park and Ride Car Park.
Train
Gloucester station is a 5 minute walk from the ground, and is well sign-posted. Virgin Trains, Great Western and Central Trains all serve Gloucester from the Midlands, and there are direct services from all regions.

Maps

Area Map

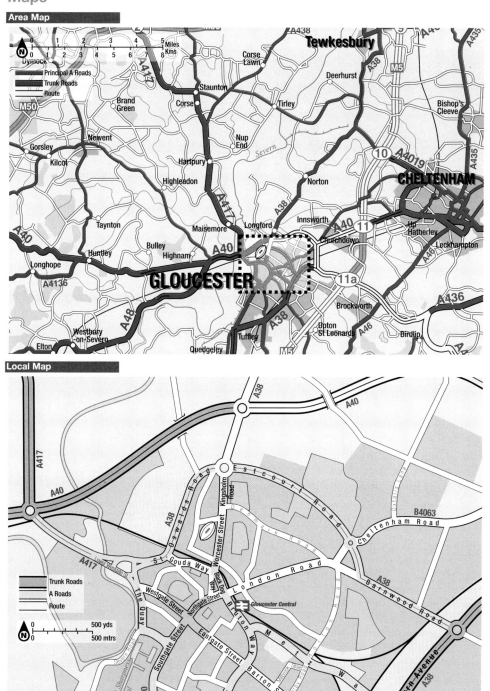

Local Map

Leicester Tigers

Season Summary 2005/06

Position	Won	Drawn	Lost	For	Against	Bonus Points	Total Points
2	**14**	**3**	**5**	**518**	**415**	**6**	**68**

Despite being out-classed in the Premiership final, Pat Howard will reflect on the 2005/06 season with a great deal of satisfaction. After an indifferent start, Tigers ended the season as the competition's form side. The Heineken Cup quarter-final defeat to Bath Rugby at the Walkers Stadium was a watershed, as Leicester went on an unbeaten run that resulted in them cruising into the Premiership semi-finals where they defeated London Irish. Much had been made of the recent retirement of influential players, but Tigers remain a force in the domestic game. Welford Road is still one of the toughest places to earn a win, while the Midlands team will be looking to appease fans by winning some silverware.

Head Coach: Pat Howard

Club Honours
Courage League / Allied Dunbar Premiership / Zurich Premiership: 1987-88, 1994-95, 1998-99 1999-2000, 2000-01, 2001-02, 2004-05 (lost in play-offs)

John Player Cup / Pilkington Cup: 1979, 1980, 1981, 1993, 1997
Heineken Cup: 2000-01 2001-02

Season Squad

Stats 2005-06

Position	Player	Height	Weight	Apps	Rep	Tries	Points
FL/H	L.Abraham	6'2"	16st 5lb	5	6	-	-
SH	S.Bemand	5'11"	13st 5lb	4	4	-	-
FH	R.Broadfoot	5'11"	13st 2lb	4	4	-	28
H	J.Buckland	5'11"	16st 11lb	6	9	1	5
H	G.Chuter	5'10"	15st 12lb	17	2	3	15
SH	N.Cole	5'11"	12st 6lb	1	2	-	-
C/FB	M.Cornwell	6'1"	15st 0lb	3	3	3	15
FL	M.Corry	6'5"	17st 10lb	13	1	-	-
L	T.Croft	6'5"	16st 4lb	2	-	-	-
L	L.Cullen	6'6"	17st 5lb	14	6	-	-
FL	B.Deacon	6'4"	17st 0lb	10	-	-	-
L	L.Deacon	6'5"	17st 10lb	14	4	1	5
C	A.Dodge	6'2"	15st 0lb	-	2	-	-
SH	H.Ellis	5'10"	13st 4lb	10	2	2	10
C	D.Gibson	5'11"	15st 6lb	8	2	-	-
FH	A.Goode	5'11"	13st 9lb	15	4	-	225
L	J.Hamilton	6'8"	19st 4lb	7	10	3	15
UB	A.Healey	5'10"	13st 9lb	14	8	1	5
C	D.Hipkiss	5'10"	14st 2lb	12	1	1	5
P	M.Holford	5'11"	16st 1lb	8	11	4	20

Position	Player	Height	Weight	Apps	Rep	Tries	Points
FH	I.Humphreys	5'11"	13st 1lb	2	1	-	15
FL	S.Jennings	6'0"	16st 1lb	16	3	1	5
BR	W.Johnson	6'4"	17st 0lb	10	4	1	5
L	B.Kay	6'6"	17st 9lb	18	2	1	5
W/C	L.Lloyd	6'4"	15st 2lb	16	5	4	20
FL	L.Moody	6'3"	16st 8lb	8	-	1	5
P	A.Moreno	6'1"	17st 5lb	6	1	-	-
P	D.Morris	6'1"	19st 10lb	8	6	1	5
FB/W	G.Murphy	6'1"	13st 3lb	13	-	2	13
C/W	S.Rabeni	6'2"	15st 0lb	2	1	-	-
P	G.Rowntree	6'0"	17st 3lb	13	-	-	-
FL	W.Skinner	5'11"	14st 2lb	3	6	2	10
C/W	O.Smith	6'1"	14st 7lb	17	4	2	10
H	E.Taukafa	5'11"	17st 0lb	1	6	1	5
W/C	A.Tuilagi	6'1"	17st 7lb	14	4	5	25
BR	H.Tuilagi	6'1"	18st 10lb	-	2	1	5
W	T.Varndell	6'3"	14st 13lb	18	3	14	70
FH/FB	S.Vesty	6'0"	14st 2lb	15	5	2	27
P	J.White	6'1"	18st 0lb	13	2	-	-

Leicester Tigers

Last Season Form 2005/06

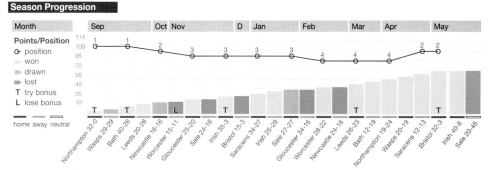

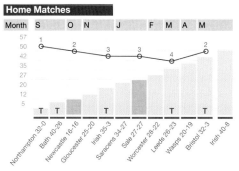

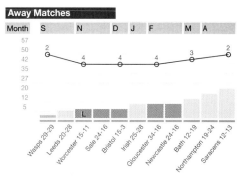

Premiership Stats

		Home	Away	Neutral
Tries	58	40	16	2
Coversions	39	25	12	2
Penalty goals	69	34	33	2
Drop goals	1	1	0	0
Kick %	68%	66%	69%	80%
Yellow/Red cards	18/1	6/1	12/0	0/0
Powerplay tries	7	4	3	0
Shorthand tries	2	1	1	0

Powerplay tries are scored when your side are playing with a man or more advantage due to yellow or red cards.

Shorthand tries are scored when your side are playing with a man or more fewer due to yellow or red cards.

Team Performance

Position	Team	% total points won	% won at home	% won away
1	Sale			
2	**Leicester**	22%	22%	24%
3	Irish			
4	Wasps			
5	Gloucester	26%	27%	24%
6	Northampton			
7	Newcastle			
8	Worcester	22%	23%	20%
9	Bath			
10	Saracens			
11	Bristol	30%	28%	32%
12	Leeds			

Leicester Tigers

Top Scorer

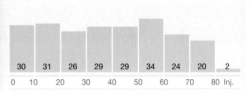

Points Facts

Total points	% team points	Home	Away	Neutral
▶ 225	▶ 39	▶ 144	▶ 71	▶ 10

Points by Time Period

30	31	26	29	29	34	24	20	2
0	10	20	30	40	50	60	70	80 Inj.

Team Tries and Points

Tries by Time Period

- scored
- conceded

9	6	9	9	6	4	4	10	1
0	10min	20min	30min	40min	50min	60min	70min	80 Injury time
2	5	4	6	2	3	1	6	0

Tries by Halves

- scored
- conceded

	Total	1st half	2nd half	1st half %	2nd half %
scored	▶ 58	▶ 33	▶ 25	▶ 57%	▶ 43%
conceded	▶ 29	▶ 17	▶ 12	▶ 59%	▶ 41%

How Points were Scored

- tries: 290
- conversions: 78
- pen goals: 207
- drop goals: 3

How Points were Conceded

- tries: 145
- conversions: 44
- pen goals: 255
- drop goals: 24

Tries Scored by Player

- backs: 35
- forwards: 21

Tries Conceded by Player

- backs: 17
- forwards: 11

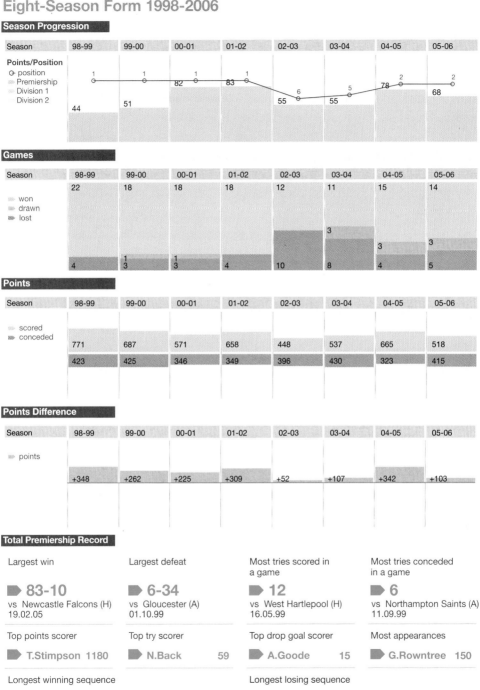

Leicester Tigers

Eight-Season Form 1998-2006

Season Progression

Season	98-99	99-00	00-01	01-02	02-03	03-04	04-05	05-06
Points/Position								

Points/Position
- position
- Premiership
- Division 1
- Division 2

Positions: 1, 1, 1, 1, 6, 5, 2, 2

Points: 44, 51, 82, 83, 55, 55, 78, 68

Games

Season	98-99	99-00	00-01	01-02	02-03	03-04	04-05	05-06
won	22	18	18	18	12	11	15	14
drawn		1	1			3	3	3
lost	4	3	3	4	10	8	4	5

Points

Season	98-99	99-00	00-01	01-02	02-03	03-04	04-05	05-06
scored	771	687	571	658	448	537	665	518
conceded	423	425	346	349	396	430	323	415

Points Difference

Season	98-99	99-00	00-01	01-02	02-03	03-04	04-05	05-06
points	+348	+262	+225	+309	+52	+107	+342	+103

Total Premiership Record

Largest win
83-10
vs Newcastle Falcons (H)
19.02.05

Largest defeat
6-34
vs Gloucester (A)
01.10.99

Most tries scored in a game
12
vs West Hartlepool (H)
16.05.99

Most tries conceded in a game
6
vs Northampton Saints (A)
11.09.99

Top points scorer
T.Stimpson 1180

Top try scorer
N.Back 59

Top drop goal scorer
A.Goode 15

Most appearances
G.Rowntree 150

Longest winning sequence
17 wins from 26.12.99 to 06.09.00

Longest losing sequence
5 defeats from 04.10.03 to 01.11.03

Leicester Tigers EFL

ENHANCED FIXTURE LIST
[does not include play-off data]

Guinness Premiership 2006-07 | **Premiership History**

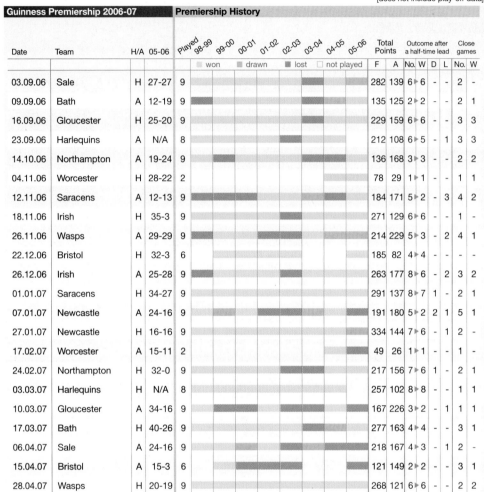

Date	Team	H/A	05-06	Played	98-99	99-00	00-01	01-02	02-03	03-04	04-05	05-06	Total Points F	Total Points A	Outcome after a half-time lead No.	W	D	L	Close games No.	W
					■ won		■ drawn		■ lost		□ not played		F	A	No.	W	D	L	No.	W
03.09.06	Sale	H	27-27	9									282	139	6►6		-	-	2	-
09.09.06	Bath	A	12-19	9									135	125	2►2		-	-	2	1
16.09.06	Gloucester	H	25-20	9									229	159	6►6		-	-	3	3
23.09.06	Harlequins	A	N/A	8									212	108	6►5		-	1	3	3
14.10.06	Northampton	A	19-24	9									136	168	3►3		-	-	2	2
04.11.06	Worcester	H	28-22	2									78	29	1►1		-	-	1	1
12.11.06	Saracens	A	12-13	9									184	171	5►2		-	3	4	2
18.11.06	Irish	H	35-3	9									271	129	6►6		-	-	1	-
26.11.06	Wasps	A	29-29	9									214	229	5►3		-	2	4	1
22.12.06	Bristol	H	32-3	6									185	82	4►4		-	-	-	-
26.12.06	Irish	A	25-28	9									263	177	8►6		-	2	3	2
01.01.07	Saracens	H	34-27	9									291	137	8►7	1	-		2	1
07.01.07	Newcastle	A	24-16	9									191	180	5►2	2	1		5	1
27.01.07	Newcastle	H	16-16	9									334	144	7►6		-	1	2	-
17.02.07	Worcester	A	15-11	2									49	26	1►1		-	-	1	-
24.02.07	Northampton	H	32-0	9									217	156	7►6	1	-		2	1
03.03.07	Harlequins	H	N/A	8									257	102	8►8		-	-	1	1
10.03.07	Gloucester	A	34-16	9									167	226	3►2		-	1	1	1
17.03.07	Bath	H	40-26	9									277	163	4►4		-	-	3	1
06.04.07	Sale	A	24-16	9									218	167	4►3		-	1	2	-
15.04.07	Bristol	A	15-3	6									121	149	2►2		-	-	3	1
28.04.07	Wasps	H	20-19	9									268	121	6►6		-	-	2	2

Club Information

Useful Information

Founded
1888

Address
Welford Road Stadium
Aylestone Road
Leicester LE2 7TR

Capacity
16,815 (12,411 seated)

Main switchboard
08701 283 430

Website
www.leicestertigers.com

Travel Information

Car
From M1 (North and South) and M69 (East): Exit the motorway at Junction 21 (M1). Follow the signs for the city centre via Narborough Road (A5460). After 3 miles, at the crossroad junction with Upperton Road, turn right. The stadium is 1/2 mile ahead (past Leicester City Football ground on the right).
From A6 (South): Follow the signs for the city centre, coming in via London Road. At the main set of lights opposite the entrance to the railway station (on the right), turn left onto the Waterloo Way. The stadium is 1/2 mile further on.
From A47 (East): Follow signs for the city centre, coming in via Uppingham Road. At the St Georges Retail Park roundabout, take the second exit into St Georges Way (A594). Carry on past the Leicester Mercury offices on the right, and then filter off right into Waterloo Way just before the Railway Station. The stadium is 1/2 mile further on.

Train
Leicester Station is a ten minute walk away, along Waterloo Way.

Leicester Tigers

Maps

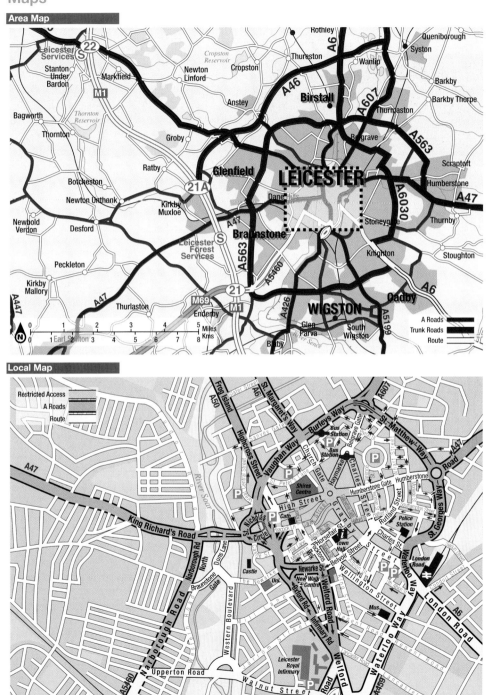

Area Map

Leicester Services 22 S
Stanton Under Bardon
Markfield
Newton Linford
Cropston Reservoir
Cropston
Rothley
Thurcaston
Queniborough
Syston
Wanlip
M1
Bagworth
Thornton Reservoir
Anstey
A46
Birstall
A607
Barkby
Barkby Thorpe
Thornton
Groby
Thurmaston
A563
Bagrave
Scraptoft
Ratby
Glenfield
LEICESTER
Humberstone
Botcheston
21A
Dane Hills
A47
Newton Unthank
Kirkby Muxloe
A6030
Stoneygate
Thurnby
Newbold Verdon
Desford
A47
Braunstone
A563
Knighton
Stoughton
Leicester Forest Services S
Peckleton
A5460
Kirkby Mallory
A47
Thurlaston
21
M69
M1
Enderby
WIGSTON
Oadby
A6
A5199
A447
Earl Shilton
Glen Parva
South Wigston
Blaby
River Sence

A Roads
Trunk Roads
Route

0 1 2 3 4 5 Miles
0 1 2 3 4 5 6 7 8 Kms
N

Local Map

Restricted Access
A Roads
Route

A50
A6
Frog Island
St Margaret's Way
Burleys Way
A607
St Matthew's Way
A47
Sanvey Gate
Highcross Street
Vaughan Way
Church Gate
Bus Station
Belgrave Gate
St Georges Way
London Road
River Soar
A47
St Peter's
Shires Centre
Haymarket
Charles Street
Humberstone Gate
Humberstone
Rutland Street
Police Station
King Richard's Road
St Nicholas Circle
High Street
Cath
Granby Street
Charles St
London Road
Narborough Rd North
Duns Lane
Castle
Horsefair St
Town Hall
Belvoir Street
Wellington Street
Waterloo Way
A6
Braunstone Gate
The Newarke
Newarke St
New Walk Centre
Uni.
Oxford Rd
Welford Road
Infirmary Rd
Mus.
London Road
Western Boulevard
A5460
Upperton Road
Leicester Royal Infirmary
Walnut Street
Welford Road
Waterloo Way
A450

143

London Irish

Season Summary 2005/06

Position	Won	Drawn	Lost	For	Against	Bonus Points	Total Points
3	14	0	8	493	454	10	66

If the Premiership title was decided by a style of play, London Irish would have been worthy champions in 2005/06. In a remarkable close season turn around, Brian Smith's side went from the lowest try-scoring Premiership side to the competition's most prolific. Key to that success was an ambition to play open, attacking rugby which suited the Exiles' talented and pacey back line. While players such as Tipsy Ojo and Delon Armitage set the Premiership alight, it was Mike Catt who was to prove most influential for Irish. The veteran World Cup winner enjoyed an Indian summer of a season, winning an England recall and sparking everything that was good about Irish.

Director of Rugby: Brian Smith

Club Honours
Powergen Cup: 2002

Season Squad

Stats 2005-06

Position	Player	Height	Weight	Apps	Rep	Tries	Points	Position	Player	Height	Weight	Apps	Rep	Tries	Points
W/FB	D.Armitage	6'1"	12st 8lb	21	1	8	40	FH	R.Laidlaw	5'10"	13st 2lb	1	1	-	17
W/C	J.Bishop	6'1"	13st 10lb	9	2	1	5	BR	J.Leguizamon	6'2"	16st 1lb	10	6	1	5
L	B.Casey	6'7"	19st 3lb	21	1	2	10	FL	O.Magne	6'2"	15st 0lb	11	-	2	10
C/FH	M.Catt	5'10"	13st 8lb	19	1	2	33	C	N.Mordt	6'1"	14st 12lb	6	1	1	5
H	D.Coetzee	6'1"	17st 5lb	8	2	-	-	8	P.Murphy	6'5"	17st 3lb	12	8	2	10
P	M.Collins	5'10"	17st 9lb	2	11	-	-	W	T.Ojo	5'11"	13st 1lb	8	3	7	35
BR	D.Danaher	6'4"	16st 3lb	13	1	1	5	H	D.Paice	6'1"	15st 12lb	4	9	2	10
FL	K.Dawson	6'1"	15st 3lb	11	4	1	5	C	R.Penney	6'0"	14st 7lb	12	-	1	5
SH	D.Edwards	5'8"	12st 9lb	1	3	-	-	P	F.Rautenbach	6'2"	18st 0lb	13	2	-	-
FH	B.Everitt	5'9"	12st 13lb	9	4	-	109	L/BR	K.Roche	6'7"	18st 2lb	20	1	1	5
W	D.Feau'nati	6'1"	17st 5lb	5	-	2	10	H	R.Russell	5'10"	15st 4lb	6	7	-	-
H	A.Flavin	5'10"	16st 7lb	5	3	-	-	P	R.Skuse	5'11"	18st 2lb	7	6	-	-
FH	R.Flutey	5'11"	13st 9lb	16	-	7	112	W/FB	S.Staniforth	6'2"	15st 11lb	7	-	3	15
C	P.Franze	6'1"	15st 6lb	2	1	-	-	C	J.Storey	6'3"	14st 5lb	-	1	-	-
FH	S.Geraghty	5'11"	13st 0lb	2	5	1	5	L	R.Strudwick	6'5"	17st 0lb	2	11	1	5
BR	P.Gustard	6'4"	17st 0lb	2	9	1	5	W/FB	S.Tagicakibau	6'3"	14st 12lb	9	1	4	20
P	R.Hardwick	5'11"	18st 10lb	3	1	-	-	FL	R.Thorpe	6'1"	15st 7lb	1	2	-	-
P	N.Hatley	6'1"	18st 11lb	21	2	-	-	C	G.Tiesi	6'1"	13st 12lb	2	4	1	5
SH	P.Hodgson	5'8"	12st 9lb	15	5	2	10	P	T.Warren	6'1"	17st 0lb	-	1	-	-
FB	M.Horak	6'3"	14st 6lb	10	2	1	5	P	D.Wheatley	6'2"	18st 12lb	-	2	-	-
L	N.Kennedy	6'8"	17st 10lb	12	3	-	-	SH	B.Willis	5'9"	13st 8lb	7	7	-	-

London Irish

Last Season Form 2005/06

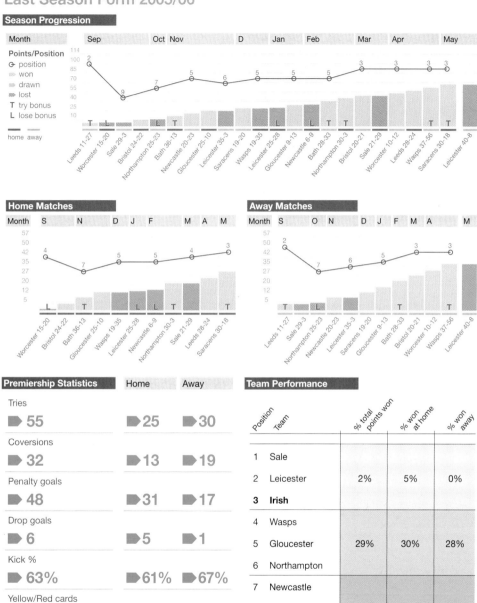

London Irish

Top Scorer

Riki Flutey

Points Facts

Total points	% team points	Home	Away
▶112	▶22	▶47	▶65

Points by Time Period

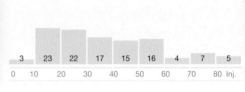

3	23	22	17	15	16	4	7	5
0	10	20	30	40	50	60	70	80 Inj.

Team Tries and Points

Tries by Time Period

- scored
- conceded

5	10	11	11	3	5	4	5	1
0	10min	20min	30min	40min	50min	60min	70min	80 Injury time
8	2	9	2	9	1	6	10	2

Tries by Halves

- scored
- conceded

	Total	1st half	2nd half	1st half %	2nd half %
scored	▶55	▶37	▶18	▶67%	▶33%
conceded	▶49	▶21	▶28	▶43%	▶57%

How Points were Scored

- tries: 275
- conversions: 64
- pen goals: 144
- drop goals: 18

How Points were Conceded

- tries: 245
- conversions: 66
- pen goals: 177
- drop goals: 6

Tries Scored by Player

- backs: 41
- forwards: 14

Tries Conceded by Player

- backs: 31
- forwards: 16

London Irish

Eight-Season Form 1998-2006

Season Progression

Season	98-99	99-00	00-01	01-02	02-03	03-04	04-05	05-06

Points/Position
○ position
▬ Premiership
  Division 1
  Division 2

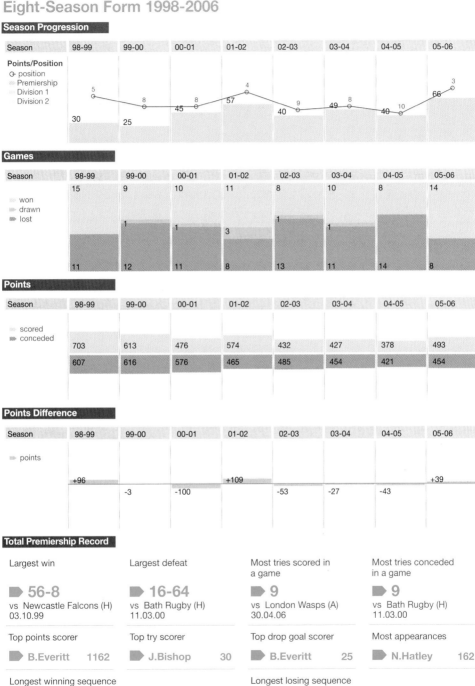

98-99: 5, 30
99-00: 8, 25
00-01: 8, 45
01-02: 4, 57
02-03: 9, 40
03-04: 8, 49
04-05: 10, 40
05-06: 3, 66

Games

Season	98-99	99-00	00-01	01-02	02-03	03-04	04-05	05-06
won	15	9	10	11	8	10	8	14
drawn		1	1	3	1	1		
lost	11	12	11	8	13	11	14	8

Points

Season	98-99	99-00	00-01	01-02	02-03	03-04	04-05	05-06
scored	703	613	476	574	432	427	378	493
conceded	607	616	576	465	485	454	421	454

Points Difference

Season	98-99	99-00	00-01	01-02	02-03	03-04	04-05	05-06
points	+96	-3	-100	+109	-53	-27	-43	+39

Total Premiership Record

Largest win
▶ **56-8**
vs Newcastle Falcons (H)
03.10.99

Largest defeat
▶ **16-64**
vs Bath Rugby (H)
11.03.00

Most tries scored in a game
▶ **9**
vs London Wasps (A)
30.04.06

Most tries conceded in a game
▶ **9**
vs Bath Rugby (H)
11.03.00

Top points scorer
▶ B.Everitt 1162

Top try scorer
▶ J.Bishop 30

Top drop goal scorer
▶ B.Everitt 25

Most appearances
▶ N.Hatley 162

Longest winning sequence
▶ **7 wins** from 19.12.98 to 07.02.99

Longest losing sequence
▶ **8 defeats** from 01.11.97 to 14.02.98

London Irish EFL

ENHANCED FIXTURE LIST
[does not include play-off data]

Guinness Premiership 2006-07 / Premiership History

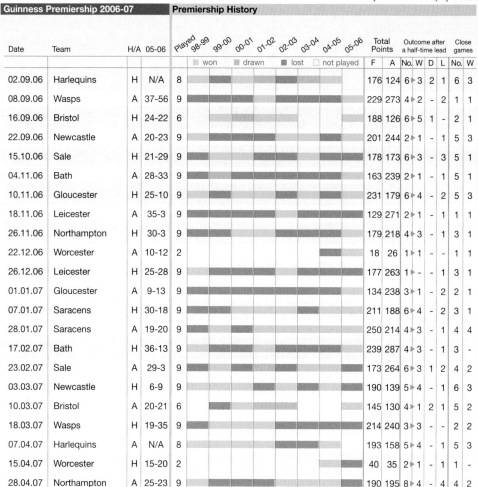

Date	Team	H/A	05-06	Played	98-99	99-00	00-01	01-02	02-03	03-04	04-05	05-06	Total Points F	Total Points A	Outcome after a half-time lead No.	W	D	L	Close games No.	W
02.09.06	Harlequins	H	N/A	8									176	124	6	3	2	1	6	3
08.09.06	Wasps	A	37-56	9									229	273	4	2	-	2	1	1
16.09.06	Bristol	H	24-22	6									188	126	6	5	1	-	2	1
22.09.06	Newcastle	A	20-23	9									201	244	2	1	-	1	5	3
15.10.06	Sale	H	21-29	9									178	173	6	3	-	3	5	1
04.11.06	Bath	A	28-33	9									163	239	2	1	-	1	5	1
10.11.06	Gloucester	H	25-10	9									231	179	6	4	-	2	5	3
18.11.06	Leicester	A	35-3	9									129	271	2	1	-	1	1	1
26.11.06	Northampton	H	30-3	9									179	218	4	3	-	1	3	1
22.12.06	Worcester	A	10-12	2									18	26	1	1	-	-	1	1
26.12.06	Leicester	H	25-28	9									177	263	1	-	-	1	3	1
01.01.07	Gloucester	A	9-13	9									134	238	3	1	-	2	2	1
07.01.07	Saracens	H	30-18	9									211	188	6	4	-	2	3	1
28.01.07	Saracens	A	19-20	9									250	214	4	3	-	1	4	4
17.02.07	Bath	H	36-13	9									239	287	4	3	-	1	3	-
23.02.07	Sale	A	29-3	9									173	264	6	3	1	2	4	2
03.03.07	Newcastle	H	6-9	9									190	139	5	4	-	1	6	3
10.03.07	Bristol	A	20-21	6									145	130	4	1	2	1	5	2
18.03.07	Wasps	H	19-35	9									214	240	3	3	-	-	2	2
07.04.07	Harlequins	A	N/A	8									193	158	5	4	-	1	5	3
15.04.07	Worcester	H	15-20	2									40	35	2	1	-	1	1	-
28.04.07	Northampton	A	25-23	9									190	195	8	4	-	4	4	2

Legend: ■ won ■ drawn ■ lost □ not played

Club Information

Useful Information

Founded
1898
Address
Madejski Stadium
Reading
Berkshire
RG2 OFL
Capacity
24,105 (all seated)
Main switchboard
0118 987 9730
Website
www.london-irish.com

Travel Information

Car
Approaching on the M4, exit at junction 11 onto the A33 towards Reading. When you reach a roundabout, take the 2nd exit onto the Reading Relief Road, the stadium is on your left.
For parking, carry on past the stadium and turn left onto Northern Way and follow the signs for the car parks.

Train
Trains run from London Paddington and London Waterloo to Reading station. A shuttle bus runs from Reading station to the ground on matchdays, costing £2 for adults and £1 for children.

Coach
National Express coaches run from London Victoria station approx every half hour.
Visit www.nationalexpress.com for further information.

London Irish

Maps

Area Map

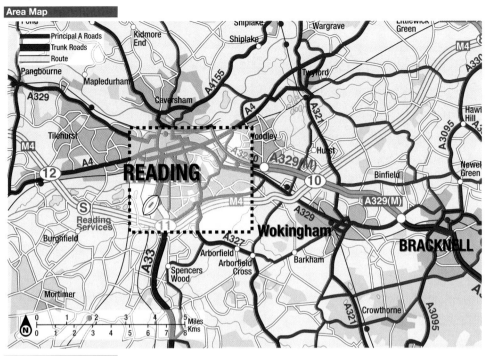

Local Map

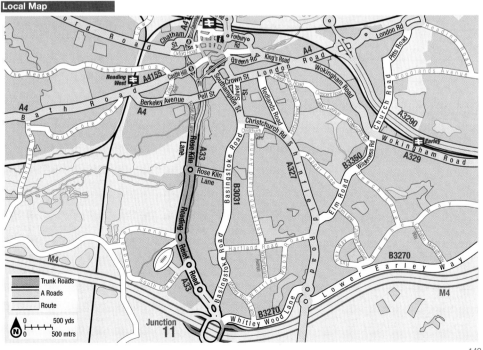

149

London Wasps

Season Summary 2005/06

Position	Won	Drawn	Lost	For	Against	Bonus Points	Total Points
4	12	3	7	527	447	10	64

London Wasps' vice-like grip on the Premiership ended with Sale Sharks' first Premiership league title. For a club whose name has become a byword for winning, the 2005/06 Premiership campaign was ultimately a disappointment. In previous victorious Premiership campaigns, Wasps were the masters of peaking for the season's climax, but captain Lawrence Dallaglio and his side looked tired this term, eventually having to settle for fourth place. Winning the Powergen Cup in a rather one-sided game against Llanelli Scarlets ensured that Ian McGeechan's side did at least add some silverware, but even the celebrations at Twickenham couldn't mask what was a far from satisfactory Premiership campaign.

Director of Rugby: Ian McGeechan

Club Honours
Courage League / Zurich Premiership: 1989-90, 1996-97, 2002-03, 2003-04, 2004-05
Tetley's Bitter Cup: 1998-99, 1999-2000
Heineken Cup: 2003-04
Parker Pen Shield: 2002-03
Powergen Cup: 2005-06

Season Squad

Stats 2005-06

Position	Player	Height	Weight	Apps	Rep	Tries	Points	Position	Player	Height	Weight	Apps	Rep	Tries	Points
C	S.Abbott	6'0"	14st 2lb	20	1	-	-	FH	A.King	6'0"	14st 6lb	11	4	-	55
H	J.Barrett	5'10"	16st 4lb	3	3	-	-	FB	R.Laird	6'0"	14st 2lb	-	1	-	-
W	N.Baxter	6'2"	13st 12lb	1	1	2	10	L/BR	D.Leo	6'6"	17st 8lb	8	2	-	-
SH	H.Biljon	5'11"	13st 2lb	-	1	-	-	W	J.Lewsey	5'10"	13st 9lb	9	1	3	15
L	R.Birkett	6'3"	17st 1lb	17	2	1	5	BR	M.Lock	6'2"	16st 2lb	6	4	-	-
P	P.Bracken	6'2"	18st 7lb	11	5	-	-	P	A.McKenzie	6'3"	18st 12lb	5	4	-	-
FH	J.Brooks	5'9"	13st 9lb	1	5	-	-	FL	J.O'Connor	5'10"	15st 10lb	7	3	-	-
FL	G.Chamberlain	6'2"	14st 2lb	-	1	-	-	P	T.Payne	6'0"	18st 3lb	21	-	1	5
L	M.Corker	6'6"	17st 6lb	-	1	-	-	L	M.Purdy	6'6"	17st 8lb	3	2	-	-
8	L.Dallaglio	6'3"	17st 8lb	16	2	-	-	SH	E.Reddan	5'7"	12st 8lb	15	3	1	5
P	J.Dawson	5'10"	18st 7lb	8	3	-	-	FL	T.Rees	5'11"	15st 10lb	10	3	4	20
SH	M.Dawson	5'10"	14st 2lb	6	8	1	5	W	P.Sackey	6'1"	14st 4lb	23	-	8	40
C	A.Erinle	6'3"	17st 4lb	12	7	2	10	L	S.Shaw	6'7"	19st 0lb	12	3	1	5
W	T.Evans	6'1"	14st 8lb	1	-	-	-	L	G.Skivington	6'6"	17st 6lb	12	-	1	5
SH	W.Fury	6'0"	13st 7lb	-	1	-	-	FH/FB	J.Staunton	6'0"	15st 1lb	12	3	2	33
H	B.Gotting	6'0"	16st 7lb	2	7	-	-	P	J.Va'a	6'0"	21st 3lb	1	8	-	-
BR	J.Hart	6'4"	17st 10lb	11	2	2	10	FB	M.Van Gisbergen	5'10"	13st 13lb	19	-	3	211
BR	J.Haskell	6'3"	17st 6lb	1	4	-	-	W	T.Voyce	6'0"	14st 13lb	18	1	10	50
C	R.Hoadley	6'0"	13st 13lb	7	5	2	10	H	J.Ward	6'0"	17st 8lb	8	4	-	-
SH	J.Honeyben	6'0"	14st 4lb	2	1	-	-	C	F.Waters	6'0"	14st 10lb	4	7	1	5
H	R.Ibanez	6'0"	15st 10lb	10	5	4	20	FL	J.Worsley	6'5"	17st 6lb	12	1	4	20

London Wasps

Last Season Form 2005/06

Season Progression

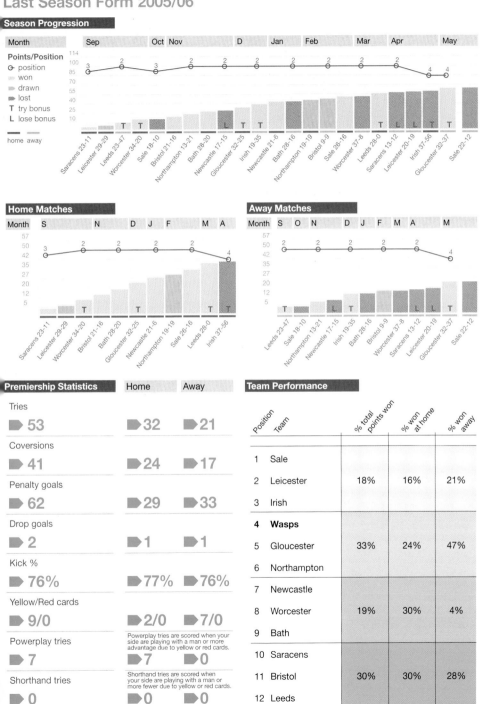

Month: Sep | Oct | Nov | D | Jan | Feb | Mar | Apr | May

Points/Position: 114, 100, 85, 70, 55, 40, 25, 10

- ⊙ position
- won
- drawn
- lost
- T try bonus
- L lose bonus

home away

Position values: 3, 2, 3, 2, 2, 2, 2, 2, 2, 2, 4, 4

Saracens 23-11 · Leicester 29-29 · Leeds 23-47 · Worcester 34-20 · Sale 18-10 · Bristol 21-16 · Northampton 13-21 · Bath 28-20 · Newcastle 17-15 · Gloucester 32-25 · Irish 19-35 · Newcastle 21-6 · Bath 28-16 · Northampton 19-19 · Bristol 9-9 · Sale 26-16 · Worcester 37-8 · Leeds 28-0 · Saracens 13-12 · Leicester 20-19 · Irish 37-56 · Gloucester 32-37 · Sale 22-12

Home Matches

Month: S | N | D | J | F | M | A

57, 50, 42, 35, 27, 20, 12, 5

Position values: 3, 2, 2, 2, 2, 4

Saracens 23-11 · Leicester 29-29 · Worcester 34-20 · Bristol 21-16 · Bath 28-20 · Gloucester 32-25 · Newcastle 21-6 · Northampton 19-19 · Sale 26-16 · Leeds 28-0 · Irish 37-56

Away Matches

Month: S | O | N | D | J | F | M | A | M

57, 50, 42, 35, 27, 20, 12, 5

Position values: 2, 2, 2, 2, 2, 4

Leeds 23-47 · Sale 18-10 · Northampton 13-21 · Newcastle 17-15 · Irish 19-35 · Bath 28-16 · Bristol 9-9 · Worcester 37-8 · Saracens 13-12 · Leicester 20-19 · Gloucester 32-37 · Sale 22-12

Premiership Statistics

	Home	Away
Tries	32	21
53		
Coversions	24	17
41		
Penalty goals	29	33
62		
Drop goals	1	1
2		
Kick %	77%	76%
76%		
Yellow/Red cards	2/0	7/0
9/0		
Powerplay tries	7	0
7		
Shorthand tries	0	0
0		

Powerplay tries are scored when your side are playing with a man or more advantage due to yellow or red cards.

Shorthand tries are scored when your side are playing with a man or more fewer due to yellow or red cards.

Team Performance

Position	Team	% total points won	% won at home	% won away
1	Sale			
2	Leicester	18%	16%	21%
3	Irish			
4	**Wasps**			
5	Gloucester	33%	24%	47%
6	Northampton			
7	Newcastle			
8	Worcester	19%	30%	4%
9	Bath			
10	Saracens			
11	Bristol	30%	30%	28%
12	Leeds			

London Wasps

Top Scorer

Points Facts

Total points	% team points	Home	Away
▶211	▶39	▶101	▶110

Points by Time Period

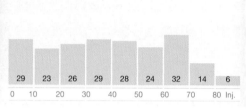

29	23	26	29	28	24	32	14	6
0	10	20	30	40	50	60	70	80 Inj.

Team Tries and Points

Tries by Time Period

- scored
- conceded

10	3	5	5	6	10	4	7	3
0	10min	20min	30min	40min	50min	60min	70min	80 Injury time
11	4	3	5	7	6	0	7	0

Tries by Halves

- scored
- conceded

▶53	▶23	▶30	▶43%	▶57%
Total	1st half	2nd half	1st half %	2nd half %
▶43	▶23	▶20	▶53%	▶47%

How Points were Scored

- tries: 265
- conversions: 82
- pen goals: 186
- drop goals: 6

How Points were Conceded

- tries: 215
- conversions: 62
- pen goals: 186
- drop goals: 6

Tries Scored by Player

- backs: 35
- forwards: 18

Tries Conceded by Player

- backs: 31
- forwards: 10

London Wasps

Eight-Season Form 1998-2006

Season Progression

Season	98-99	99-00	00-01	01-02	02-03	03-04	04-05	05-06
Points/Position								

Points/Position
○ position
▬ Premiership
▬ Division 1
▬ Division 2

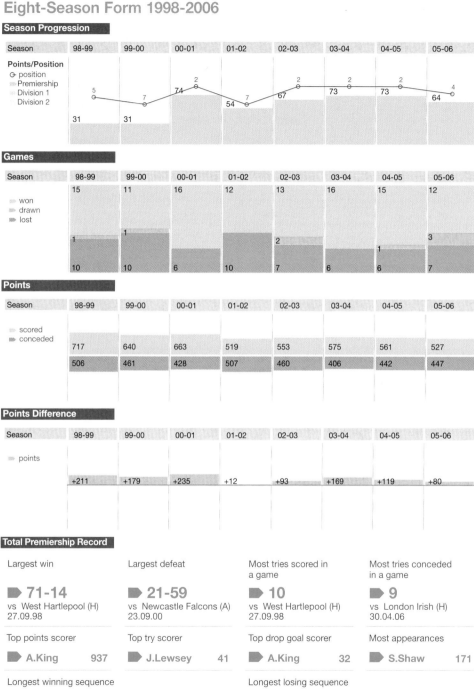

5   7   74 / 2   54 / 7   67 / 2   73 / 2   73 / 2   64 / 4

31   31

Games

Season	98-99	99-00	00-01	01-02	02-03	03-04	04-05	05-06
won	15	11	16	12	13	16	15	12
drawn	1	1			2		1	3
lost	10	10	6	10	7	6	6	7

Points

Season	98-99	99-00	00-01	01-02	02-03	03-04	04-05	05-06
scored	717	640	663	519	553	575	561	527
conceded	506	461	428	507	460	406	442	447

Points Difference

Season	98-99	99-00	00-01	01-02	02-03	03-04	04-05	05-06
points	+211	+179	+235	+12	+93	+169	+119	+80

Total Premiership Record

Largest win	Largest defeat	Most tries scored in a game	Most tries conceded in a game
71-14	**21-59**	**10**	**9**
vs West Hartlepool (H) 27.09.98	vs Newcastle Falcons (A) 23.09.00	vs West Hartlepool (H) 27.09.98	vs London Irish (H) 30.04.06

Top points scorer	Top try scorer	Top drop goal scorer	Most appearances
A.King 937	J.Lewsey 41	A.King 32	S.Shaw 171

Longest winning sequence	Longest losing sequence
11 wins from 21.11.03 to 18.04.04	**6 defeats** from 08.09.01 to 11.11.01

London Wasps EFL

ENHANCED FIXTURE LIST
[does not include play-off data]

Guinness Premiership 2006-07 — Premiership History

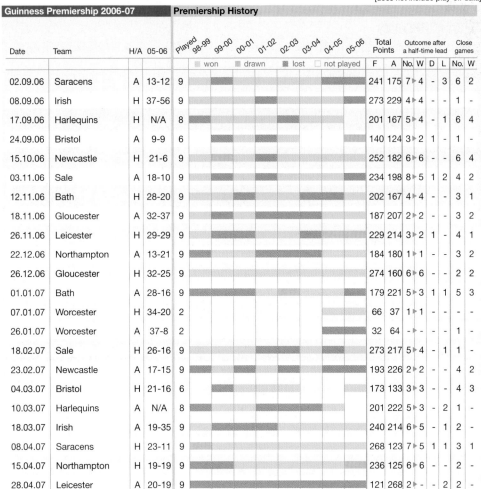

Legend: ■ won   ■ drawn   ■ lost   □ not played

Date	Team	H/A	05-06	Played	F	A	No.	W	D	L	No.	W
02.09.06	Saracens	A	13-12	9	241	175	7	4	-	3	6	2
08.09.06	Irish	H	37-56	9	273	229	4	4	-	-	1	-
17.09.06	Harlequins	H	N/A	8	201	167	5	4	-	1	6	4
24.09.06	Bristol	A	9-9	6	140	124	3	2	1	-	1	-
15.10.06	Newcastle	H	21-6	9	252	182	6	6	-	-	6	4
03.11.06	Sale	A	18-10	9	234	198	8	5	1	2	4	2
12.11.06	Bath	H	28-20	9	202	167	4	4	-	-	3	1
18.11.06	Gloucester	A	32-37	9	187	207	2	2	-	-	3	2
26.11.06	Leicester	H	29-29	9	229	214	3	2	1	-	4	1
22.12.06	Northampton	A	13-21	9	184	180	1	1	-	-	3	2
26.12.06	Gloucester	H	32-25	9	274	160	6	6	-	-	2	2
01.01.07	Bath	A	28-16	9	179	221	5	3	1	1	5	3
07.01.07	Worcester	H	34-20	2	66	37	1	1	-	-	-	-
26.01.07	Worcester	A	37-8	2	32	64	-	-	-	-	1	-
18.02.07	Sale	H	26-16	9	273	217	5	4	-	1	1	-
23.02.07	Newcastle	A	17-15	9	193	226	2	2	-	-	4	2
04.03.07	Bristol	H	21-16	6	173	133	3	3	-	-	4	3
10.03.07	Harlequins	A	N/A	8	201	222	5	3	-	2	1	-
18.03.07	Irish	A	19-35	9	240	214	6	5	-	1	2	-
08.04.07	Saracens	H	23-11	9	268	123	7	5	1	1	3	1
15.04.07	Northampton	H	19-19	9	236	125	6	6	-	-	2	-
28.04.07	Leicester	A	20-19	9	121	268	2	-	-	2	2	-

Column groups: **Played** (98-99, 99-00, 00-01, 01-02, 02-03, 03-04, 04-05, 05-06) · **Total Points** (F / A) · **Outcome after a half-time lead** (No. / W / D / L) · **Close games** (No. / W)

Club Information

Useful Information

Founded
1867
Address
Adam's Park
Hillbottom Road
Sands
High Wycombe
Buckinghamshire
HP12 4HJ
Capacity
10,200 (all seated)
Main switchboard
0208 993 8298
Website
www.wasps.co.uk

Travel Information

Car
From North
Approaching on the M1, exit onto the M25 at junction 6a (anti-clockwise). Continue on the M25 until junction 16 (M40), then head to junction 4 for the A404 High Wycombe. When you reach the junction take the slip road and turn right, taking the exit for the A4010 John Hall Way. Continue on this road, which becomes New Road, until you reach a mini roundabout with a left turn on to Lane End Road. Take this left turning and continue straight ahead onto Hillbottom Road, which leads to Causeway Stadium.

Train
Train services run from London Marylebone to High Wycombe.

154

London Wasps

Maps

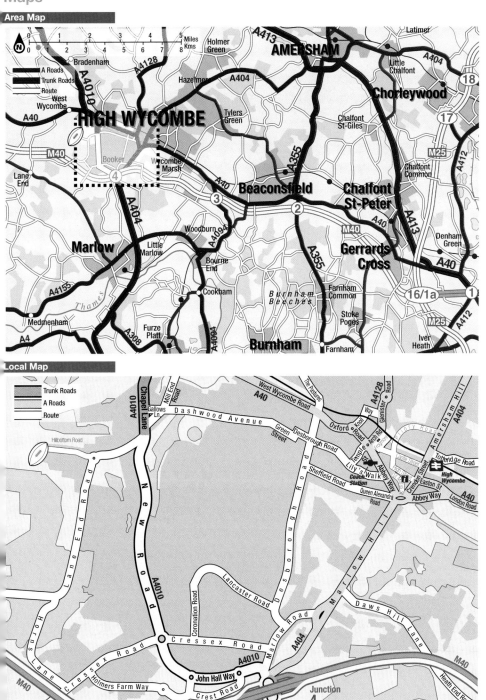

Local Map

155

NEC Harlequins

Season Summary 2005/06 (National Division One)

Position	Won	Drawn	Lost	For	Against	Bonus Points	Total Points
1	**25**	**0**	**1**	**1001**	**337**	**21**	**121**

NEC Harlequins returned to the Premiership at the first attempt after completely dominating National Division One, losing only once along the way. Key to this success was the club's ability to retain the majority of their big name players, while the signing of former All Blacks legend Andrew Mehrtens gave Quins the direction and impetus they lacked during 2004/05's relegation season. With Dean Richards back at the helm of a Premiership club and a plethora of summer signings, Quins will be looking to challenge for silverware in their return season.

Director of Rugby: Andy Friend

Club Honours
John Player Cup / Pilkington Cup: 1988, 1991
European Shield / Parker Pen Challenge Cup: 2001, 2004
National Division One: 2006
Powergen National Trophy: 2006

Season Squad

Stats 2005-06

Position	Player	Height	Weight	Apps	Rep	Tries	Points	Position	Player	Height	Weight	Apps	Rep	Tries	Points
W	C.Amesbury	N/A	N/A	4	2	3	15	P	M.Lambert	6'3"	19st 1lb	-	3	-	-
BR	P.Bouza	6'4"	15st 10lb	2	10	1	5	C	T.Masson	N/A	N/A	8	2	3	15
FB	M.Brown	6'0"	14st 5lb	7	6	7	37	FH	A.Mehrtens	5'10"	13st 2lb	16	4	1	194
L	K.Burke	6'6"	19st 3lb	-	6	-	-	L	S.Miall	6'4"	16st 6lb	26	-	3	15
BR	D.Clayton	N/A	N/A	-	1	-	-	W	U.Monye	6'1"	13st 4lb	16	2	16	80
P	A.Croall	6'0"	16st 7lb	2	3	-	-	P	R.Nebbett	5'11"	17st 8lb	20	3	-	-
C	M.Deane	5'10"	13st 8lb	9	12	2	10	H	J.Richards	5'9"	15st 10lb	9	12	-	-
8	T.Diprose	6'5"	17st 8lb	5	1	1	5	W	K.Richards	N/A	N/A	-	1	-	-
FB	G.Duffy	6'1"	14st 2lb	24	1	6	30	BR	C.Robshaw	6'2"	14st 7lb	6	4	2	10
BR	N.Easter	6'4"	18st 2lb	23	2	16	80	L	G.Robson	N/A	N/A	-	3	-	-
L	J.Evans	6'7"	16st 2lb	24	1	6	30	P	A.Rogers	6'3"	18st 5lb	4	1	2	10
H	T.Fuga	5'11"	14st 8lb	16	3	3	15	FL	L.Sherriff	6'4"	15st 10lb	14	6	4	20
C	W.Greenwood	6'4"	15st 12lb	15	1	4	22	SH	S.So'oialo	5'10"	14st 6lb	19	1	6	30
BR	T.Guest	6'4"	16st 0lb	7	10	5	25	C	J.Turner-Hall	N/A	N/A	4	1	-	-
W/C	G.Harder	6'1"	14st 9lb	6	3	4	20	SH	I.Vass	5'11"	15st 2lb	7	7	1	5
H	J.Hayter	6'2"	15st 10lb	1	4	1	5	FL	A.Vos	6'5"	16st 1lb	23	-	1	5
L	J.Inglis	N/A	N/A	-	1	-	-	P	L.Ward	N/A	N/A	7	17	-	-
FH	A.Jarvis	6'2"	13st 0lb	10	9	3	138	FB/W	T.Williams	5'11"	13st 2lb	13	5	12	60
P	C.Jones	6'0"	16st 7lb	18	-	5	25	P	M.Worsley	6'0"	17st 2lb	1	1	-	-
SH/W	S.Keogh	5'9"	12st 9lb	24	1	18	90								

NEC Harlequins

Last Season Form 2005/06

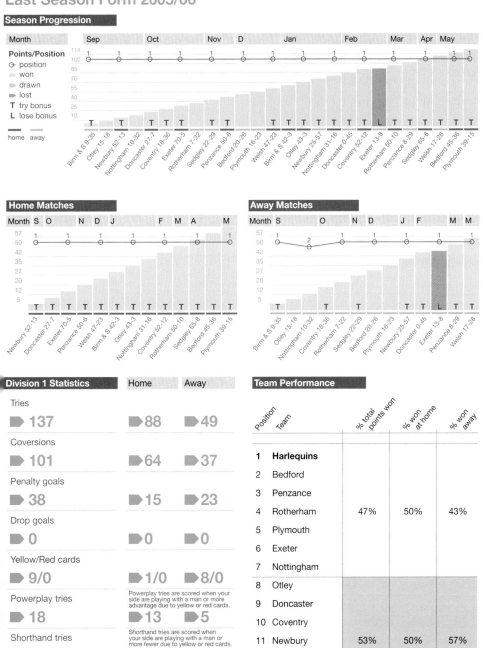

Season Progression

| Month | Sep | Oct | Nov | D | Jan | Feb | Mar | Apr | May |

Points/Position
- ○ position
- won
- drawn
- lost
- T try bonus
- L lose bonus

home away

Birm & S 9-35, Otley 15-18, Newbury 52-13, Nottingham 10-32, Doncaster 27-7, Coventry 18-36, Exeter 70-5, Rotherham 7-22, Sedgley 22-29, Penzance 50-6, Bedford 20-26, Plymouth 16-23, Welsh 47-23, Birm & S 42-3, Otley 43-3, Newbury 25-57, Nottingham 31-16, Doncaster 0-45, Coventry 52-12, Exeter 13-8, Rotherham 50-10, Penzance 8-29, Sedgley 65-8, Welsh 17-28, Bedford 45-36, Plymouth 39-15

Home Matches

| Month | S | O | N | D | J | F | M | A | M |

Newbury 52-13, Doncaster 27-7, Exeter 70-5, Penzance 50-6, Welsh 47-23, Birm & S 42-3, Otley 43-3, Nottingham 31-16, Coventry 52-12, Rotherham 50-10, Sedgley 65-8, Bedford 45-36, Plymouth 39-15

Away Matches

| Month | S | O | N | D | J | F | M | M |

Birm & S 9-35, Otley 15-18, Nottingham 10-32, Coventry 18-36, Rotherham 7-22, Sedgley 22-29, Bedford 20-26, Plymouth 16-23, Newbury 25-57, Doncaster 0-45, Exeter 13-8, Penzance 8-29, Welsh 17-28

Division 1 Statistics

	Home	Away
Tries	88	49
137		
Coversions	64	37
101		
Penalty goals	15	23
38		
Drop goals	0	0
0		
Yellow/Red cards	1/0	8/0
9/0		
Powerplay tries	13	5
18		
Shorthand tries	1	2
3		

Powerplay tries are scored when your side are playing with a man or more advantage due to yellow or red cards.

Shorthand tries are scored when your side are playing with a man or more fewer due to yellow or red cards.

Team Performance

Position	Team	% total points won	% won at home	% won away
1	**Harlequins**			
2	Bedford			
3	Penzance			
4	Rotherham	47%	50%	43%
5	Plymouth			
6	Exeter			
7	Nottingham			
8	Otley			
9	Doncaster			
10	Coventry			
11	Newbury	53%	50%	57%
12	Welsh			
13	Sedgley			
14	Birm & S			

NEC Harlequins

Top Scorer

Points Facts

Total points	% team points	Home	Away
▶194	▶19	▶84	▶110

Points by Time Period

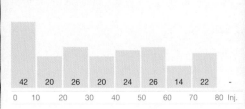

42	20	26	20	24	26	14	22	-
0	10	20	30	40	50	60	70	80 Inj.

Team Tries and Points

Tries by Time Period

- scored
- conceded

16	19	12	21	16	12	17	24	0
0	10min	20min	30min	40min	50min	60min	70min	80 Injury time
2	5	6	6	5	6	3	8	0

Tries by Halves

- scored
- conceded

	Total	1st half	2nd half	1st half %	2nd half %
scored	▶137	▶68	▶69	▶50%	▶50%
conceded	▶41	▶19	▶22	▶46%	▶54%

How Points were Scored

- tries: 685
- conversions: 202
- pen goals: 114
- drop goals: 0

How Points were Conceded

- tries: 205
- conversions: 42
- pen goals: 87
- drop goals: 3

Tries Scored by Player

- backs: 86
- forwards: 50

Tries Conceded by Player

- backs: 26
- forwards: 14

NEC Harlequins

Eight-Season Form 1998-2006

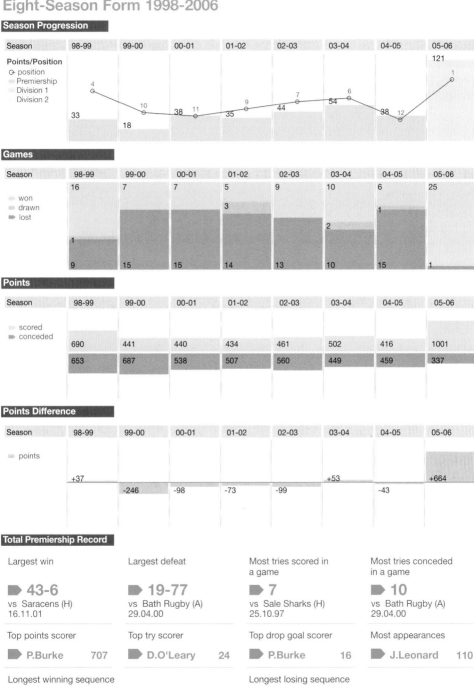

Season Progression

Season	98-99	99-00	00-01	01-02	02-03	03-04	04-05	05-06
Points/Position								121

Points/Position
- position
- Premiership
- Division 1
- Division 2

98-99: 33, position 4
99-00: 18, position 10
00-01: 38, position 11
01-02: 35, position 9
02-03: 44, position 7
03-04: 54, position 6
04-05: 38, position 12
05-06: 121, position 1

Games

Season	98-99	99-00	00-01	01-02	02-03	03-04	04-05	05-06
won	16	7	7	5	9	10	6	25
drawn				3		2	1	
lost	9	15	15	14	13	10	15	1

won: 1 (98-99 additional)

Points

Season	98-99	99-00	00-01	01-02	02-03	03-04	04-05	05-06
scored	690	441	440	434	461	502	416	1001
conceded	653	687	538	507	560	449	459	337

Points Difference

Season	98-99	99-00	00-01	01-02	02-03	03-04	04-05	05-06
points	+37	-246	-98	-73	-99	+53	-43	+664

Total Premiership Record

Largest win	Largest defeat	Most tries scored in a game	Most tries conceded in a game
43-6	**19-77**	**7**	**10**
vs Saracens (H) 16.11.01	vs Bath Rugby (A) 29.04.00	vs Sale Sharks (H) 25.10.97	vs Bath Rugby (A) 29.04.00
Top points scorer	Top try scorer	Top drop goal scorer	Most appearances
P.Burke 707	D.O'Leary 24	P.Burke 16	J.Leonard 110

Longest winning sequence	Longest losing sequence
6 wins from 17.10.98 to 21.11.98	**9 defeats** from 08.05.04 to 05.11.04

NEC Harlequins EFL

Guinness Premiership 2006-07 | **Premiership History**

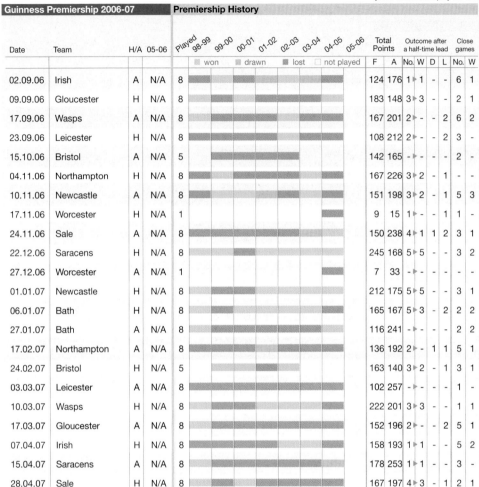

Legend: ■ won   ■ drawn   ■ lost   ☐ not played

Date	Team	H/A	05-06	Played	Total Points F	A	Outcome after a half-time lead No.	W	D	L	Close games No.	W
02.09.06	Irish	A	N/A	8	124	176	1	1	-	-	6	1
09.09.06	Gloucester	H	N/A	8	183	148	3	3	-	-	2	1
17.09.06	Wasps	A	N/A	8	167	201	2	-	-	2	6	2
23.09.06	Leicester	H	N/A	8	108	212	2	-	-	2	3	-
15.10.06	Bristol	A	N/A	5	142	165	-	-	-	-	2	-
04.11.06	Northampton	H	N/A	8	167	226	3	2	-	1	-	-
10.11.06	Newcastle	A	N/A	8	151	198	3	2	-	1	5	3
17.11.06	Worcester	H	N/A	1	9	15	1	-	-	1	1	-
24.11.06	Sale	A	N/A	8	150	238	4	1	1	2	3	1
22.12.06	Saracens	H	N/A	8	245	168	5	5	-	-	3	2
27.12.06	Worcester	A	N/A	1	7	33	-	-	-	-	-	-
01.01.07	Newcastle	H	N/A	8	212	175	5	5	-	-	3	1
06.01.07	Bath	H	N/A	8	165	167	5	3	-	2	2	2
27.01.07	Bath	A	N/A	8	116	241	-	-	-	-	2	2
17.02.07	Northampton	A	N/A	8	136	192	2	-	1	1	5	1
24.02.07	Bristol	H	N/A	5	163	140	3	2	-	1	3	1
03.03.07	Leicester	A	N/A	8	102	257	-	-	-	-	1	-
10.03.07	Wasps	H	N/A	8	222	201	3	3	-	-	1	1
17.03.07	Gloucester	A	N/A	8	152	196	2	-	-	2	5	1
07.04.07	Irish	H	N/A	8	158	193	1	1	-	-	5	2
15.04.07	Saracens	A	N/A	8	178	253	1	1	-	-	3	-
28.04.07	Sale	H	N/A	8	167	197	4	3	-	1	2	1

(Played history year columns: 98-99, 99-00, 00-01, 01-02, 02-03, 03-04, 04-05, 05-06)

Club Information

Useful Information

Founded
1866
Address
Twickenham Stoop
Langhorn Drive
Twickenham
Middlesex
TW2 7SX
Stadium capacity
12,700
Main switchboard
020 8410 6000
Website
www.quins.co.uk

Travel Information

Car
From the M4:
Leave the M4 at Junction 3. Take the 3rd exit of the Roundabout for the A312, towards Feltham (A3006). Continue along the A312 for 4.5 miles. At the A305 / A316 roundabout, turn left onto the A316. Follow the A316 Chertsey Road, over three roundabouts. Continue for 2 miles. With Twickenham Rugby Stadium on your left, Quins' ground is on the right. U-turn at the RFU roundabout. Enter the Stoop via Langhorn Drive, 450 yards on your left.

Train
Twickenham station is served by trains from London Waterloo and Reading, with more services and routes accessible via Clapham Junction. After the match (and after a warming pint or two in the East Stand) there are plenty of trains to return you home safely. Upon leaving the station, turn right towards Twickenham Rugby Stadium and left at the mini-roundabout. Take the first left into Court Way and then turn left into Craneford Way and continue on until you reach the stadium. The Twickenham Stoop is at the end of the road on the right.

NEC Harlequins

Maps

Area Map

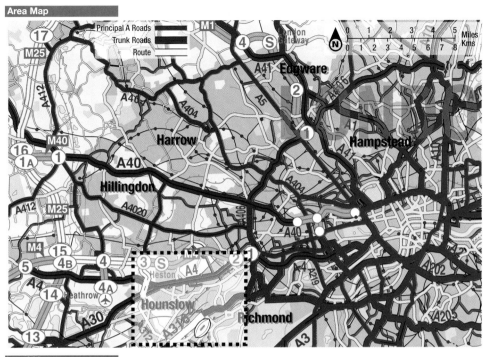

Local Map

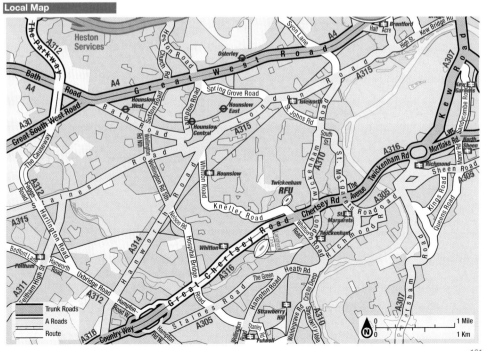

161

Newcastle Falcons

Season Summary 2005/06

Position	Won	Drawn	Lost	For	Against	Bonus Points	Total Points
7	**9**	**1**	**12**	**416**	**433**	**9**	**47**

The 2005/06 season was a landmark for long-serving Newcastle Falcon's director of rugby Rob Andrew, who celebrated 10 years at the helm of the club. Andrew, though, had little to celebrate, as his side once again flattered to deceive in the Premiership. Without the services of playmaker Jonny Wilkinson for most of the campaign and lacking in fire power, Newcastle were always going to struggle. However, it wasn't all doom and gloom. The coming-of-age of talented youngsters Toby Flood and Matthew Tait, the return of Wilkinson and the emergence of some promising young players gave reason for optimism.

Director of Rugby: Rob Andrew

Club Honours
Allied Dunbar Premiership: 1997-98
John Player Cup / Powergen Cup: 1976, 1977, 2001, 2004

Season Squad

Position	Player	Height	Weight	Apps	Rep	Tries	Points	Position	Player	Height	Weight	Apps	Rep	Tries	Points
P	G.Anderson	6'0"	18st 8lb	1	-	-	-	P	R.Morris	6'2"	18st 11lb	20	2	1	5
L	A.Buist	6'6"	17st 0lb	8	4	-	-	C	J.Noon	5'10"	13st 5lb	12	3	2	10
FB	M.Burke	6'0"	14st 10lb	20	-	8	142	P	T.Paoletti	6'0"	20st 0lb	1	5	-	-
SH	H.Charlton	5'11"	14st 4lb	9	5	-	-	L/FL	G.Parling	6'5"	16st 5lb	16	2	1	5
BR	C.Charvis	6'3"	16st 10lb	13	-	-	-	P	I.Peel	5'11"	18st 0lb	1	1	-	-
SH	L.Dickson	5'11"	12st 6lb	-	3	-	-	L	A.Perry	6'7"	18st 7lb	19	-	-	-
8	P.Dowson	6'3"	16st 10lb	2	-	-	-	W	O.Phillips	5'11"	14st 7lb	5	-	2	10
W/FB	A.Elliott	6'3"	14st 9lb	12	1	8	42	FB/C	J.Shaw	6'0"	15st 2lb	5	4	2	10
FL/L	O.Finegan	6'6"	18st 12lb	13	4	1	5	8	J.Smithson	6'2"	11st 13lb	2	1	-	-
FH/FB	T.Flood	6'2"	15st 0lb	12	4	1	7	C/W	M.Tait	5'11"	13st 4lb	16	-	2	10
L	S.Grimes	6'5"	17st 3lb	4	5	-	-	H	M.Thompson	6'2"	18st 0lb	5	12	-	-
SH	J.Grindal	5'9"	13st 4lb	13	7	-	-	FH	D.Walder	5'10"	12st 9lb	11	2	2	56
L	L.Gross	6'9"	19st 8lb	2	4	-	-	P	M.Ward	5'11"	18st 9lb	19	3	-	-
FL	C.Harris	6'0"	17st 0lb	12	1	1	5	FH	J.Wilkinson	5'10"	13st 5lb	4	3	1	56
W/C	J.Hoyle	6'1"	13st 4lb	3	-	1	5	C	M.Wilkinson	6'3"	17st 0lb	-	1	-	-
8	G.Irvin	N/A	N/A	-	1	-	-	P	J.Williams	6'0"	15st 5lb	2	6	-	-
H	A.Long	5'11"	16st 3lb	17	4	1	5	FL	E.Williamson	6'2"	14st 9lb	-	1	-	-
W	T.May	5'10"	14st 5lb	18	-	4	23	P	D.Wilson	6'1"	18st 7lb	-	7	-	-
C	M.Mayerhofler	6'0"	15st 2lb	14	1	-	-	FL	B.Woods	6'2"	16st 5lb	10	7	1	5
FL	M.McCarthy	6'4"	17st 0lb	9	10	3	15								

Newcastle Falcons

Last Season Form 2005/06

Season Progression

Month: Sep, Oct, Nov, D, Jan, Feb, Mar, Apr, May

Points/Position
- G position
- won
- drawn
- lost
- T try bonus
- L lose bonus

home away

Matches: Sale 26-25, Bristol 14-16, Northampton 9-16, Bath 16-27, Leicester 16-16, Gloucester 27-20, Irish 20-23, Saracens 27-18, Wasps 17-15, Leeds 10-13, Worcester 21-15, Wasps 21-6, Saracens 21-16, Irish 6-9, Gloucester 9-13, Leicester 24-16, Bath 20-18, Northampton 13-32, Bristol 23-7, Sale 32-21, Worcester 35-27, Leeds 54-19

Home Matches

Month: S, N, J, F, M, A, M

Matches: Bristol 14-16, Bath 16-27, Irish 20-23, Wasps 17-15, Worcester 21-15, Saracens 21-16, Gloucester 9-13, Leicester 24-16, Northampton 13-32, Sale 32-21, Leeds 54-19

Away Matches

Month: S, O, N, D, J, F, M, A

Matches: Sale 26-25, Northampton 9-16, Leicester 16-16, Gloucester 27-20, Saracens 27-18, Leeds 10-13, Wasps 21-6, Irish 6-9, Bath 20-18, Bristol 23-7, Worcester 35-27

Premiership Statistics

		Home	Away
Tries	42	23	19
Coversions	25	15	10
Penalty goals	45	29	16
Drop goals	7	3	4
Kick %	63%	68%	57%
Yellow/Red cards	9/1	3/0	6/1
Powerplay tries	3	2	1
Shorthand tries	3	1	2

Powerplay tries are scored when your side are playing with a man or more advantage due to yellow or red cards.

Shorthand tries are scored when your side are playing with a man or more fewer due to yellow or red cards.

Team Performance

Position	Team	% total points won	% won at home	% won away
1	Sale			
2	Leicester	34%	32%	37%
3	Irish			
4	Wasps			
5	Gloucester	20%	16%	26%
6	Northampton			
7	**Newcastle**			
8	Worcester	18%	19%	16%
9	Bath			
10	Saracens			
11	Bristol	28%	33%	21%
12	Leeds			

Newcastle Falcons

Top Scorer

Matthew Burke

Points Facts

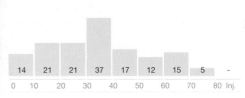

Total points	% team points	Home	Away
▶ 142	▶ 34	▶ 80	▶ 62

Points by Time Period

14	21	21	37	17	12	15	5	-
0	10	20	30	40	50	60	70	80 Inj.

Team Tries and Points

Tries by Time Period

- scored
- conceded

3	4	7	4	2	8	7	5	2
0	10min	20min	30min	40min	50min	60min	70min	80 Injury time
6	4	3	8	8	5	5	5	0

Tries by Halves

- scored
- conceded

	Total	1st half	2nd half	1st half %	2nd half %
scored	▶ 42	▶ 18	▶ 24	▶ 43%	▶ 57%
conceded	▶ 44	▶ 21	▶ 23	▶ 48%	▶ 52%

How Points were Scored

tries:	210
conversions:	50
pen goals:	135
drop goals:	21

How Points were Conceded

tries:	220
conversions:	60
pen goals:	150
drop goals:	3

Tries Scored by Player

backs:	33
forwards:	9

Tries Conceded by Player

backs:	29
forwards:	15

Newcastle Falcons

Eight-Season Form 1998-2006

Season Progression

Season	98-99	99-00	00-01	01-02	02-03	03-04	04-05	05-06
Position	8	9	6	6	10	9	7	7
Points	28	19	57	56	40	45	47	47

Points/Position
- ⊙ position
- Premiership
- Division 1
- Division 2

Games

Season	98-99	99-00	00-01	01-02	02-03	03-04	04-05	05-06
won	14	6	11	12	8	7	9	9
drawn		2		1		2	2	1
lost	12	14	11	9	14	13	11	12

Points

Season	98-99	99-00	00-01	01-02	02-03	03-04	04-05	05-06
scored	719	377	554	490	388	497	475	416
conceded	639	630	568	458	545	525	596	433

Points Difference

Season	98-99	99-00	00-01	01-02	02-03	03-04	04-05	05-06
points	+80	-253	-14	+32	-157	-28	-121	-17

Total Premiership Record

Largest win	**Largest defeat**	**Most tries scored in a game**	**Most tries conceded in a game**

56-10
vs Rotherham Titans (H)
09.11.03

10-83
vs Leicester Tigers (A)
19.02.05

8
vs Leeds Tykes (H)
06.05.06

11
vs Leicester Tigers (A)
19.02.05

Top points scorer — J.Wilkinson 1307

Top try scorer — G.Armstrong 35

Top drop goal scorer — J.Wilkinson 19

Most appearances — J.Noon 132

Longest winning sequence — **12 wins** from 23.08.97 to 10.03.98

Longest losing sequence — **7 defeats** from 03.11.02 to 03.01.03

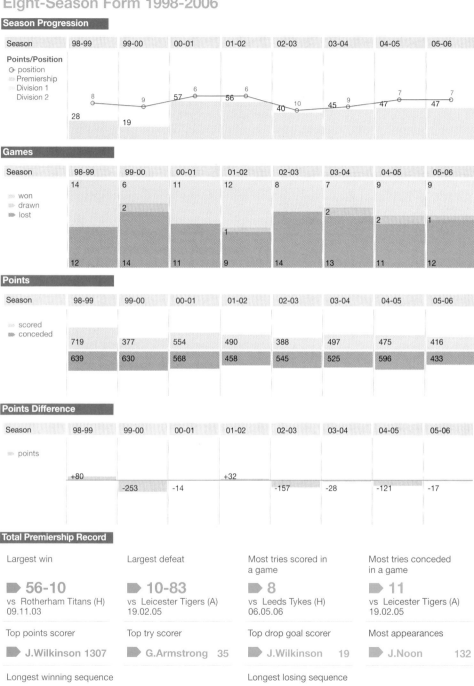

Newcastle Falcons EFL

ENHANCED FIXTURE LIST
[does not include play-off data]

Guinness Premiership 2006-07 | Premiership History

Premiership History legend: won / drawn / lost / not played (seasons 98-99, 99-00, 00-01, 01-02, 02-03, 03-04, 04-05, 05-06)

Date	Team	H/A	05-06	Played	Total Points F	Total Points A	Outcome after a half-time lead No.	W	D	L	Close games No.	W
03.09.06	Northampton	A	9-16	9	150	257	3►1		-	2	3	1
08.09.06	Worcester	H	21-15	2	37	36	1►1		-	-	2	1
17.09.06	Saracens	A	27-18	9	166	268	-►-		-	-	5	1
22.09.06	Irish	H	20-23	9	244	201	7►4		-	3	5	2
15.10.06	Wasps	A	21-6	9	182	252	1►-		1	-	6	1
03.11.06	Bristol	H	14-16	6	161	126	2►2		-	-	2	-
10.11.06	Harlequins	H	N/A	8	198	151	5►3		1	1	5	1
17.11.06	Sale	A	26-25	9	185	285	3►2		-	1	1	-
25.11.06	Bath	A	20-18	9	137	199	3►2		-	1	2	-
22.12.06	Gloucester	A	27-20	9	187	275	3►1		-	2	3	1
26.12.06	Sale	H	32-21	9	245	151	7►7		-	-	4	4
01.01.07	Harlequins	A	N/A	8	175	212	2►2		-	-	3	2
07.01.07	Leicester	H	24-16	9	180	191	4►3		-	1	5	2
27.01.07	Leicester	A	16-16	9	144	334	2►-		1	1	2	1
18.02.07	Bristol	A	23-7	6	109	159	1►1		-	-	-	-
23.02.07	Wasps	H	17-15	9	226	193	7►6		-	1	4	2
03.03.07	Irish	A	6-9	9	139	190	3►2		-	1	6	3
09.03.07	Saracens	H	21-16	9	254	171	6►6		-	-	6	4
16.03.07	Worcester	A	35-27	2	57	44	1►1		-	-	-	-
06.04.07	Northampton	H	13-32	9	230	215	4►4		-	-	3	3
13.04.07	Gloucester	H	9-13	9	245	189	5►4		-	1	5	1
28.04.07	Bath	H	16-27	9	175	161	6►4		-	2	7	4

Club Information

Useful Information

Founded
1995
(Gosforth formed in 1877)

Address
Kingston Park
Brunton Road
Kenton Bank Foot
Newcastle NE13 8AF

Capacity
10,000

Main switchboard
0191 214 5588

Website
www.newcastle-falcons.co.uk

Travel Information

Car
From South:
Take the M1 and turn right onto the M62 at junction 42, towards the A1. Follow the A1 all the way into Newcastle, heading for the junction for Newcastle Airport. When you reach that junction, take the Kingston Park exit then continue straight ahead over two mini roundabouts. After passing under a bridge, turn right into Brunton Road then continue until you see the ground on your left.
From West:
Follow the A69 until it joins the A1, and follow signs for the Newcastle Airport junction. Then as route for South.

Train
GNER and Virgin Trains run services to Newcastle Central. From there, catch the Tyne and Wear Metro to Kingston Park station.

Air
Newcastle International Airport is a short cab ride from the stadium.

Newcastle Falcons

Maps

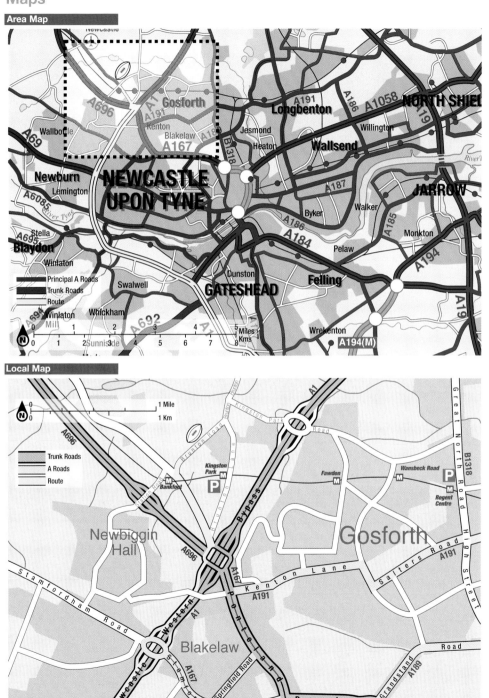

Northampton Saints

Season Summary 2005/06

Position	Won	Drawn	Lost	For	Against	Bonus Points	Total Points
6	10	1	11	464	488	11	53

Saints fans waited in anticipation for All Black Carlos Spencer to pull on a Northampton shirt and they certainly weren't disappointed, as Spencer wowed the Franklin's Gardens crowd with his electric pace and breathtaking skills, ensuring he was voted Saints Player of the Year. Despite inconsistent form in the Premiership, Saints rose to the occasion with perhaps the performance of the season against Saracens in February, where they put on an outstanding display of rugby. Northampton fans will enjoy Heineken Cup rugby at Franklin's Gardens next season and Saints will face French Champions and last season's beaten finalists Biarritz in the quest for European glory.

Head Coach: Budge Pountney

Club Honours
Heineken Cup: 1999-2000

Season Squad

Stats 2005-06

Position	Player	Height	Weight	Apps	Rep	Tries	Points	Position	Player	Height	Weight	Apps	Rep	Tries	Points
P	P.Barnard	6'0"	17st 8lb	9	1	1	5	L	M.Lord	6'4"	17st 2lb	17	5	-	-
L	S.Boome	6'3"	17st 0lb	1	2	-	-	C	S.Mallon	6'3"	14st 11lb	4	1	2	10
8	D.Browne	6'5"	16st 3lb	39	-	2	10	FH	L.Myring	6'0"	14st 3lb	1	-	1	5
P	C.Budgen	5'8"	17st 10lb	11	8	1	5	P	C.Noon	5'11"	18st 3lb	1	2	-	-
FB/W	J.Clarke	6'3"	14st 1lb	22	-	6	30	FB	J.Pritchard	5'9"	13st 5lb	1	1	-	4
W	B.Cohen	6'2"	15st 10lb	13	1	7	35	C	D.Quinlan	6'4"	16st 2lb	14	1	1	5
C	R.Davies	5'9"	14st 0lb	3	4	2	10	L	A.Rae	6'5"	15st 8lb	1	1	-	-
W	P.Diggin	5'8"	13st 2lb	3	1	-	-	FB	B.Reihana	6'0"	13st 7lb	21	-	5	206
BR	M.Easter	6'3"	16st 0lb	4	2	2	10	H	D.Richmond	5'11"	15st 6lb	10	4	-	-
P	S.Emms	5'11"	17st 8lb	1	7	-	-	SH	M.Robinson	5'10"	13st 8lb	18	4	2	10
FL	D.Fox	6'0"	15st 10lb	11	7	2	10	W	J.Rudd	6'2"	17st 0lb	11	3	1	5
L	D.Gerard	6'6"	19st 0lb	5	11	-	-	BR/L	G.Seely	6'4"	17st 0lb	2	1	-	-
H	M.Grove	6'3"	17st 2lb	-	1	-	-	P	T.Smith	5'10"	16st 3lb	19	-	-	-
P	L.Harbut	5'10"	17st 7lb	-	3	-	-	BR	M.Soden	6'2"	16st 4lb	2	2	-	-
FL	S.Harding	6'1"	16st 4lb	10	7	1	5	FH	C.Spencer	6'1"	15st 0lb	21	-	4	34
H	D.Hartley	6'1"	17st 11lb	4	8	-	-	P	B.Sturgess	6'1"	17st 10lb	3	3	-	-
SH	J.Howard	5'9"	12st 7lb	4	9	-	-	H	S.Thompson	6'2"	18st 2lb	9	4	3	15
C/FH	R.Kydd	5'11"	14st 3lb	3	3	-	-	BR	P.Tupai	6'4"	17st 10lb	11	1	1	5
W	S.Lamont	6'2"	15st 0lb	12	2	6	30	C	A.Vilk	5'11"	15st 6lb	3	4	1	5
FL	B.Lewitt	6'3"	15st 0lb	6	7	-	-								

Northampton Saints

Last Season Form 2005/06

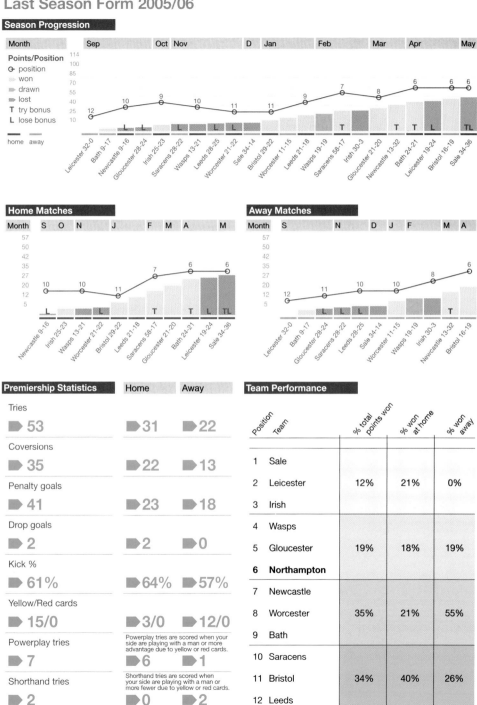

Season Progression

Month: Sep | Oct | Nov | D | Jan | Feb | Mar | Apr | May

Points/Position
- ○ position
- won
- drawn
- lost
- T try bonus
- L lose bonus

home away

Positions: 12, 10, 9, 10, 11, 11, 9, 7, 8, 6, 6, 6

Matches: Leicester 32-0, Bath 9-17, Newcastle 9-16, Gloucester 28-24, Irish 25-23, Saracens 28-22, Wasps 13-21, Leeds 28-25, Worcester 21-22, Sale 34-14, Bristol 29-22, Worcester 11-15, Leeds 21-18, Wasps 19-19, Saracens 58-17, Irish 30-3, Gloucester 21-20, Newcastle 13-32, Bath 24-21, Leicester 19-24, Bristol 16-19, Sale 34-36

Home Matches

Month: S | O | N | J | F | M | A | M

Positions: 10, 10, 11, 7, 6, 6

Matches: Newcastle 9-16, Irish 25-23, Wasps 13-21, Worcester 21-22, Bristol 29-22, Leeds 21-18, Saracens 58-17, Gloucester 21-20, Bath 24-21, Leicester 19-24, Sale 34-36

Away Matches

Month: S | | N | D | J | F | | M | A

Positions: 12, 11, 10, 10, 8, 6

Matches: Leicester 32-0, Bath 9-17, Gloucester 28-24, Saracens 28-22, Leeds 28-25, Sale 34-14, Worcester 11-15, Wasps 19-19, Irish 30-3, Newcastle 13-32, Bristol 16-19

Premiership Statistics

	Home	Away
Tries	31	22
53		
Coversions	22	13
35		
Penalty goals	23	18
41		
Drop goals	2	0
2		
Kick %	64%	57%
61%		
Yellow/Red cards	3/0	12/0
15/0		
Powerplay tries	6	1
7		
Shorthand tries	0	2
2		

Powerplay tries are scored when your side are playing with a man or more advantage due to yellow or red cards.

Shorthand tries are scored when your side are playing with a man or more fewer due to yellow or red cards.

Team Performance

Position	Team	% total points won	% won at home	% won away
1	Sale			
2	Leicester	12%	21%	0%
3	Irish			
4	Wasps			
5	Gloucester	19%	18%	19%
6	**Northampton**			
7	Newcastle			
8	Worcester	35%	21%	55%
9	Bath			
10	Saracens			
11	Bristol	34%	40%	26%
12	Leeds			

Northampton Saints

Top Scorer

Bruce Reihana

Points Facts

Total points	% team points	Home	Away
▶206	▶45	▶131	▶75

Points by Time Period

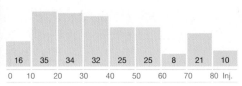

16	35	34	32	25	25	8	21	10
0	10	20	30	40	50	60	70	80 Inj.

Team Tries and Points

Tries by Time Period

- scored
- conceded

7	4	6	7	3	8	7	10	1
0	10min	20min	30min	40min	50min	60min	70min	80 Injury time
7	7	8	6	5	4	6	6	1

Tries by Halves

- scored
- conceded

	Total	1st half	2nd half	1st half %	2nd half %
scored	53	24	29	45%	55%
conceded	50	28	22	56%	44%

How Points were Scored

- tries: 265
- conversions: 70
- pen goals: 123
- drop goals: 6

How Points were Conceded

- tries: 250
- conversions: 64
- pen goals: 162
- drop goals: 12

Tries Scored by Player

- backs: 38
- forwards: 14

Tries Conceded by Player

- backs: 37
- forwards: 12

Northampton Saints

Eight-Season Form 1998-2006

Season Progression

Season	98-99	99-00	00-01	01-02	02-03	03-04	04-05	05-06

Points/Position
- position
- Premiership
- Division 1
- Division 2

	2	5	4	5	3	3	11	6
	38	35	59	56	62	70	40	53

Games

Season	98-99	99-00	00-01	01-02	02-03	03-04	04-05	05-06
won	19	13	13	12	13	15	8	10
drawn				1		1		1
lost	7	9	9	9	9	6	14	11

Points

Season	98-99	99-00	00-01	01-02	02-03	03-04	04-05	05-06
scored	754	551	518	506	512	574	410	464
conceded	556	480	463	426	376	416	473	488

Points Difference

Season	98-99	99-00	00-01	01-02	02-03	03-04	04-05	05-06
points	+198	+71	+55	+80	+136	+158	-63	-24

Total Premiership Record

Largest win	Largest defeat	Most tries scored in a game	Most tries conceded in a game
42-0	**12-54**	**9**	**7**
vs Rotherham (H) 10.02.01	vs London Wasps (H) 09.05.00	vs Newcastle Falcons (H) 27.03.99	vs London Irish (A) 18.11.01

Top points scorer	Top try scorer	Top drop goal scorer	Most appearances
P.Grayson 1238	B.Cohen 45	P.Grayson 9	G.Seely 133

Longest winning sequence	Longest losing sequence
7 wins from 05.11.99 to 26.01.00	**9 defeats** from 18.09.04 to 28.11.04

Northampton Saints EFL

ENHANCED FIXTURE LIST
[does not include play-off data]

Guinness Premiership 2006-07 **Premiership History**

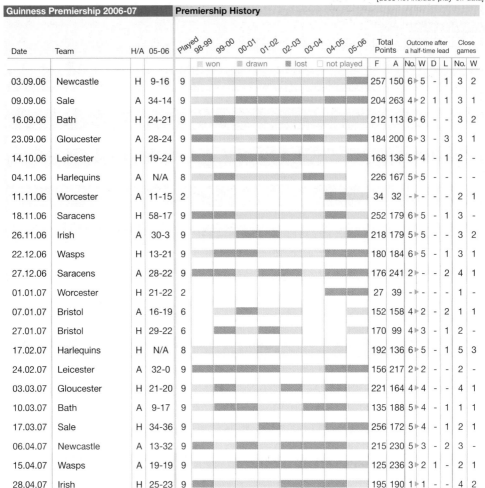

Date	Team	H/A	05-06	Played	98-99	99-00	00-01	01-02	02-03	03-04	04-05	05-06	F	A	No.	W	D	L	No.	W
03.09.06	Newcastle	H	9-16	9									257	150	6	5	-	1	3	2
09.09.06	Sale	A	34-14	9									204	263	4	2	1	1	3	1
16.09.06	Bath	H	24-21	9									212	113	6	6	-	-	3	2
23.09.06	Gloucester	A	28-24	9									184	200	6	3	-	3	3	1
14.10.06	Leicester	H	19-24	9									168	136	5	4	-	1	2	-
04.11.06	Harlequins	A	N/A	8									226	167	5	5	-	-	-	-
11.11.06	Worcester	A	11-15	2									34	32	-	-	-	-	2	1
18.11.06	Saracens	H	58-17	9									252	179	6	5	-	1	3	-
26.11.06	Irish	A	30-3	9									218	179	5	5	-	-	3	2
22.12.06	Wasps	H	13-21	9									180	184	6	5	-	1	3	1
27.12.06	Saracens	A	28-22	9									176	241	2	-	-	2	4	1
01.01.07	Worcester	H	21-22	2									27	39	-	-	-	-	1	-
07.01.07	Bristol	A	16-19	6									152	158	4	2	-	2	1	1
27.01.07	Bristol	H	29-22	6									170	99	4	3	-	1	2	-
17.02.07	Harlequins	H	N/A	8									192	136	6	5	-	1	5	3
24.02.07	Leicester	A	32-0	9									156	217	2	2	-	-	2	-
03.03.07	Gloucester	H	21-20	9									221	164	4	4	-	-	4	1
10.03.07	Bath	A	9-17	9									135	188	5	4	-	1	1	1
17.03.07	Sale	H	34-36	9									256	172	5	4	-	1	2	1
06.04.07	Newcastle	A	13-32	9									215	230	5	3	-	2	3	-
15.04.07	Wasps	A	19-19	9									125	236	3	2	1	-	2	1
28.04.07	Irish	H	25-23	9									195	190	1	1	-	-	4	2

Key: ▨ won ▨ drawn ▨ lost ☐ not played

(Total Points columns: F / A. Outcome after a half-time lead: No. / W / D / L. Close games: No. / W.)

Club Information

Useful Information

Founded
1880
Address
Franklin's Gardens
Weedon Road
Northampton
NN5 5BG
Capacity
13,591 (11,500 seated)
Main switchboard
01604 751543
Website
www.northamptonsaints.
co.uk

Travel Information

Car
From North:
Approaching on the M1, exit at junction 16 and take the A45 onto Weedon Road, which is signposted 'Town Centre'. Turn left into Ross Road and follow signs for the car park.
From South:
Approaching on the M1, exit at junction 15a and follow signs for Sixfields. Turn left to join the A45 onto Weedon Road. Then as route for North.

Train
Silverlink trains run from Milton Keynes Central or Coventry to Northampton station.
Silverlink Trains also run directly from London Euston to Northampton station.
From Northampton station, turn right and continue walking until you pass the bus station and enter a shopping area. Turn left, then left again down Abbey Street into the Northampton Saints Car Park.

Northampton Saints

Maps

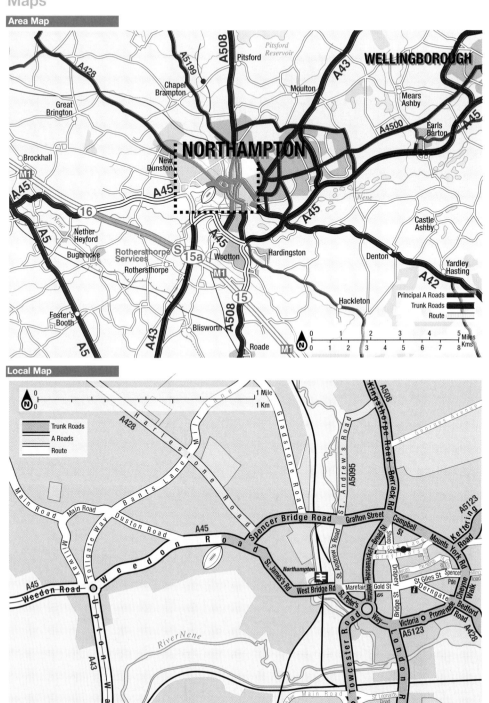

Area Map legend:
- Principal A Roads
- Trunk Roads
- Route

Pitsford Reservoir, Pitsford, Chapel Brampton, Moulton, WELLINGBOROUGH, Mears Ashby, Great Brington, Earls Barton, A508, A5199, A428, A43, A45, A4500, NORTHAMPTON, New Dunston, Brockhall, M1, A45, Nene, Castle Ashby, 16, Nether Heyford, Bugbrooke, Rothersthorpe Services, Rothersthorpe, 15a, Wootton, Hardingstone, Denton, Yardley Hasting, A42, A5, M1, 15, Foster's Booth, A508, A43, Blisworth, Hackleton, Roade, M1

0 1 2 3 4 5 Miles
0 1 2 3 4 5 6 7 8 Kms

Local Map

0 1 Mile
0 1 Km

Local Map legend:
- Trunk Roads
- A Roads
- Route

Harlestone Road, Mill Lane, A428, Gladstone Road, Bants Lane, Kingsthorpe Road, A508, St Georges Avenue, St Andrews Road, A5095, Barrack Rd, Main Road, Duston Road, Spencer Bridge Road, Grafton Street, Campbell St, Mounts, A5123, Kettering Road, Tollgate Way, Weedon Road, A45, St Andrew's Rd, Sheep St, Broad St, Greyfriars, York Rd, Northampton, St James's Rd, Horsemarket, Drapery, Spencer Pde, Cheyne Walk, Millway, A45, Weedon Road, West Bridge Rd, Marefair, Gold St, St Giles St, Derngate, Bedford Road, St Peter's Way, Horseshoe St, Victoria, Promenade, A428, Upton Way, River Nene, Towcester Road, London Road, A5123, A43, Main Road, St Leonards Road

173

Sale Sharks

Season Summary 2005/06

Position	Won	Drawn	Lost	For	Against	Bonus Points	Total Points
1	16	1	5	573	444	8	74

An emphatic win over Tigers at Twickenham saw the north west side winning their first league title and making Premiership history finishing top of the league and going on to claim the Premiership title. Although Sharks were forced to play periods of the season without key players due to international commitments, they proved they had quality players to stand in for the likes of Charlie Hodgson and Mark Cueto, only losing five Premiership games throughout their campaign. Head Coach Kingsley Jones has retained all his key players and has recruited well for the coming season – including Newport Gwent's John Bryant and Leeds' Chris Bell – as he looks to emulate the success achieved in 2005/06.

Director of Rugby: Philippe Saint-Andre

Club Honours
Parker Pen Shield: 2002, 2005
Guinness Premiership Champions: 2006

Season Squad

Stats 2005-06

Position	Player	Height	Weight	Apps	Rep	Tries	Points	Position	Player	Height	Weight	Apps	Rep	Tries	Points
BR	P.Anglesea	6'3"	16st 4lb	-	4	-	-	FL	M.Lund	6'3"	16st 9lb	19	1	4	20
8	N.Bonner-Evans	6'4"	18st 0lb	7	4	-	-	SH	S.Martens	5'11"	14st 7lb	14	2	3	15
H	N.Briggs	5'10"	14st 13lb	-	1	-	-	C/W	C.Mayor	6'2"	15st 0lb	5	10	5	25
H	S.Bruno	5'9"	16st 9lb	6	9	1	5	W	M.Riley	6'2"	14st 4lb	-	1	-	-
FL	J.Carter	6'3"	17st 0lb	2	1	-	-	W	O.Ripol Fortuny	5'9"	12st 6lb	13	2	4	20
8	S.Chabal	6'3"	17st 0lb	17	1	3	15	P	E.Roberts	N/A	N/A	1	2	-	-
SH	V.Courrent	5'9"	13st 12lb	12	5	3	82	FB	J.Robinson	5'8"	13st 4lb	23	-	4	29
P	B.Coutts	6'3"	18st 0lb	9	2	-	-	L	D.Schofield	6'6"	18st 0lb	17	3	3	15
W	M.Cueto	6'0"	14st 9lb	16	-	6	30	C/W	E.Seveali'i	5'10"	14st 0lb	14	-	3	15
L	C.Day	6'6"	16st 10lb	9	10	-	-	P	A.Sheridan	6'5"	18st 10lb	8	2	-	-
P	L.Faure	6'1"	18st 0lb	6	4	-	-	P	B.Stewart	6'2"	18st 0lb	14	9	-	-
L	I.Fernandez Lobbe	6'5"	17st 4lb	12	6	3	15	C/W/BR	E.Taione	6'4"	19st 6lb	1	4	-	-
SH	B.Foden	6'0"	13st 7lb	1	7	1	5	C	M.Taylor	6'1"	15st 0lb	20	-	1	5
W	S.Hanley	6'4"	15st 12lb	7	1	4	20	H/FL	A.Titterrell	5'8"	14st 9lb	19	5	2	10
FL	M.Hills	6'1"	14st 7lb	-	2	-	-	C	R.Todd	5'11"	16st 0lb	11	4	1	5
FH	C.Hodgson	5'10"	12st 13lb	15	1	2	248	P	S.Turner	6'0"	17st 9lb	10	12	-	-
L/BR	C.Jones	6'7"	16st 1lb	19	1	2	10	W/C	N.Wakley	6'2"	15st 0lb	-	2	-	-
P	M.Jones	5'7"	19st 0lb	-	1	-	-	FL/L	J.White	6'5"	18st 6lb	16	2	-	-
FH	D.Larrechea	6'0"	14st 3lb	11	2	1	32	SH	R.Wigglesworth	5'9"	13st 3lb	6	12	1	19
L/BR	B.Lloyd	6'5"	15st 13lb	-	1	-	-								

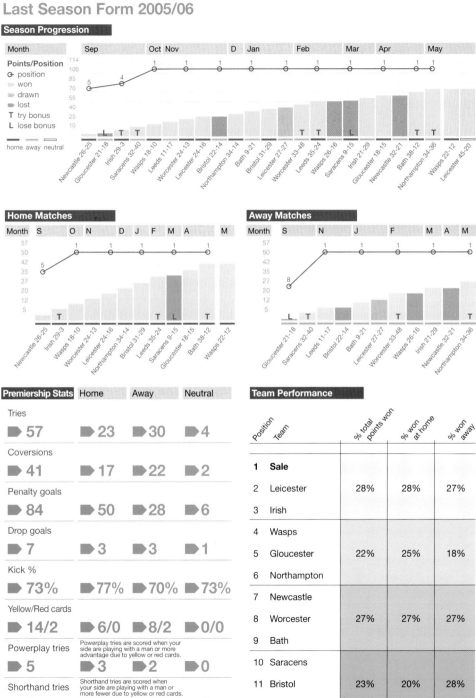

Sale Sharks

Last Season Form 2005/06

Season Progression

Month: Sep | Oct Nov | D | Jan | Feb | Mar | Apr | May

Points/Position
- ○ position
- ⟹ won
- ⟹ drawn
- ⟹ lost
- T try bonus
- L lose bonus

home away neutral

Newcastle 26-25, Gloucester 21-18, Irish 29-3, Saracens 32-40, Wasps 18-10, Leeds 11-17, Worcester 24-13, Leicester 24-16, Bristol 22-14, Northampton 34-14, Bath 9-21, Bristol 31-29, Leicester 27-27, Worcester 33-48, Leeds 35-24, Wasps 26-16, Saracens 9-15, Irish 21-29, Gloucester 18-15, Newcastle 32-21, Bath 38-12, Northampton 34-36, Wasps 22-12, Leicester 45-20

Home Matches

Month: S | O N | D J F M A | M

Newcastle 26-25, Irish 29-3, Wasps 18-10, Worcester 24-13, Leicester 24-16, Northampton 34-14, Bristol 31-29, Leeds 35-24, Saracens 9-15, Gloucester 18-15, Bath 38-12, Wasps 22-12

Away Matches

Month: S | N | J | F | M A | M

Gloucester 21-18, Saracens 32-40, Leeds 11-17, Bristol 22-14, Bath 9-21, Leicester 27-27, Worcester 33-48, Wasps 26-16, Irish 21-29, Newcastle 32-21, Northampton 34-36

Premiership Stats

	Home	Away	Neutral
Tries			
⟹ 57	⟹ 23	⟹ 30	⟹ 4
Coversions			
⟹ 41	⟹ 17	⟹ 22	⟹ 2
Penalty goals			
⟹ 84	⟹ 50	⟹ 28	⟹ 6
Drop goals			
⟹ 7	⟹ 3	⟹ 3	⟹ 1
Kick %			
⟹ 73%	⟹ 77%	⟹ 70%	⟹ 73%
Yellow/Red cards			
⟹ 14/2	⟹ 6/0	⟹ 8/2	⟹ 0/0
Powerplay tries			
⟹ 5	⟹ 3	⟹ 2	⟹ 0
Shorthand tries			
⟹ 0	⟹ 0	⟹ 0	⟹ 0

Powerplay tries are scored when your side are playing with a man or more advantage due to yellow or red cards.

Shorthand tries are scored when your side are playing with a man or more fewer due to yellow or red cards.

Team Performance

Position	Team	% total points won	% won at home	% won away
1	Sale			
2	Leicester	28%	28%	27%
3	Irish			
4	Wasps			
5	Gloucester	22%	25%	18%
6	Northampton			
7	Newcastle			
8	Worcester	27%	27%	27%
9	Bath			
10	Saracens			
11	Bristol	23%	20%	28%
12	Leeds			

175

Sale Sharks

Top Scorer

Points Facts

Total points	% team points	Home	Away	Neutral
248	39	157	68	23

Points by Time Period

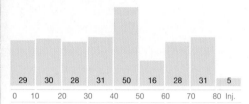

29	30	28	31	50	16	28	31	5
0	10	20	30	40	50	60	70	80 Inj.

Team Tries and Points

Tries by Time Period

- scored
- conceded

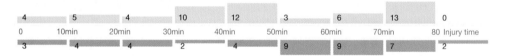

4	5	4	10	12	3	6	13	0
0	10min	20min	30min	40min	50min	60min	70min	80 Injury time
3	4	4	2	4	9	9	7	2

Tries by Halves

- scored
- conceded

	Total	1st half	2nd half	1st half %	2nd half %
scored	57	23	34	40%	60%
conceded	44	13	31	30%	70%

How Points were Scored

- tries: 285
- conversions: 82
- pen goals: 252
- drop goals: 21

How Points were Conceded

- tries: 220
- conversions: 58
- pen goals: 186
- drop goals: 12

Tries Scored by Player

- backs: 39
- forwards: 18

Tries Conceded by Player

- backs: 33
- forwards: 10

Sale Sharks

Eight-Season Form 1998-2006

Season Progression

Season	98-99	99-00	00-01	01-02	02-03	03-04	04-05	05-06

Points/Position
- position
- Premiership
- Division 1
- Division 2

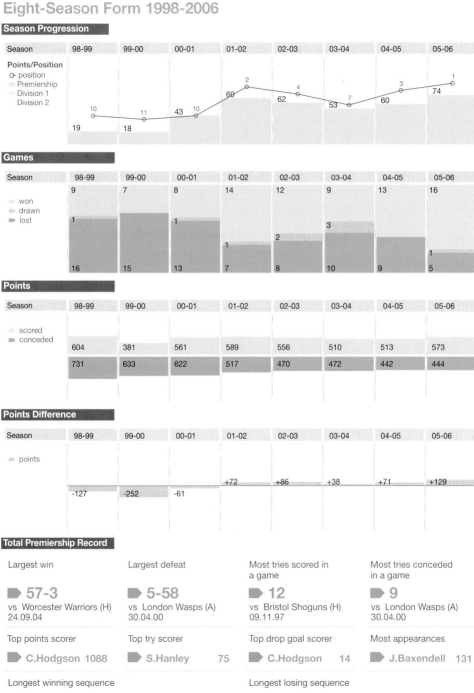

Season Progression values: 98-99: 19 (position 10); 99-00: 18 (position 11); 00-01: 43 (position 10); 01-02: 69 (position 2); 02-03: 62 (position 4); 03-04: 53 (position 7); 04-05: 60 (position 3); 05-06: 74 (position 1)

Games

Season	98-99	99-00	00-01	01-02	02-03	03-04	04-05	05-06
won	9	7	8	14	12	9	13	16
drawn	1		1	1	2	3		1
lost	16	15	13	7	8	10	9	5

Points

Season	98-99	99-00	00-01	01-02	02-03	03-04	04-05	05-06
scored	604	381	561	589	556	510	513	573
conceded	731	633	622	517	470	472	442	444

Points Difference

Season	98-99	99-00	00-01	01-02	02-03	03-04	04-05	05-06
points	-127	-252	-61	+72	+86	+38	+71	+129

Total Premiership Record

Largest win

▶ **57-3**
vs Worcester Warriors (H)
24.09.04

Largest defeat

▶ **5-58**
vs London Wasps (A)
30.04.00

Most tries scored in a game

▶ **12**
vs Bristol Shoguns (H)
09.11.97

Most tries conceded in a game

▶ **9**
vs London Wasps (A)
30.04.00

Top points scorer

▶ C.Hodgson 1088

Top try scorer

▶ S.Hanley 75

Top drop goal scorer

▶ C.Hodgson 14

Most appearances

▶ J.Baxendell 131

Longest winning sequence

▶ **6 wins** from 08.05.04 to 03.10.04

Longest losing sequence

▶ **7 defeats** from 20.12.98 to 14.02.99

Guinness Premiership 2006-07 | **Premiership History**

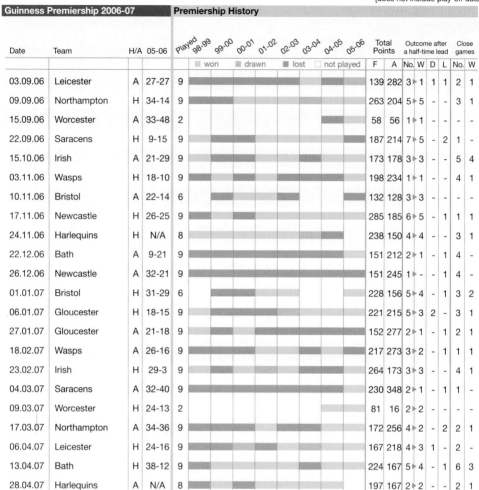

Legend: ■ won ■ drawn ■ lost ☐ not played

Date	Team	H/A	05-06	Played	98-99	99-00	00-01	01-02	02-03	03-04	04-05	05-06	Total Points F	A	Outcome after a half-time lead No.	W	D	L	Close games No.	W
03.09.06	Leicester	A	27-27	9									139	282	3▶1	1	1		2	1
09.09.06	Northampton	H	34-14	9									263	204	5▶5	-	-		3	1
15.09.06	Worcester	A	33-48	2									58	56	1▶1	-	-		-	-
22.09.06	Saracens	H	9-15	9									187	214	7▶5	-	2		1	-
15.10.06	Irish	A	21-29	9									173	178	3▶3	-	-		5	4
03.11.06	Wasps	H	18-10	9									198	234	1▶1	-	-		4	1
10.11.06	Bristol	A	22-14	6									132	128	3▶3	-	-		-	-
17.11.06	Newcastle	H	26-25	9									285	185	6▶5	-	1		1	1
24.11.06	Harlequins	H	N/A	8									238	150	4▶4	-	-		3	1
22.12.06	Bath	A	9-21	9									151	212	2▶1	-	1		4	-
26.12.06	Newcastle	A	32-21	9									151	245	1▶-	-	1		4	-
01.01.07	Bristol	H	31-29	6									228	156	5▶4	-	1		3	2
06.01.07	Gloucester	H	18-15	9									221	215	5▶3	2	-		3	1
27.01.07	Gloucester	A	21-18	9									152	277	2▶1	-	1		2	1
18.02.07	Wasps	A	26-16	9									217	273	3▶2	-	1		1	1
23.02.07	Irish	H	29-3	9									264	173	3▶3	-	-		4	1
04.03.07	Saracens	A	32-40	9									230	348	2▶1	-	1		1	-
09.03.07	Worcester	H	24-13	2									81	16	2▶2	-	-		-	-
17.03.07	Northampton	A	34-36	9									172	256	4▶2	-	2		2	1
06.04.07	Leicester	H	24-16	9									167	218	4▶3	1	-		2	-
13.04.07	Bath	H	38-12	9									224	167	5▶4	-	1		6	3
28.04.07	Harlequins	A	N/A	8									197	167	2▶2	-	-		2	1

Club Information

Useful Information

Founded
1861
Address
Edgeley Park
Hardcastle Road
Edgeley
Stockport
SK3 9DD
Capacity
10,641 (3,132 seated)
Main switchboard
0161 283 8888
Website
www.salesharks.com

Travel Information

Car
From South:
Leave the M6 at junction 19 (towards Manchester Airport, Stockport A55), then turn right at the roundabout onto the A556. After approx four miles you reach a roundabout, turn right onto the M56 (towards Manchester). After approx a further seven miles, exit the M56 and join the M60 (signposted Stockport, Sheffield). Leave the M60 at junction 1 and follow the signs to Cheadle and Stockport County FC at the roundabout. Continue straight ahead at the first set of traffic lights, then right at the next set (keep following signs for Stockport County FC). After a mile, turn left onto the B5465 Edgeley Road, then after another mile turn right into Dale Street. Take the second turning on the left into Hardcastle Road to reach the stadium.

From North:
From the M62 join the M60 and continue south. Leave the M60 at junction 1, then as route for South.

Train
Stockport station is approx half a mile from the stadium. Arriva Trains Northern run services from Sheffield to Stockport. From London, Virgin Trains run from London Euston to directly to Stockport.

Maps

Area Map

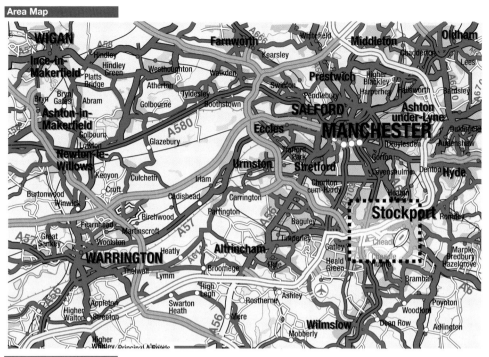

Local Map

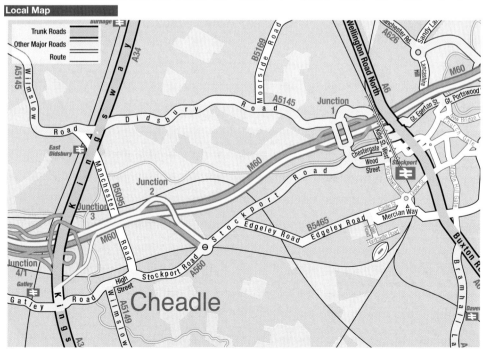

Saracens

Season Summary 2005/06

Position	Won	Drawn	Lost	For	Against	Bonus Points	Total Points
10	8	1	13	433	483	12	46

Eight successive Premiership defeats saw Saracens plunge to 11th in the league and only four points above bottom club Leeds in February, ending Steve Diamond's reign. However, thanks to the arrival of Australian coach Eddie Jones, the Vicarage Road side pulled themselves from the brink of relegation, finding some form during the latter part of the season. A memorable win against Sale marked a turning point in their campaign, triggering a run of four successive wins for the men in black, easing them into 10th place. The Watford side was boosted by the news that French international Thomas Castaignede had signed a one-year contract extension.

Director of Rugby: Alan Gaffney

Club Honours
Pilkington Cup: 1998

Season Squad

Stats 2005-06

Position	Player	Height	Weight	Apps	Rep	Tries	Points	Position	Player	Height	Weight	Apps	Rep	Tries	Points
FL	S.Armitage	5'9"	16st 8lb	2	1	3	15	P	N.Lloyd	6'0"	16st 9lb	4	10	-	-
C	P.Bailey	6'0"	12st 8lb	6	1	-	-	P	H.Mitchell	N/A	N/A	2	2	1	5
8	D.Barrell	6'4"	15st 0lb	-	1	-	-	C	A.Powell	5'11"	14st 4lb	2	5	2	10
C	M.Bartholomeusz	5'9"	13st 8lb	12	-	2	10	L	S.Raiwalui	6'6"	18st 13lb	17	2	-	-
SH	K.Bracken	5'11"	13st 0lb	12	4	-	-	BR	T.Randell	6'2"	17st 4lb	7	5	-	-
P	B.Broster	5'11"	16st 9lb	6	9	-	-	SH	M.Rauluni	5'10"	13st 7lb	2	13	1	5
H	S.Byrne	5'10"	15st 6lb	12	5	-	-	BR	B.Russell	6'3"	15st 10lb	9	9	1	5
H	M.Cairns	5'11"	16st 0lb	10	11	2	10	L	T.Ryder	6'5"	16st 9lb	7	2	-	-
FH	T.Castaignede	5'9"	13st 3lb	9	1	4	20	BR	A.Sanderson	6'2"	16st 1lb	4	1	-	-
L	K.Chesney	6'6"	18st 4lb	14	8	1	5	FB	D.Scarbrough	6'1"	13st 3lb	19	1	7	35
SH	A.Dickens	5'10"	12st 9lb	8	5	-	-	BR	D.Seymour	5'11"	14st 2lb	9	7	-	-
L	I.Fullarton	6'7"	16st 12lb	6	1	-	-	BR	B.Skirving	6'4"	16st 12lb	14	1	2	10
C	D.Harris	5'10"	15st 12lb	4	6	1	5	C	K.Sorrell	5'11"	13st 8lb	21	-	2	10
W	R.Haughton	6'2"	13st 7lb	9	2	3	15	W	T.Vaikona	6'2"	16st 2lb	15	1	2	10
FH	G.Jackson	5'11"	13st 6lb	22	-	3	238	P	C.Visagie	6'1"	18st 0lb	14	1	-	-
C	B.Johnston	6'3"	16st 7lb	13	1	3	15	BR	H.Vyvyan	6'6"	16st 0lb	21	-	-	-
H	A.Kyriacou	5'11"	15st 2lb	-	3	-	-	P	K.Yates	5'11"	17st 12lb	18	2	-	-
FH	N.Little	6'0"	15st 0lb	-	1	-	-								

Saracens

Last Season Form 2005/06

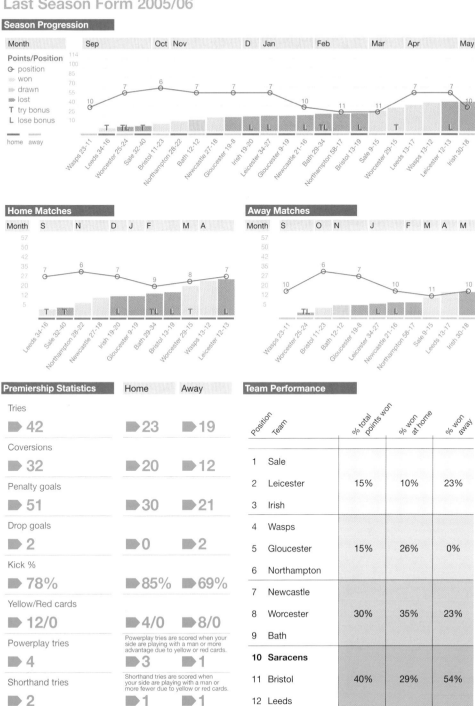

Season Progression

| Month | Sep | Oct | Nov | D | Jan | Feb | Mar | Apr | May |

Points/Position
- G position
- won
- drawn
- lost
- T try bonus
- L lose bonus

home   away

Wasps 23-11, Leeds 34-16, Worcester 25-24, Sale 32-40, Bristol 11-23, Northampton 28-22, Bath 12-12, Newcastle 27-18, Gloucester 19-8, Irish 19-20, Leicester 34-27, Gloucester 9-19, Newcastle 21-16, Bath 29-34, Northampton 58-17, Bristol 13-19, Sale 9-15, Worcester 29-15, Leeds 13-17, Wasps 13-12, Leicester 12-13, Irish 30-18

Home Matches

| Month | S | N | D | J | F | M | A |

Leeds 34-16, Sale 32-40, Northampton 28-22, Newcastle 27-18, Irish 19-20, Gloucester 9-19, Bath 29-34, Bristol 13-19, Worcester 29-15, Wasps 13-12, Leicester 12-13

Away Matches

| Month | S | O | N | J | F | M | A | M |

Wasps 23-11, Worcester 25-24, Bristol 11-23, Bath 12-12, Gloucester 19-8, Leicester 34-27, Newcastle 21-16, Northampton 58-17, Sale 9-15, Leeds 13-17, Irish 30-18

Premiership Statistics

	Home	Away
Tries	42	23	19
Coversions	32	20	12
Penalty goals	51	30	21
Drop goals	2	0	2
Kick %	78%	85%	69%
Yellow/Red cards	12/0	4/0	8/0
Powerplay tries	4	3	1
Shorthand tries	2	1	1

Powerplay tries are scored when your side is playing with a man or more advantage due to yellow or red cards.

Shorthand tries are scored when your side is playing with a man or more fewer due to yellow or red cards.

Team Performance

Position	Team	% total points won	% won at home	% won away
1	Sale			
2	Leicester	15%	10%	23%
3	Irish			
4	Wasps			
5	Gloucester	15%	26%	0%
6	Northampton			
7	Newcastle			
8	Worcester	30%	35%	23%
9	Bath			
10	**Saracens**			
11	Bristol	40%	29%	54%
12	Leeds			

181

Saracens

Top Scorer

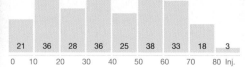

Points Facts

Total points	% team points	Home	Away
▶ 238	▶ 56	▶ 135	▶ 103

Points by Time Period

21	36	28	36	25	38	33	18	3
0	10	20	30	40	50	60	70	80 Inj.

Team Tries and Points

Tries by Time Period

- scored
- conceded

5	5	1	6	6	6	8	5	0
0	10min	20min	30min	40min	50min	60min	70min	80 Injury time
4	5	8	9	3	4	2	12	1

Tries by Halves

- scored
- conceded

	Total	1st half	2nd half	1st half %	2nd half %
scored	▶ 42	▶ 17	▶ 25	▶ 40%	▶ 60%
conceded	▶ 48	▶ 26	▶ 22	▶ 54%	▶ 46%

How Points were Scored

- tries: 210
- conversions: 64
- pen goals: 153
- drop goals: 6

How Points were Conceded

- tries: 240
- conversions: 60
- pen goals: 168
- drop goals: 15

Tries Scored by Player

- backs: 30
- forwards: 10

Tries Conceded by Player

- backs: 37
- forwards: 9

Eight-Season Form 1998-2006

Season Progression

Season	98-99	99-00	00-01	01-02	02-03	03-04	04-05	05-06

Points/Position
- ⊙ position
- Premiership
- Division 1
- Division 2

	98-99	99-00	00-01	01-02	02-03	03-04	04-05	05-06
position	3	4	5	10	8	10	5	10
points	33	37	58	34	42	39	57	46

Games

Season	98-99	99-00	00-01	01-02	02-03	03-04	04-05	05-06
won	16	14	12	7	8	8	12	8
drawn	1					1	2	1
lost	9	8	10	15	14	13	8	13

Points

Season	98-99	99-00	00-01	01-02	02-03	03-04	04-05	05-06
scored	748	729	589	425	499	397	384	433
conceded	583	514	501	671	587	543	428	483

Points Difference

Season	98-99	99-00	00-01	01-02	02-03	03-04	04-05	05-06
points	+165	+215	+88	-246	-88	-146	-44	-50

Total Premiership Record

Largest win	Largest defeat	Most tries scored in a game	Most tries conceded in a game
▶ **59-5**	▶ **13-55**	▶ **9**	▶ **7**
vs Rotherham (H) 24.09.00	vs London Irish (H) 22.11.01	vs Bedford Blues (A) 16.04.00	vs Newcastle Falcons (A) 15.05.02

Top points scorer	Top try scorer	Top drop goal scorer	Most appearances
▶ **G.Johnson** 363	▶ **T.Castaignede** 25	▶ **A.Goode** 9	▶ **K.Chesney** 153

Longest winning sequence	Longest losing sequence
▶ **7 wins** from 29.04.98 to 11.10.98	▶ **9 defeats** from 26.11.05 to 26.02.06

Guinness Premiership 2006-07 | **Premiership History**

Date	Team	H/A	05-06	Played	98-99 · 99-00 · 00-01 · 01-02 · 02-03 · 03-04 · 04-05 · 05-06	Total Points F	A	Outcome after a half-time lead No.	W	D	L	Close games No.	W
02.09.06	Wasps	H	13-12	9	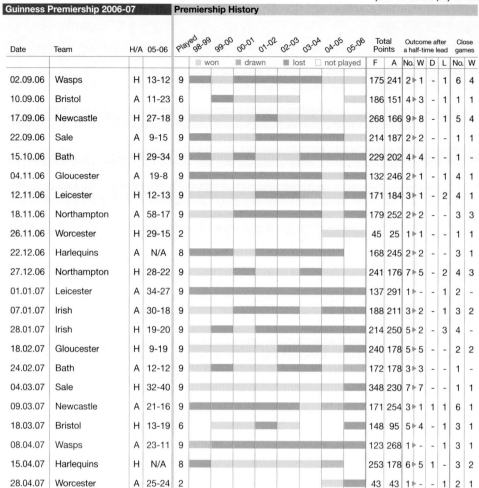	175	241	2 ▸ 1	-	-	1	6	4
10.09.06	Bristol	A	11-23	6		186	151	4 ▸ 3	-	-	1	1	1
17.09.06	Newcastle	H	27-18	9		268	166	9 ▸ 8	-	-	1	5	4
22.09.06	Sale	A	9-15	9		214	187	2 ▸ 2	-	-	-	1	1
15.10.06	Bath	H	29-34	9		229	202	4 ▸ 4	-	-	-	1	-
04.11.06	Gloucester	A	19-8	9		132	246	2 ▸ 1	-	-	1	4	1
12.11.06	Leicester	H	12-13	9		171	184	3 ▸ 1	-	-	2	4	1
18.11.06	Northampton	A	58-17	9		179	252	2 ▸ 2	-	-	-	3	3
26.11.06	Worcester	H	29-15	2		45	25	1 ▸ 1	-	-	-	1	1
22.12.06	Harlequins	A	N/A	8		168	245	2 ▸ 2	-	-	-	3	1
27.12.06	Northampton	H	28-22	9		241	176	7 ▸ 5	-	-	2	4	3
01.01.07	Leicester	A	34-27	9		137	291	1 ▸ -	-	-	1	2	-
07.01.07	Irish	A	30-18	9		188	211	3 ▸ 2	-	-	1	3	2
28.01.07	Irish	H	19-20	9		214	250	5 ▸ 2	-	-	3	4	-
18.02.07	Gloucester	H	9-19	9		240	178	5 ▸ 5	-	-	-	2	2
24.02.07	Bath	A	12-12	9		172	178	3 ▸ 3	-	-	-	1	-
04.03.07	Sale	H	32-40	9		348	230	7 ▸ 7	-	-	-	1	1
09.03.07	Newcastle	A	21-16	9		171	254	3 ▸ 1	1	1	1	6	1
18.03.07	Bristol	H	13-19	6		148	95	5 ▸ 4	-	-	1	3	1
08.04.07	Wasps	A	23-11	9		123	268	1 ▸ -	-	-	1	3	1
15.04.07	Harlequins	H	N/A	8		253	178	6 ▸ 5	1	-	-	3	2
28.04.07	Worcester	A	25-24	2		43	43	1 ▸ -	-	-	1	2	1

Legend: ■ won ■ drawn ■ lost ☐ not played

Club Information

Useful Information

Founded
1876
Address
Vicarage Road Stadium
Vicarage Road
Watford
Herts
WD1 8ER
Capacity
22,100 (all seated)
Main switchboard
01923 475222
Website
www.saracens.com

Travel Information

Car
From North:
Leave the M1 at junction 5, taking the third exit from the roundabout and follow signs to Watford Town Centre. When joining the ring road get into the middle lane, before moving into the left lane after the second set of traffic lights. Follow signs for Watford General Hospital, which is next to Vicarage Road.

From West:
Leave the M25 at junction 19, and follow the A411 Hempstead Road, signposted Watford. Go straight over the first roundabout, then left at the second. Follow the signs towards Watford General Hospital, which is next to Vicarage Road.

Train
Watford High Street station is approx 10 minutes walk from the stadium. North London Railway trains run from London Euston station.

Tube
Watford tube station is approx 20 minutes walk from the stadium, on the Metropolitan Line.

Maps

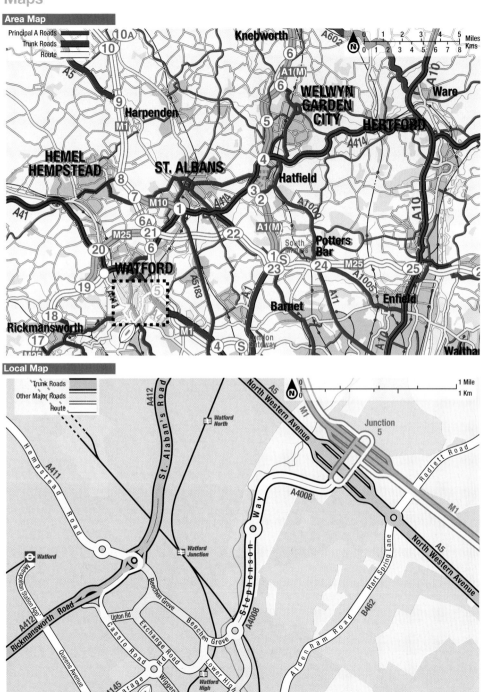

Area Map

Principal A Roads
Trunk Roads
Route

10A
10
A5
9
Harpenden
M1
HEMEL HEMPSTEAD
8
7
M10
A41
6A
M25
21
20
6
19
WATFORD
18
Rickmansworth
17
M25

Knebworth
A602
6
A1(M)
6
WELWYN GARDEN CITY
5
HERTFORD
A414
4
ST. ALBANS
Hatfield
3
A414
2
A1000
1
A1(M)
South Mimms
22
Potters Bar
1 S
23
24
M25
25
A1
A5183
5
A1005
Enfield
Barnet
A11
M1
4
London Gateway
S
Waltham

Ware
A10
A10
A10

0 1 2 3 4 5 Miles
0 1 2 3 4 5 6 7 8 Kms
N

Local Map

Trunk Roads
Other Major Roads
Route

A412
St. Alban's Road
Watford North
A5
North Western Avenue
M1
Junction 5
Radlett Road

Hempstead Road
A411
A412
A4008
M1
A5

Watford
Metropolitan Station Approach
Watford Junction
Stephenson Way
A4008
North Western Avenue

A412 Rickmansworth Road
Beechen Grove
Upton Rd
Exchange Road
Beechen Grove
A4008
Hart Spring Lane
B462
Aldenham Road

Queens Avenue
Cassio Road
Wiggenhall Rd
Lower High Street
Watford High Street
A4145
Vicarage

0 1 Mile
0 1 Km
N

Worcester Warriors

Season Summary 2005/06

Position	Won	Drawn	Lost	For	Against	Bonus Points	Total Points
8	**9**	**1**	**12**	**451**	**494**	**9**	**47**

In their second season in the top flight and under the watchful eye of John Brain and new head coach Anthony Eddy, Worcester were fourth in the league at Christmas and on course for finishing in the top half. However, with Pat Sanderson sidelined for much of the season with a back injury, Warriors struggled to replicate that kind of form in the second half of the season, winning only three league games in 2006. Andy Gomarsall jostled for a place with Matt Powell to form the half back pairing with Shane Drahm, with Powell ending the season the favoured of the two. Warriors finished the season in a creditable eighth position, one place higher than their first year in the Premiership.

Head Coach: Anthony Eddy
Director of Rugby: John Brain

Club Honours
N/A

Season Squad

Stats 2005-06

Position	Player	Height	Weight	Apps	Rep	Tries	Points
P	C.Black	5'11"	17st 2lb	-	1	-	-
L	R.Blaze	6'7"	18st 0lb	1	2	-	-
FH	J.Brown	5'10"	11st 2lb	5	2	-	30
L	T.Collier	6'6"	21st 3lb	1	5	-	-
FB	T.Delport	6'2"	14st 6lb	16	2	4	20
FH	S.Drahm	5'9"	12st 10lb	17	3	3	233
H	C.Fortey	5'11"	17st 8lb	15	4	-	-
P	L.Fortey	5'10"	16st 3lb	2	6	-	-
L	C.Gillies	6'7"	17st 8lb	20	-	-	-
SH	A.Gomarsall	5'10"	14st 4lb	13	5	1	5
W	C.Hallam	N/A	N/A	-	1	-	-
FL	T.Harding	6'0"	15st 4lb	7	4	1	5
W	A.Havili	5'7"	15st 10lb	14	-	6	30
BR	D.Hickey	6'3"	15st 12lb	17	2	2	10
H	G.Hickie	5'10"	15st 10lb	1	8	-	-
C	B.Hinshelwood	6'2"	15st 10lb	7	-	-	-
P	C.Horsman	6'2"	17st 6lb	6	-	-	-
BR	K.Horstmann	6'3"	16st 9lb	19	2	3	15
W	J.Hylton	6'0"	13st 5lb	4	3	-	-
H	A.Keylock	N/A	N/A	-	-	-	-
FB/W	N.Le Roux	5'8"	11st 13lb	13	1	2	10
C	T.Lombard	6'2"	13st 5lb	21	-	2	10
P	M.MacDonald	6'1"	20st 5lb	1	3	-	-
W/C	M.Maguire	6'1"	14st 11lb	1	-	-	-
L	P.Murphy	6'7"	17st 6lb	21	1	1	5
L	E.O'Donoghue	6'6"	17st 4lb	1	8	-	-
W	U.Oduoza	6'3"	14st 4lb	3	-	-	-
SH	M.Powell	5'10"	13st 9lb	7	10	-	-
C	D.Rasmussen	6'2"	14st 12lb	17	2	2	10
SH	N.Runciman	5'9"	11st 11lb	2	-	1	5
BR	P.Sanderson	6'2"	14st 8lb	11	-	2	10
P	T.Taumoepeau	6'0"	18st 0lb	14	5	-	-
C	G.Trueman	6'0"	14st 2lb	4	4	1	5
BR	J.Tu'amoheloa	5'10"	14st 6lb	7	-	-	-
C/W	M.Tucker	6'0"	15st 10lb	7	-	-	-
BR	S.Vaili	6'4"	17st 6lb	5	11	2	10
H	A.Van Niekerk	5'10"	16st 12lb	6	3	-	-
FH/C	S.Whatling	5'10"	15st 0lb	3	6	-	3
P	T.Windo	6'0"	16st 12lb	21	-	3	15

Worcester Warriors

Last Season Form 2005/06

Season Progression

Month: Sep | Oct | Nov | D | Jan | Feb | Mar | Apr | May

Points/Position
- ○ position
- won
- drawn
- lost
- T try bonus
- L lose bonus

home away

Positions: 6, 5, 5, 6, 4, 6, 6, 6, 9, 8, 8

L L L L T L T TL

Gloucester 15-15, Irish 15-20, Saracens 25-24, Wasps 34-20, Leeds 22-15, Leicester 15-11, Sale 24-13, Bristol 24-15, Northampton 21-22, Bath 18-36, Newcastle 21-15, Northampton 11-15, Bristol 23-26, Sale 33-48, Leicester 28-22, Leeds 21-15, Wasps 37-8, Saracens 29-15, Irish 10-12, Gloucester 27-16, Newcastle 35-27, Bath 25-22

Home Matches

Month: S | O | N | D | J | F | M | A

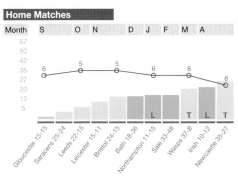

Positions: 6, 5, 5, 6, 6, 8

L T L T

Gloucester 15-15, Saracens 25-24, Leeds 22-15, Leicester 15-11, Bristol 24-15, Bath 18-36, Northampton 11-15, Sale 33-48, Wasps 37-8, Irish 10-12, Newcastle 35-27

Away Matches

Month: S | N | J | F | M | A | M

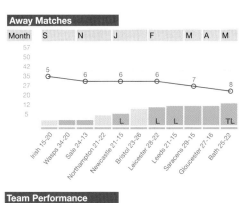

Positions: 5, 6, 6, 6, 7, 8

L L L TL

Irish 15-20, Wasps 34-20, Sale 24-13, Northampton 21-22, Newcastle 21-15, Bristol 23-26, Leicester 28-22, Leeds 21-15, Saracens 29-15, Gloucester 27-16, Bath 25-22

Premiership Statistics

		Home	Away
Tries	40	22	18
Coversions	28	15	13
Penalty goals	61	35	26
Drop goals	4	0	4
Kick %	70%	69%	71%
Yellow/Red cards	15/2	6/1	9/1
Powerplay tries	8	5	3
Shorthand tries	0	0	0

Powerplay tries are scored when your side are playing with a man or more advantage due to yellow or red cards.

Shorthand tries are scored when your side are playing with a man or more fewer due to yellow or red cards.

Team Performance

Position	Team	% total points won	% won at home	% won away
1	Sale			
2	Leicester	20%	15%	27%
3	Irish			
4	Wasps			
5	Gloucester	24%	25%	22%
6	Northampton			
7	Newcastle			
8	**Worcester**	24%	23%	24%
9	Bath			
10	Saracens			
11	Bristol	32%	37%	27%
12	Leeds			

Worcester Warriors

Top Scorer

Points Facts

	Total points	% team points	Home	Away
	233	54	117	116

Points by Time Period

29	16	44	36	26	23	34	15	10
0	10	20	30	40	50	60	70	80 Inj.

Team Tries and Points

Tries by Time Period

- scored
- conceded

5	3	6	6	5	4	4	7	0
0	10min	20min	30min	40min	50min	60min	70min	80 Injury time
7	5	6	7	9	9	7	5	1

Tries by Halves

- scored
- conceded

	Total	1st half	2nd half	1st half %	2nd half %
	40	20	20	50%	50%
	56	25	31	45%	55%

How Points were Scored

- tries: 200
- conversions: 56
- pen goals: 183
- drop goals: 12

How Points were Conceded

- tries: 280
- conversions: 64
- pen goals: 144
- drop goals: 6

Tries Scored by Player

- backs: 22
- forwards: 14

Tries Conceded by Player

- backs: 41
- forwards: 15

Worcester Warriors

Eight-Season Form 1998-2006

Season Progression

Season	98-99	99-00	00-01	01-02	02-03	03-04	04-05	05-06
Points/Position			112	108	114	125		
○ position	3	3	2	2	2	1	9	8
Premiership								47
Division 1	34	38					42	
Division 2								

Games

Season	98-99	99-00	00-01	01-02	02-03	03-04	04-05	05-06
won	18	19	23	23	23	26	9	9
drawn								1
lost	8	7	2	3	3		13	12

Points

Season	98-99	99-00	00-01	01-02	02-03	03-04	04-05	05-06
scored	716	865	844	941	1185	1119	365	451
conceded	409	450	387	364	431	340	493	494

Points Difference

Season	98-99	99-00	00-01	01-02	02-03	03-04	04-05	05-06
points	+307	+415	+457	+577	+754	+779	-128	-43

Total Premiership Record

Largest win	Largest defeat	Most tries scored in a game	Most tries conceded in a game
33-7	**3-57**	**5**	**8**
vs Harlequins (H) 02.10.04	vs Sale Sharks (A) 24.09.04	vs Harlequins (H) 02.10.04	vs Sale Sharks (A) 24.09.04

Top points scorer	Top try scorer	Top drop goal scorer	Most appearances
S.Drahm 233	**A.Havili** 6	**J.Brown** 5	**T.Windo** 43

Longest winning sequence	Longest losing sequence
3 wins from 04.02.05 to 25.02.05	**4 defeats** from 10.10.04 to 13.11.04

Worcester Warriors `EFL`

ENHANCED FIXTURE LIST
[does not include play-off data]

Guinness Premiership 2006-07 — Premiership History

Date	Team	H/A	05-06	Played	98-99	99-00	00-01	01-02	02-03	03-04	04-05	05-06	Total Points F	A	Outcome after a half-time lead No.	W	D	L	Close games No.	W
					▪ won		▪ drawn		▪ lost		☐ not played									
02.09.06	Bristol	H	24-15	1									24	15	1	1	-	-	-	-
08.09.06	Newcastle	A	21-15	2									36	37	1	1	-	-	2	1
15.09.06	Sale	H	33-48	2									56	58	1	1	-	-	-	-
23.09.06	Bath	A	25-22	2									32	43	1	-	-	1	1	-
13.10.06	Gloucester	H	15-15	2									28	33	1	-	-	1	2	-
04.11.06	Leicester	A	28-22	2									29	78	-	-	-	-	1	-
11.11.06	Northampton	H	11-15	2									32	34	1	1	-	-	2	1
17.11.06	Harlequins	A	N/A	1									15	9	-	-	-	-	1	1
26.11.06	Saracens	A	29-15	2									25	45	1	-	-	1	1	-
22.12.06	Irish	H	10-12	2									26	18	1	1	-	-	-	-
27.12.06	Harlequins	H	N/A	1									33	7	1	1	-	-	-	-
01.01.07	Northampton	A	21-22	2									39	27	2	2	-	-	1	1
07.01.07	Wasps	A	34-20	2									37	66	1	-	-	1	-	-
26.01.07	Wasps	H	37-8	2									64	32	2	2	-	-	1	1
17.02.07	Leicester	H	15-11	2									26	49	1	1	-	-	1	1
24.02.07	Gloucester	A	27-16	2									32	55	-	-	-	-	-	-
03.03.07	Bath	H	18-36	2									40	62	1	-	-	1	1	-
09.03.07	Sale	A	24-13	2									16	81	-	-	-	-	-	-
16.03.07	Newcastle	H	35-27	2									44	57	1	1	-	-	-	-
08.04.07	Bristol	A	23-26	1									26	23	1	1	-	-	1	1
15.04.07	Irish	A	15-20	2									35	40	-	-	-	-	1	1
28.04.07	Saracens	H	25-24	2									43	43	1	-	-	1	2	1

Club Information

Useful Information

Founded
1871
Address
Sixways
Pershore Lane
Hindlip
Worcester
WR3 8ZE
Capacity
10,000 (3,700 seated)
Main switchboard
01905 454183
Website
www.wrfc.co.uk

Travel Information

Car
M5 Junction 7 (Worcester South) and follow AA signs for Park & Ride, County Hall (Countryside Centre). For a 15:00 kick off, buses start at 12:30 then every few minutes until 14:25. For a 20:00 kick off, buses start at 18:20 then every few minutes until 19:25.
M5 Junction 6 (Worcester North) and follow AA signs for Park & Ride, Blackpole (Blackpole East Trading Estate). For a 15:00 kick off, buses start at 12:30 then every few minutes until 14:25. For a 20:00 kick off, buses start at 18:20 then every few minutes until 19:25.
M5 Junction 6 (Worcester North) and follow AA signs for Park & Walk, Shire Business Park.

Train
Worcester Shrub Hill Station. Orange Bus Route 31 to City Bus station (every 10 minutes), then transfer to Rugby Special Service at frequent intervals (Stand F). A taxi to Sixways is about £8.00.
Worcester Foregate Street Station. Rugby Special Bus Service from outside the station every 10 minutes. For a 15:00 kick off, buses start to leave the station at 12:30 then every few minutes until 14:05 to the ground. For a 20:00 kick off, buses leave the station at 18:00 then every few minutes until 19:05.

Worcester Warriors

Maps

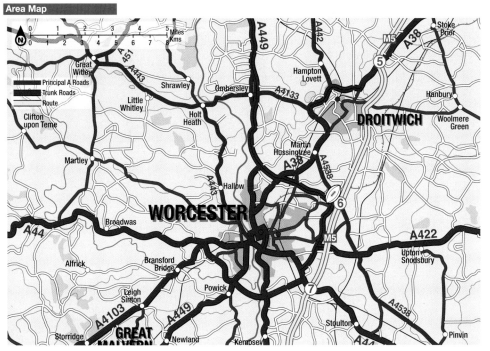

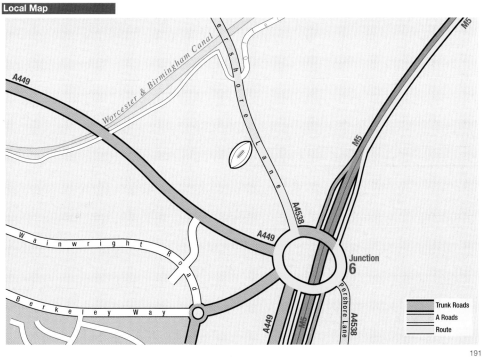

Premiership Fixture Grid 2006/07

AWAY \ HOME	Worcester	Saracens	Sale Sharks	Northampton	Newcastle	NEC Harlequins	London Wasps	London Irish	Leicester Tigers	Gloucester	Bristol Rugby	Bath Rugby
Bath Rugby	3-Mar	15-Oct	13-Apr	16-Sep	28-Apr	6-Jan	12-Nov	17-Feb	17-Mar	2-Sep	27-Dec	
Bristol Rugby	2-Sep	18-Mar	1-Jan	27-Jan	3-Nov	24-Feb	4-Mar	16-Sep	22-Dec	28-Apr		17-Nov
Gloucester	13-Oct	18-Feb	6-Jan	3-Mar	13-Apr	9-Sep	26-Dec	10-Nov	16-Sep		24-Nov	7-Apr
Leicester Tigers	17-Feb	12-Nov	6-Apr	14-Oct	7-Jan	23-Sep	26-Nov	26-Dec		10-Mar	15-Apr	9-Sep
London Irish	22-Dec	28-Jan	23-Feb	28-Apr	22-Sep	7-Apr	8-Sep		18-Nov	1-Jan	10-Mar	4-Nov
London Wasps	26-Jan	2-Sep	3-Nov	22-Dec	23-Feb	10-Mar		18-Mar	28-Apr	18-Nov	24-Sep	1-Jan
NEC Harlequins	27-Dec	15-Apr	24-Nov	17-Feb	10-Nov		17-Sep	2-Sep	3-Mar	17-Mar	15-Oct	27-Jan
Newcastle	16-Mar	17-Sep	17-Nov	3-Sep		1-Jan	15-Oct	3-Mar	27-Jan	22-Dec	18-Feb	25-Nov
Northampton	11-Nov	27-Dec	9-Sep		6-Apr	4-Nov	15-Apr	26-Nov	24-Feb	23-Sep	7-Jan	10-Mar
Sale Sharks	15-Sep	4-Mar		17-Mar	26-Dec	28-Apr	18-Feb	15-Oct	3-Sep	27-Jan	10-Nov	22-Dec
Saracens	28-Apr		22-Sep	18-Nov	9-Mar	22-Dec	8-Apr	7-Jan	1-Jan	4-Nov	10-Sep	24-Feb
Worcester		26-Nov	9-Mar	1-Jan	8-Sep	17-Nov	7-Jan	15-Apr	4-Nov	24-Nov	8-Apr	23-Sep